CHIRON

MARTIN LASS (New York, Australia) is a professional astrologer and has studied and worked with Chiron for thirteen years. He has written for *Well Being, Woman Spirit,* and a variety of other holistic and alternative journals, has lectured and conducted numerous seminars internationally in many diverse areas of alternative healing and spirituality, and is an accredited associate of the Concourse of Wisdom School of Philosophy and Healing, in Houston, TX.

Lass is also a professional violinist, entertainer, and composer and has performed worldwide alongside the likes of Julio Iglesias, Yehudi Menuhin, and Luciano Pavarotti. He recently released his tenth solo CD, *Sonnet.*

CHIRON

⚷

Healing Body & Soul

MARTIN LASS

Llewellyn Publications
Woodbury, Minnesota

First Edition
First Printing, 2005

Series design and format by Donna Burch
Cover art © Photodisc
Cover design by Ellen Dahl
Edited by Andrea Neff
Llewellyn is a registered trademark of Llewellyn Worldwide, Ltd.

The quotation on page 1 is reproduced by permission of Timothy Freke and Peter Gandy.

The Melanie Reinhart quotation on page 4 is reproduced by permission of Penguin Books, Ltd.

Chart wheels were produced by the Kepler program by permission of Cosmic Patterns Software, Inc. (www.AstroSoftware.com)

Library of Congress Cataloging-in-Publication Data

Lass, Martin.
        Chiron : healing body & soul / Martin Lass.
            p.   cm.
        Includes bibliographical references and index.
        ISBN 0-7387-0717-1
            1. Chiron (Asteroid)—Miscellanea. 2. Astrology. I. Title.

        BF1724.2.C48L37 2005
        133.5'398—dc22   2005044100

Llewellyn Worldwide does not participate in, endorse, or have any authority or responsibility concerning private business transactions between our authors and the public.
    All mail addressed to the author is forwarded but the publisher cannot, unless specifically instructed by the author, give out an address or phone number.
    Any Internet references contained in this work are current at publication time, but the publisher cannot guarantee that a specific location will continue to be maintained. Please refer to the publisher's website for links to authors' websites and other sources.

Llewellyn Publications
A Division of Llewellyn Worldwide, Ltd.
2143 Wooddale Drive, Dept. 0-7387-0717-1
Woodbury, MN 55125-2989, U.S.A.
www.llewellyn.com

Printed in the United States of America

The gift is in the wound.

*Love is the beginning and the end
of our journey of wounding and healing.*

Contents

Charts

Tables

Acknowledgments

Thank you to my friend and teacher, Rickie Hilder, for introducing me to Chiron—not just as a cold planetary object, but as a living guide. Thank you to my innumerable clients over the years who have illuminated Chiron for me so that I could then return the favor and assist in the healing of their lives; without their help, this book would not exist. Thank you to my family for putting up with my dark nights of the soul while delving into my 12th-house Chiron. Thank you to Stephanie Clement for actively helping me cut and polish what was at first a very rough and jagged stone, the result being the shining jewel of this book, as given to me from above. Thank you to the late Lois Rodden, without whose fierce dedication, astrologers would not have in their possession one of the most powerful research tools in AstroDatabank software. Most importantly, thank you to Chiron for gradually awakening me to a conception of the cosmos that is so vast and so unified that it often brings tears of inspiration; thank you to Chiron for showing me that there is nothing in the universe except love.

Preface

My journey with Chiron began in 1992 when, while browsing the shelves of the Theosophical Society bookstore in Sydney, Australia, the ultimate cliché happened: a book fell off the shelves and landed at my feet. I looked around, half expecting Shirley MacLaine to come around the corner! Not seeing her, I picked up the book and looked at the title—*Chiron and the Healing Journey* by Melanie Reinhart. Not interested in asteroids at the time, I simply put the book back and went on my merry way. Little did I know at the time that this event would be the first in a series of synchronicities marking Chiron's forceful entry into my life.

Having studied astrology since the age of twelve and having practiced professionally for many years, I felt as though there was still something missing—a key that would unlock the astrology chart and bring together what seemed at the time to be a whole lot of disconnected pieces. Interestingly, I felt that my life at the time was also a collection of such pieces—disconnected, disjointed, unrelated, and misshapen.

In the midst of this inner and outer turmoil, I remember calling out to whoever might have been listening in the greater cosmos: Why was my life so fragmented? Why did I feel so alone? Why did I feel like an outsider—like an alien on an alien planet? Why did I feel as though there was something missing, something that seemed just out of my grasp, something that might otherwise bring together the scattered pieces of my life?

A few weeks later, a psychic friend of mine[1] called me out of the blue, saying that she had some messages for me from her spiritual guides. She wouldn't tell me the messages on the phone, so we arranged to meet later in the week.

In the intervening days, I had a powerful dream.[2] In the dream, a woman was dying in my arms. It may have been my wife, my mother, my daughter, or a lover . . . it didn't matter, except that it was female. In the midst of my anguish, she died. Nearly overcome with emotional pain, I "dived down" toward the pain, into the darkness of my psyche. As I approached the source of the pain, it became almost too much to bear. At that moment, though, the woman came alive again, and my pain was transformed into pure love. With my chest almost bursting with this love, I awoke, tears streaming down my face. In hindsight, I recognized that a great healing had taken place. I had recovered my disowned feminine side.

A few days later, my psychic friend came to visit. Among other things, she told me that I needed to know about Chiron and to work with its energies. She said Chiron was the "wounded healer." She said that Chiron was all about recovering and healing the lost pieces of our lives—our disowned and unloved parts.

As she spoke about Chiron, I felt some of the pieces of *my* life come together—the bookstore cliché, my quest for the missing key to unifying astrology charts, the feeling of being an outsider, the disconnectedness of my life, and, of course, my recent dream. An underlying connection and pattern began to emerge, and, somewhere in the recesses of my mind, I felt a door open—a door to a new yet somehow ancient and more direct understanding of the living world. Although I did not know where this would lead me, I knew at that moment, without knowing exactly why, that I had found the key I had been searching for.

The upshot of it all was that, for the first time, I looked at where Chiron sat in my own natal chart—its sign, house, aspects, travel, and current transits.[3] I was floored, to say the

---

1. Birth data: July 13, 1940, 8:00 AM, AEST −10:00, Sydney, Australia, 33°S52', 151°E13'. Note the Chiron-Sun conjunction.

2. Natal birth data (Martin Lass): August 6, 1958, 8:33 PM, CST +6:00, Chicago, Illinois, 42°N06', 087°W44'. Transit data: July 8, 1992, 4:00 AM, AEST −10:00, Sydney, Australia, 33°S52', 151°E13'.

3. Chiron was retrograde in Aquarius in the 12th house, opposing my Sun (5th/6th-house cusp), and participated in a yod of Chiron, Saturn (9th house), and Venus (4th house), with Venus as the focal point.

least! It answered many questions about the way I felt about myself and about my life—particularly in relation to feeling unloved and in relation to the way in which I expressed my woundedness.

In the ensuing months, I would also see that placing Chiron into the astrological picture would answer the many questions I had concerning how to unify the otherwise disconnected pieces of the astrology chart. What were previously collections of clinical, dry, disconnected planetary influences were transformed into living, breathing, dynamic pictures of people's lives.

Perhaps the most striking feature of this series of synchronicities, though, lay in my Chiron transits. At the time of the aforementioned meeting, a conjunction of Chiron and Mercury was transiting my natal Sun-Uranus conjunction and I was fast approaching my Chiron half-Return. Moreover, shortly after this meeting, I experienced a spontaneous and cathartic past-life memory of the loss of a loved one. When I later examined the transits, I found that transiting Chiron was exactly conjunct my natal Uranus, and transiting Venus was exactly conjunct my natal Sun.[4] I needed no more convincing! In the ensuing years, it became apparent that Chiron had chosen me to be an emissary—a spokesman for its healing messages.

The journey of the last decade and more has been an enlightening one, with Chiron as my primary planetary guide. It has been a journey of delving deeply into my own wounds and issues, as mirrored by Chiron in my natal chart. This is only half the story, though. The other half has been the miraculous journey of *healing*—not only for me, but also for the many people close to me, as well as for the many clients with whom I have worked. True to its astrological glyph, Chiron was (and is) certainly the key.

As wondrous as those early years were, I did not suspect at the time how vast a picture Chiron would eventually paint. Nor did I realize how relevant (and obvious, in retrospect!) it was that Chiron was discovered exactly when it was.

In short, Chiron's discovery augurs a *new paradigm*—a new way of looking at ourselves and at the world around us. It augurs a revolution in *consciousness* and consciousness's connection to health and disease and function and dysfunction—a revolution the likes of which the world has not known in over two thousand years. With this somewhat sweeping statement (!), let us begin our exploration of Chiron . . .

---

4. Natal birth data (Martin Lass): August 6, 1958, 8:33 PM, CST +6:00, Chicago, Illinois, 42°N06', 087°W44'. Transit data: July 26, 1992, 11:00 AM, AEST −10:00, Townsville, Australia, 19°S16', 146°E48'.

CHAPTER ONE

The Chiron Paradigm

Suddenly everything changed before me.
Reality was opened out in a moment.
I saw the boundless view.
All became dissolved in Light—
united within one joyous love.

Yet the Light cast a shadow,
Grim and terrible,
Which, passing downwards,
Became like restless water,
Chaotically tossing forth spume like smoke.
And I heard an unspeakable lament—
an inarticulate cry of separation.
The Light then uttered a Word,
Which calmed the chaotic waters.
  —The Hermetica[1]

---

1. *The Hermetica* is a collection of second- and third-century Alexandrine texts in Latin, Greek, and Coptic, referred to as *Corpus Hermeticum.* New translation by Timothy Freke and Peter Gandy, *The Hermetica: The Lost Wisdom of the Pharoahs,* pp. 37–38. See bibliography.

The Brink of a New Paradigm

It has been said that nothing is as powerful as an idea whose time has come. The greatest advances in the consciousness of the human race have come from just such ideas, presented at the time humanity was ready to hear them and embrace them. The discovery in 1977 of the "planet" Chiron represented a threshold of this kind. It represented the beginning of a new paradigm—a new way of seeing ourselves and seeing the world around us—that we will call the *Chiron Paradigm.*

Chiron's primary themes are *wounding* and *healing,* taken in their broadest sense—physical, emotional, mental, and spiritual—and covering the full gamut of life from the physical to the metaphysical and from the terrestrial to the celestial.

What, according to the Chiron Paradigm, is meant by wounding and healing? In everyday terms, our life from birth consists of a series of events, circumstances, and experiences, each of which we perceive and judge in one of three ways: either things are considered more painful than pleasureful (negativity/depression/resentment), more pleasureful than painful ("positivity"/elation/infatuation), or neither more painful nor pleasureful (indifference). The origins of these perceptions of life lie primarily in the physical senses, the nervous system, and the brain's interpretation of the messages of the senses.

I say "primarily" because we can also look at life from a higher *transpersonal* perspective, beyond the limitations and modalities of the senses. In fact, according to the Chiron Paradigm, such a higher perspective is the essence of healing.

In any case, when things in our lives are considered bad, wrong, painful, traumatic, dysfunctional, and/or unjust—whether physically, emotionally, mentally, or spiritually—this is what we are calling *wounding.* The traces left by such experiences (and by our judgments of these experiences) are what we will call *wounds.* This is the first half of Chiron's nature, as seen in the astrological tapestry.

If this is so, then, in ordinary terms, the *healing* journey consists of revealing, identifying, and dissolving/resolving the issues associated with our wounds. This is the second half of Chiron's nature. To summarize Chiron's perspective, *the whole of life is nothing more or less than a journey of wounding and healing.*

From a far broader perspective—astronomical, metaphysical, and spiritual—the Chiron Paradigm asserts that our wounding and healing journey is synonymous with the *descent* and *re-ascent* of consciousness through the cosmos. It is synonymous with *creation* (the Fall, the wounding) and subsequent *evolution* (the Ascension, the healing). Our everyday lives are but a hologram of this larger cosmic picture. As above, so below.

Chiron asserts that the healing journey—in our everyday lives, as well as in the broader life of humanity—consists of *awakening to the perfection of our lives*, no more, no less. It asserts that there lies a gift within every wound, waiting to be discovered. In fact, Chiron itself epitomizes the gift in the wound inasmuch as this dark horse planet's innate gifts and wisdom lie hidden beneath an unsuspecting and seemingly painful exterior.

In order to fully understand and appreciate the preceding assertions, we must expand our vision well beyond the astrological considerations of Chiron, the planet. In this day and age, it is ever more important that astrology moves toward *consilience*, i.e., toward the cross-disciplinary unification of all knowledge. The survival and credibility of astrology rests upon this. However, before mapping out the grand unified plan of the cosmos and solving the mysteries of life (!), we must begin with our rogue comet friend and his astrological considerations.

Early Studies of Chiron

Such noted astrologers as Erminie Lantero, Zane Stein, Richard Nolle, Melanie Reinhart, and Barbara Hand Clow undertook the early studies of Chiron. In these studies, the theme of wounding (taken, as always, in its broadest sense) was emphasized. Although its partner theme—healing—was broached and it was clear that the healing journey was Chiron's challenge, it was unclear in these early days exactly what the healing journey entailed. In my opinion, the clearest picture was presented by Hand Clow: the healing journey was mirrored in the outward planetary journey from Saturn to Uranus—in the "Rainbow Bridge"—and healing was considered the process of rejoining our lower earthly nature (mirrored in the inner planets) with our higher celestial nature (mirrored in the outer planets).

True enough! However, in these early studies, our potential healing path was mapped in terms of more traditional and established psychological and archetypal paradigms, leading to many inadequacies and contradictions. Sometimes, new ideas cannot be measured against old contexts, but require an entirely new paradigm. The difficulties encountered during these early studies were aptly summed up in Reinhart's 1989 book on Chiron:[2]

2. Melanie Reinhart, *Chiron and the Healing Journey* (London: Arkana, 1989), p. 5.

This book *[Chiron and the Healing Journey]* is in the nature of a mosaic; the long process of researching and writing it has been rather like the experience of trying to piece together a jigsaw for which initially there was no picture, and eventually several different pictures! The reader will find many irreconcilables sitting here side by side, sometimes with no attempt to resolve them. The archetypal nature of Chiron himself is also thus: the opposites of horse and human being are yoked uncomfortably into one form, awaiting the more inclusive synthesis that only a journey into the depths of his own inner nature can bring. Latching on to ready-made philosophies does not necessarily work where Chiron is involved, for this archetypal pattern suggests the need, and brings the opportunity, for each of us to make our own personal and unique quest for the meaning of our lives. During this process, we inevitably come up against many imponderables, paradoxes, and unanswerable questions.

How true! However, over the last decade and a half, a new context into which Chiron's revolutionary ideas can be properly placed has emerged. In short, Chiron's new paradigm is coming into view. With it comes the requirement to turn many consensus views concerning psychology, physiology, spirituality, astrology, metaphysics, mythology, religion, and more on their heads. At the same time, the Chiron Paradigm is gradually reconnecting us to wisdom that was already known in our distant past, but that was subsequently forgotten.

In the early days, Chiron tended to be associated more with wounding and pain and less with its partner theme of healing. To delve into one's natal Chiron brought a certain dread and reluctance. The gift of doing so, though, has been the gradual emergence of a new paradigm of healing—a new understanding of what healing is and how to attain it.

Alongside many other astrologers, my aim over the last decade and more has been to discover and present the balancing half of the equation, i.e., a new paradigm of healing. When both sides of the picture—the wounding and the healing—are seen equally and as equally necessary to our journey, then all contradictions, dilemmas, and paradoxes are resolved; all seemingly unanswerable questions are answered; a larger context emerges; we approach the "inclusive synthesis" that Reinhart projected. In fact, the Chiron Paradigm asserts that the ongoing process of discovering both sides of any given issue *is* the healing journey. This is one of Chiron's greatest messages and tools.

Although our healing journey must necessarily begin as a personal and inner journey—by facing our inner darkness and pain—as we heal, a larger picture emerges. We begin to see that our personal journey is mirrored in ever larger contexts and that these contexts constitute the framework of the cosmogonic cycles of Creation and evolution. We begin to realize that healing is synonymous with the evolution of consciousness—personally, collectively, and cosmically.

The Gift in the Wound

The Chiron Paradigm asserts that the gift is in the wound. Other ways of expressing this are:

There is a blessing in every crisis.

Every cloud has a silver lining.

There are benefits to every negative situation.

Every void has a value.

Every thing and every happening is a service of love.

Through the darkness lies the light.

Beyond the pain, love lies.

Let's look at this from an everyday perspective. When painful, traumatic, adverse, and/or negative experiences befall us, we tend to see the negative sides more than the positive (if we see the positive at all). As we have said, the reason for this lies in the nature of the senses, the nervous system, and the brain. Said another way, in such circumstances, we tend to *express* the negative and *repress* the positive. Such is the face of Chiron, as initially seen in the natal chart (in synergy with many other factors, not the least of which is the Moon, as we shall see in the material that follows).

What we do *not* see at the time are the benefits, blessings, lessons, gifts, and service of these painful and traumatic experiences. We fail to see the balancing sides. The healing journey consists of discovering and embracing these balancing sides. This can take anything from a second to a lifetime. Hindsight is a great gift in this respect. As we discover and uncover the hidden balancing sides, so a larger picture is revealed—a picture that contains our gift. The gift is a piece of the puzzle of the meaning and purpose of our lives.

The Chiron Paradigm also asserts that there is nothing to fix, change, or get rid of in our lives. *All is perfect as it is.* However, our failure to see this at first (or our out-and-out denial) takes us on the *journey* of our lives. Along the way, we become the person we are meant to become. That is, we manifest our service to ourselves (in terms of learning our lessons and evolving our consciousness) and to others (in terms of how we contribute to others' lives). Our gradual awakening to, and embracing of, this service *is* the healing journey, *is* the evolution of consciousness. In this lies a larger perfection with a capital P.

Such assertions inevitably bring us to the idea of an ordered universe—a universe with a higher plan and purpose. Although one cannot scientifically argue this case (yet!) with those who are so wounded as to deny a higher order or higher power, our personal healing journey will inevitably (and inexorably) awaken us to just such a higher order. This is Chiron's promise. Moreover, herein lies the hope for the eventual unification of science and spirituality/religion. We can expedite this process (if we so wish) by putting Chiron's musings, as seen astrologically, into ever larger contexts. We will hint at some of these contexts in what follows.

Chiron Astrology

Given the preceding, we arrive at the essence of the argument: Chiron, in the natal chart, points to the place of our greatest wounds—the things we feel are the most missing, wrong, unjust, painful, and/or lacking in our lives. It encompasses all the things that we feel, consciously or unconsciously, should or should not have happened. It is reflected in all the things in our lives and in ourselves that we feel need changing, "fixing," or getting rid of, or that we would prefer to run away from, avoid, or ignore. In this place, we harbor bottled-up negative emotions, judgments, blame, resentments, injustices, traumatic memories, past-life issues, and "rooms" within us where we either fear to tread or that we would rather avoid, ignore, condemn, or banish altogether.

Hidden within this place of darkness, though, *lie all the balancing sides of the equation—* the benefits, blessings, lessons, gifts, and service of each and every one of our issues. Through the darkness lies the light. When we try to avoid the darkness, the darkness persists and blocks our way. Inherent within the wound itself lies the healing path. As we *approach* the wound, so its hidden aspects are illuminated, allowing growth, transformation, healing, and evolution of consciousness. If we understand the principles involved, each person's healing path can be clearly seen in the natal chart.

Perhaps the most striking symbolic example of Chiron's healing process was presented in the animated film *The Dark Crystal.*[3] Here, the dark and light sides of the psyche are personified in two races of creatures—polar opposites in every way, yin and yang, positive and

---

3. *The Dark Crystal,* 1982. Written by Jim Hensen (of *The Muppets* fame). Directed by Jim Hensen, Frank Oz, and Gary Kurtz.

negative, feminine and masculine, and so forth. The races are rejoined into one "super-race" of "light beings" when a broken shard of a magical but fractured crystal is rejoined with the whole of the crystal. The shard is symbolic of the dark, lost, disowned, denied, rejected, and/or condemned pieces of ourselves that seek to be rejoined with the whole of us.

Of all the psychologists of the last hundred years, perhaps Carl G. Jung came closest to understanding this principle of rejoining our light and dark sides (individuation). All that remained was to define the exact nature of the light and dark sides of the psyche. Chiron points the way to just such a definition.

Myths and Themes

Chiron was a *centaur*—half horse (animal, lower nature) and half man (human, higher nature). The schism between what we perceive as our wounds and their hidden benefits, blessings, lessons, gifts, and service is aptly summarized in the animal (lower) half of the centaur. In the myth, Chiron's leg was wounded, symbolizing the woundedness of our lower nature—a nature that sees one side of the world while repressing, ignoring, denying, disowning, condemning, and/or failing to acknowledge the other balancing sides. Such is the origin of blame.

As we shine a light upon our darkness, though, seeking out the balancing sides, so our lower nature is healed, transformed, unified, and rejoined with our higher human nature. Such was the ultimate destiny of Chiron when immortalized in the constellation of Sagittarius (symbolizing the greater truth, oneness, and love of the galactic core consciousness).

Chiron's message is only understood when we understand and appreciate that the world we see around us is a world of perceived *duality*. Everything in existence has an equal and opposite companion, although one side tends to be hidden from us in the beginning. As the great teacher/visionary G. I. Gurdjieff put it last century: "Every stick has two ends." Modern quantum physics concurs with this view in its conception of matter and anti-matter. Such is the eastern view, too—yin and yang, for example. However, to put it more poetically, we quote from Emerson:[4]

> Every excess causes a defect; every defect an excess. Every sweet hath its sour; every evil its good. Every faculty which is a receiver of pleasure has an equal penalty put on its abuse. It is to answer for its moderation with its life. For every grain of wit there is a grain of folly. For everything you have missed, you have gained something else; and

---

4. Ralph Waldo Emerson, *Nature and Other Writings,* edited by Peter Turner, from essay "Compensation," (Boston: Shambhala, 1994), pp. 118–19.

for everything you gain, you lose something. If riches increase, they're increased that use them. If the gatherer gathers too much, nature takes out of the man what she puts into his chest; swells the estate, but kills the owner. Nature hates monopolies and exceptions.

Why the world presents a dualistic face is, according to the Chiron Paradigm, all a matter of perception. It is all about *consciousness*. The astrology chart is, in the final analysis, a mandala of consciousness. Again, quantum physics can teach us much concerning this topic. However, that is a topic for another book!

Many other mythic, archetypal, and symbolic examples are available, some of which we will explore in the material that follows. Each reveals its secrets in the wake of the Chiron Paradigm. More than this, each mirrors and supports the Chiron Paradigm. Why and how this is so will only become apparent as we draw increasingly wide circles around our topic of study.

Astronomical Features of Chiron

So far, we have presented Chiron's new paradigm without much recourse to astronomical/astrological data. The following is a short overview of some of Chiron's astronomical/astrological features, showing how each contributes to and illuminates the basis upon which the new paradigm is built. A more detailed study of these features appears in chapter 3, "The Discovery of Chiron."

Chiron's highly elliptical orbit means that it spends considerably more time in Aries than in Libra. In short, it exaggerates Arian traits and minimizes Libran traits. Taking the view from the zodiac of the Mysteries,[5] where the Moon rules Aries and the Sun rules Libra, Aries/Moon represents our dualistic (wounded) lower nature and Libra/Sun represents our potentially unified (healed) higher nature. Thus, Chiron, on the surface, *exaggerates woundedness* and *minimizes healing*. (We must be aware, though, that woundedness and healing are, ultimately, a matter of perception. Healing is a journey of consciousness.)

Moreover, Chiron's degree of inclination from the ecliptic (declination) makes it somewhat of a rogue in the larger scheme of things, also giving Chiron an unusual perspective when compared to the other planets (barring Pluto, perhaps). Not only this, but studies show that extremes in ellipticity and declination give rise to more polarized, more extreme

---

5. The Mysteries are the combined body of knowledge and wisdom passed down in an unbroken lineage through esoteric schools, both hidden and visible, from the time of Atlantis. Reference: Dr. John F. Demartini, The Concourse of Wisdom School of Philosophy and Healing, Houston, TX.

expressions of planetary (and, hence, human) expressions. From this perspective, cometary bodies like Chiron (and Pluto, presumably) represent the solar system's more extreme emotional expressions.

Furthermore, Chiron, like Pluto, may be more correctly associated with the Kuiper Belt of astronomical objects, most of which orbit well beyond Neptune. Without going into detail here, this association means that Chiron's energetic origin may well lie outside the local Seven Ray origin of the rest of the solar system.[6] Psychologically, this means that Chiron is "far from home," isolated, abandoned, a loner, and so on. However, it also offers Chiron an "extra-solar" perspective and the potential for a reconnection to consciousness outside the "egg sac" of our solar system (solar *magnetosphere*).

In addition, like most comets, Chiron tends to "suck in" light and present an extremely dark surface (even though a comet's tail "lights up" when it approaches the Sun). This is relevant inasmuch as Chiron, on the surface of things and as previously mentioned, tends to emphasize wounding (darkness) and minimize healing (light).

Finally, although Chiron's orbit is mostly confined between Saturn and Uranus, Chiron periodically crosses the orbit of Saturn, and it periodically intrudes upon Uranus's orbital space, waving a planetary hand toward Jupiter and Neptune, respectively. This implies that Chiron's affairs span a wide scope. Moreover, it means that Chiron has the potential to bridge the affairs of these outer planets—to see life from on high, so to speak. Not only this, but it has the capacity to be a bridge between the inner and the outer planets, carrying our worldview from a "material-centric" perspective to a "spiritual-centric" one.

Jupiter's association with the Inner Child and with naïve views of the world (pre-Saturnian, pre-responsibility) and Neptune's association (in its higher octave) with unconditional love (post-Uranian, the culmination of the healing journey) are extremely relevant when deciphering Chiron's themes and the way Chiron operates. We will cover many of these aspects in later chapters. The bottom line is that we cannot fully appreciate Chiron's higher messages until we put Chiron into the larger cosmic picture, as these few preceding points have endeavored to do.

By virtue of the aforementioned astronomical features, Chiron is at once *disconnected* from the rest of the solar system and *connected* to the higher consciousness that lies further

---

6. Each solar system has its origin in a singular "cone" of light emanating from the galactic core and having seven aspects—Seven Rays—arising from the light's deflection by seven primary constellations upon its "descent" to the given solar system. From these Seven Rays arise the seven sacred planets and seven non-sacred planets in esoteric astrology. Refer to *Esoteric Astrology* by Alice Bailey (available in its entirety online at http://laluni.helloyou.ws/netnews/bk/astrology/toc.html), and to the work of Dr. John Demartini of the Concourse of Wisdom School of Philosophy and Healing, Houston TX.

"upstream" (outside our solar system) in the larger cosmic picture. Such a dichotomy makes for a very interesting proposition. In short, the answers to Chiron's own wounds lie within its very orbit, so to speak. Again, the gift is in the wound.

The Chiron Cycle

When we examine Chiron's elliptical orbit (its perihelion and aphelion in Libra and Aries, respectively), map this out over time, and then correlate this with human history, we begin to see a definite cycle. Individually, this plays out over 49- to 51-year cycles in our personal lives. The elliptical nature of Chiron's orbit means that this cycle's nodal points (major transits to its natal position in our charts) differ from person to person and from generation to generation. Individually, this traces the waxing and waning of our inclination and ability to address and deal with our wounds and issues. Taken collectively, this cycle traces the waxing and waning of humanity's collective interest in, and pursuit of, spiritual matters. (By "spiritual matters," I mean wounding and healing, taken in their broadest sense).

Moreover, when the Chiron cycle is placed against the background of the ebbing and flowing of major aspects between the outer planets (including Chiron), we begin to understand why and how Chiron was discovered when it was. The tumultuous years of the 1960s constituted the fulcrum point for the subsequent reversal (in the early 1970s) of the direction of the Chiron cycle—from waning to waxing, i.e., from movement away from the Sun and toward aphelion to movement toward the Sun and perihelion. Although beyond the scope of this book, the details of this fascinating historical and astrological drama can be found online at http://www.martinlass.com/library.htm#issues.

Chiron's Musings in Relation to Body and Mind

Although we will not cover the body/mind connection in this book, it is important to know that the Chiron Paradigm in relation to body and mind asserts that *our physiology is a perfect mirror of our consciousness*. In short, in the same way that Chiron in the astrology chart mirrors our issues and wounds, all our wounds and issues can be seen upon our countenance in the form of various states of health and disease, function and dysfunction, in our tensions and relaxations, in our excesses and deficiencies, and in our postures and expressions. Such is the holographic nature of the body/mind. The body/mind, like the astrology chart, is a *mandala* of consciousness.

Put concisely, *lopsided (unbalanced, wounded) consciousness* (in the form of exaggerations and minimizations in our perceptions of the experiences of our lives, i.e., when we exaggerate Aries/Moon dualities and minimize Libra/Sun unity) *creates lopsided physiology* (in the form of hypo- (inhibition) and hyper- (activation) reactions of the sympathetic and parasympathetic nervous systems and the immune system in general).

Conversely, as we heal our consciousness—i.e., as we seek out the balancing sides of our wounds and issues and bring unity to our consciousness—so this is reflected in the healing of the body. This view is vindicated when working with the healing side of Chiron in the natal chart. Moreover, there is now ample medical and scientific evidence to support the connection between our emotional and mental states and our body's health and disease. In fact, the latest research has discovered a connection between our emotional and mental states and the activation and inhibition of our genes, manifesting in the expression or repression of various states of disease and health.[7]

In the end, we will see that *everything is about consciousness* and *consciousness is all there is.*

Moreover, if we examine the extremes of mental and emotional disorders in our society, we can see our own predicament as in a mirror, brought into sharp relief, as though looking through a powerful microscope. Chiron in the astrology chart certainly illuminates such extremes, having definite connections to mental and emotional dysfunction and to violent crime as well as to almost mystical states of illumination.

According to the Chiron Paradigm, we each have elements of every mental and emotional disease/dysfunction ever discovered and labeled. Such are the elements of our woundedness. Fragmented mental and emotional processes are the symptoms of fragmented consciousness—the dualistic consciousness of our lower nature, of our *terrestrial* nature. Again, such is the woundedness of the horse half of the centaur Chiron.

As we bring our consciousness into greater unity—by seeking the balancing sides of our issues and wounds—we reconnect with our higher human nature, with our *celestial* nature. This is ultimately reflected in the body/mind. However, such healing goes beyond the illusion of the physical (material) world we call *reality* and reconnects us with the truth of the energetic (spiritual) world that I will call *actuality.* Again, although this goes beyond the scope of this book, there is physics to support such an assertion.

Thus, the secret to healing—whether physical, emotional, mental, or spiritual—is to bring the darknesses of our psyche into the light and reintegrate them with the whole of us.

---

7. For the connection between Chiron, its discovery, and genetic research, refer to astrologer Zane B. Stein's website, *Chiron & Friends:* http://www.geocities.com/SoHo/7969/chiron.htm.

As we do so, we become increasingly balanced—physically, emotionally, mentally, and spiritually. As we approach balanced consciousness, we gradually awaken to the perfection of our lives and, thus, to the larger plan and purpose of existence. As we have said previously, this is Chiron's promise.

Chiron's Musings in Relation to the Cosmic Plan

Must we wait for healing in order to gain a glimpse of the larger plan and purpose of existence? Yes and no. Yes, inasmuch as personal experience can never be replaced by second-hand or anecdotal evidence, even when such evidence is scientifically based; no, inasmuch as the larger plan and purpose of existence can be seen anywhere and everywhere we look. We simply need the key. Chiron hints at this key.

If we expand our view of wounding and healing from the orbit of Chiron, past the body and mind, and out into the starry cosmos, we can witness a universal law, known in ancient times and only just being rediscovered. This is the law of the *One* and the *Many*.

In short, we are, individually and collectively, *consciousness as light,* descended from oneness (pre-Big Bang) into manyness (the creation, the Fall, *the wounding*). Our path then takes us from manyness back toward oneness (evolution of consciousness, Ascension, *the healing*). This cyclic movement from oneness to manyness and back to oneness can be seen in all aspects of nature as well as in innumerable ancient texts, myths, spiritual teachings, and so forth. The cycle is also called the *cosmogonic cycle*.

The story of our descent and re-ascent—our cosmogonic journey of wounding and healing—can be seen in astronomy, the physics of light, the nature of time and space, in music, in astrology (in the zodiac of the Mysteries), in mythologies, in religions, in metaphysics, and more.

The essence of the story is that *all is astronomy.* And, *all astronomy is a dance of light* (taking light in its broadest scientific sense to mean all energy in the cosmos, whether in the form of free intangible energy, i.e., spirit, or frozen tangible energy, i.e., matter). *All is light,* not just in the metaphysical sense, but in the scientific sense, too. Moreover, *all is consciousness.*

In these last statements lies the key to deciphering Chiron's musings. Our metaphysical/spiritual journey can be traced physically and energetically in the starry heavens as well as in the physics of light thereof. In this lies the original gift of astrology.

Astrology was designed as a key that joined the two sides—the physical with the metaphysical and the celestial with the terrestrial—but it has degenerated over the centuries. Moreover, like astrology, all mythologies and religions were attempts by wise beings in antiquity to put the great cosmogonic story into a form that humanity would not and could not forget. (What better place to put it than in the skies above us?) All mythologies and religious parables are analogies of astronomical events, analogies of the descent and re-ascent of consciousness as light, analogies of our metaphysical and cosmic journey of wounding and healing. However, over time, the stories have been distorted, perverted, lost, altered, misinterpreted, and/or forgotten.

Nonetheless, the key still exists. If we examine the myths and religions of such diverse places as Mesopotamia, Egypt, Greece, Polynesia, North America, South America, Great Britain, and so on, we will see the same story written before us. The myth of Chiron is but one example of this great Story of Life—and one that is relatively intact.

In Conclusion

Everywhere we look, we can see evidence of the Story of Life—our personal and cosmic journey of wounding and healing. The Chiron myth and Chiron's astrological considerations are but two examples amidst a myriad of examples. Everything in existence is a hologram of a greater picture of existence.

Moreover, every aspect of each of our individual lives represents a holographic piece of yet larger puzzles: the puzzle of our personal life as a whole as well as that of the greater life of humanity. When we deny, disown, fail to acknowledge, ignore, try to escape from, condemn, and/or try to banish certain parts of ourselves, we are wounded; we are in denial of the larger plan and purpose of the cosmos. Such are the wounds that Chiron mirrors through our natal charts.

However, when we walk willingly into our darkness, shining a light, so to speak, we gradually recover the lost pieces of our lives. Such is the healing journey that Chiron also mirrors through our natal charts. Gradually, we become whole once more, reconnect with our higher celestial nature, and take our rightful place as co-creators of this magnificent universe.

Most importantly, Chiron's higher message is that *everything is about perception*. Seeing one side of things (duality) is wounding. Seeing all sides of things (unity) is healing. As we heal, so the world around us changes, not because we have set out to change it, fix it, or get rid of the things we do not like, but because we see things differently. In short, as we heal, we increasingly see things from the eyes of love. This is the *ultimate* gift in the wound. Surely, this is a journey worth pursuing.

Having presented a vast overview of the Chiron Paradigm, it is now necessary to come back to Earth . . . or, more accurately, back to Chiron! In the material that follows, I will present the first chapter—the cornerstone—of the Chiron Paradigm: the astronomical and astrological study. In what follows, it is my ardent wish that readers will begin to be able to pull back the curtains of their psyches—the curtains shrouding the disowned and/or unloved parts of themselves and their lives—and begin (or continue) the journey back to the truth, oneness, and love from which we all came.

CHAPTER TWO

The Mythology & Symbolism of Chiron

Why are planets named the way they are? Who decides? And how is it that their new name and the symbols associated with that new name end up corresponding to the planet's innate astrological nature, themes, and influences? More specifically, how is it that Chiron's nature, themes, and influences ended up corresponding so perfectly with the mythology of its namesake?

If one were a skeptic, one would simply say that it all amounts to a kind of collective illusion—that believing makes it so, that wishful thinking allows us to focus upon supporting evidence while blindly ignoring evidence to the contrary. If we are honest and sincere in our study, we must acknowledge that this happens all the time—even in supposedly scientific circles.

However, when the accumulated evidence—not only anecdotal evidence, but statistical evidence—repeatedly affirms and reaffirms the connection between the astrological/astronomical and the mythological, even the scientifically minded person may be stumped. There is an answer to our dilemma, though, and it comes from science as well as from ancient knowledge. The answer lies in the holographic nature of the cosmos, in the illusion of the direction of time, and in the resultant illusions of cause and effect.

The latest quantum physics not only argues that the entire universe may be a giant hologram, but it argues that there is no one-way direction to time and thus no meaning to the concepts of cause and effect *except in the illusions of our consciousness.* The Chiron Paradigm concurs with this view. In fact, the Chiron Paradigm asserts that our healing journey consists in part of dissolving *blame,* which ultimately rests upon the illusions of cause and effect.

In short, Chiron's naming and its astrological nature, themes, and influences were simply a synchronistic meeting in the timeless, spaceless fabric of the actuality that lies beyond our time- and space-bound reality. From this perspective, both the following suppositions are valid: (1) Chiron's nature, themes, and influences were derived from the Chiron myth, and (2) Chiron's unseen influence more than two thousand years ago created the Chiron mythology!

In any case, before we get too far off the track into metaphysics, we can learn a great deal about the nature, themes, and influences of planet Chiron by examining the myth of Chiron.

Chiron's grandparents were Uranus and Gaia—the Sky Father/male/spiritual and Earth Mother/female/material aspects, respectively, of the descending (unified) galactic light before its entry into the egg sac of the nascent solar system (magnetosphere). Chiron was born of an illicit union between Kronos (Saturn) and Philyra (a sea nymph) or Rhea (depending on the version of the myth). Kronos represents time, and Philyra/Rhea represents space (waters, seas, lakes, ponds, oceans, etcetera, are mythic devices for the portrayal of space). That is to say, *the birth of Chiron was the birth of the illusions of time and space at the boundary (magnetopause) of the solar egg sac.*

In these few aspects, we already recognize that Chiron is symbolic of our descent—individually and collectively—as light/consciousness from the relatively more unified galactic realms into the relatively more dualistic realms of the solar system. In astrophysics, this descent was the particle decay of light at the light interphase of the solar magnetopause. In fact, the origins of the word *Chiron* and the word *chiral*—meaning the polarization (splitting) of light into right- and left-handedness—are the same! This "moment" at the solar magnetopause was an important milestone in the journey of the great wounding (also known as the Fall or the Creation).

Our innate (and, for many, unconscious) feelings of separation from our energetic (divine) origins is mirrored in the aforementioned "genealogical" descent of light,[1] as well as by Chiron's abandonment by his mother (due to her disgust at his appearance) and his disconnection from his father (he never knew his father).

Chiron lived in a cave at the base of Mount Pelion. In mythology, the cave symbol is synonymous with the idea of the underworld. The original meaning of the underworld, according to the ancient Mysteries, was the realms of consciousness (astral realms) between the Sun and the Earth—the realms in which each one of us labors for the eventual release from our seemingly endless cycles of incarnation.[2] So, again, the Chiron myth describes our further descent (wounding) from the boundary of the solar egg sac (magnetopause) into the relatively more dualistic realms of the "lower" solar system—the planetary realms and the Earth.

Chiron was a centaur—lower half horse and upper half man. This symbolizes our dual nature: a lower animal nature and a higher human nature. The lower animal nature sees the world from a more material/dualistic perspective—left/right, positive/negative, right/wrong, pain/pleasure, yes/no, yin/yang, past/future, here/there, and so forth. The higher human nature has the potential to see the world from a more unified/spiritual perspective. As centaurs in essence, each one of us has the potential to bring together Earth (lower animal dualistic nature) and Heaven (higher human unified nature). Such is the journey of healing, i.e., the re-ascent from the dualistic realms below the Sun to the relatively more unified realm of the Sun and beyond, all the way back to the boundary of the solar system (magnetopause).

Not only this, but Chiron's half-brothers were Zeus, god of the gods and symbolic of the galactic consciousness lying outside the solar egg sac, and Hades, god of the underworld. Again, Chiron represents a symbolic intersection between Heaven and Earth—between unified and polarized consciousness.

Hercules and the Lapiths (representing the "civilized" or higher human potential) were constantly battling with the centaurs as a whole (representing the "uncivilized" or lower

---

1. The genealogical aspects (and biologically impossible twists!) of many myths—the Egyptian myths being a perfect example—can be completely explained if we understand that they describe the descent and re-ascent of light/consciousness into and out of the solar system.

2. This interpretation is based on the idea that our consciousness in incarnation does not reside in the body (the body being but a diving suit donned to explore more dualistic realms), but in the electromagnetic ionospheres (metaphysically, the astral realms) between the Earth and the Sun and between the Sun and the solar magnetopause.

animal nature). In other words, there is a constant battle going on in us and in our lives between the lower, dualistic perspectives of our animal nature (that sees one side of things while ignoring or denying the other balancing sides) and our potentially higher, more unified human nature. Again, such is the journey of healing. Moreover, the Lapiths reputedly invented the bridling of horses (lower nature), the two reins symbolizing the possibility of the rider (higher nature) taming or balancing the two sides—the dualisms, the polarities—of our perceptions of the world and of ourselves.

Chiron was wounded in the leg—in his lower animal nature. Such woundedness is symbolic of the crippled way in which our animal nature sees the world, i.e., seeing one side of things to the exclusion of the other balancing sides (this propensity having its origins in the senses, nervous system, and brain, aforementioned). In short, as we have already explored, when calamities happen, we tend initially to see more pain than pleasure, and only in hindsight do we discover the benefits, blessings, lessons, gifts, and service hidden within these calamities.

Chiron was raised and tutored by Apollo, the god of the Sun,[3] light, music, poetry, healing, truth, and prophecy. In relation to the relatively "dark" realms (underworld) between the Earth and the Sun, the Sun (and any and all sun, light, or fire gods) represents the relatively more unified light of higher consciousness.

From an astrophysics perspective, the tutoring of Chiron by Apollo (or, for that matter, any descent of an Avatar to tutor or offer salvation to humanity, whether Hermes, Jesus Christ, Krishna, Coyote, Utnapishtim, Thoth, or another) *is representative of periodic solar maximums.* During solar maximums, there is an increased output of high-energy particles of light/consciousness that challenges/assists humanity to evolve—biologically as well as spiritually. From a personal perspective, it represents the spiritual guidance that becomes available to us at dark moments in our lives.

Chiron, through the tutelage of Apollo and having become a master healer himself, taught Aesclepius, the father of medicine. In everyday translation, our wounds and issues impel us to seek healing. Not only this, but we tend to see our wounds reflected in others, sometimes inspiring a wish to heal others (hence the wounded healer symbolism). As we endeavor to heal others, so we better understand ourselves and better understand our

---

3. Some archaeologists and historians will argue that Apollo was never a sun god and that we have confused him with Helios. Whether this be true or not, Apollo was certainly the god of light, indicative of his higher spiritual nature.

predicament (as in a mirror), thus healing ourselves. As we heal, so we are inspired to pass the torch, so to speak. In this lies the perfect symbolism for the collective ascending octaves of healing and evolution of consciousness—whether of humanity or of consciousness beyond our limited planetary sphere.

In an extraordinary arrangement with Zeus, Chiron exchanged his immortality for the release of Prometheus, the god of fire. Prometheus, symbolizing the fire of the spirit and the human potential for a return to spirit (the first step of which is the attainment of Sun consciousness), was chained to a rock by Zeus and condemned to having his liver pecked out daily by a monstrous gryphon. During the night, the liver would grow back and the cycle would repeat itself seemingly endlessly.

The liver is the seat of the emotions—the seat of the lower animal nature, which sees the world in terms of dualities (as opposed to the heart center, which is the seat of our higher human nature). The daily pecking out is symbolic of our seemingly endless cycles of mortal incarnations. Chiron agreed to sacrifice his immortality—*actually, to sacrifice his seemingly endless cycles of incarnations and his attachment to the dualistic illusions of the lower nature*—in exchange for the release of Prometheus, i.e., for the release/Ascension of the human nature back to more unified realms. Such is the healing journey, as we have said.

After nine days in Hades, representing a kind of life review and reconciliation, Chiron was immortalized in the constellation of Sagittarius. Sagittarius, lying in the direction of the galactic core, beyond the time/space illusions of the solar egg sac, represents the greater truth, oneness, and love of the galactic core consciousness from which the solar system was birthed. The healing journey was complete.

Interestingly, Chiron married Thea, a water goddess, their marriage representing the reunion of soul mates—mirroring the reunion of the male/spiritual and female/material aspects of creation, which is the ultimate healing. Thea, too, ascended to the stars, becoming the constellation of the flying horse, Pegasus. In mythology, the flying horse, alongside birds, boats, chariots, and other mythic devices, represents the spirit traveling through the astral realms—the "waters" of space—on its descending (wounding) and/or ascending (healing) journey.

In conclusion, we can see that the entire Chiron myth is nothing more or less than a symbolic retelling of our personal and cosmic journey of wounding and healing. Let's keep the elements of this story in mind when we are exploring the astrological meaning of the planet Chiron, as it will illuminate many of the topics we will cover.

CHAPTER THREE

The Discovery of Chiron

Chiron's Planetary Characteristics

Although Chiron was initially considered a planetoid—a small or *minor* planet—it is now considered a "cometary body."[1] (Some astrologers, however, still call it an "asteroid.") At 190–250 miles in diameter, it is the largest periodic comet in the solar system—some 10,000 times the mass of Halley's Comet. Chiron was discovered on November 1, 1977.[2] (See Chart 1—The Birth of Chiron.)

Some astronomers have suggested that Chiron may have been "captured" by our Sun while passing through the neighborhood of our solar system and, furthermore, that it may not remain within our solar system for an indefinite time. Another suggestion is that Chiron may be a stray from the Kuiper Belt of objects that orbit beyond Neptune, some

---

1. Ken Croswell, "The Changing Face of Chiron," *New Scientist* 1731 (August 25, 1990), http://www. newscientist.com. Extract: "When astronomers discovered Chiron between the orbits of Saturn and Uranus in 1977, they thought it was an asteroid in a very strange orbit. But in the past few years, this odd object has begun to look like a gigantic comet."

2. Chiron was discovered by Charles T. Kowal of the Hale Observatories at Pasadena, California, at about 10:00 AM on November 1, 1977.

1,000 AU[3] from the Sun.[4] If this is the case, then Chiron is the largest of a group of cometary bodies strayed from the Kuiper Belt collectively referred to as *the Centaurs,* all of which have their orbits in the outer solar system.[5]

If the preceding is true, and Chiron is a "stray" from outside the solar system proper, then this has some interesting ramifications that will be explored shortly. Suffice it to say, it appears that Chiron's origin is related to the origins of Pluto (also considered a cometary body) and maybe even Neptune by way of the Kuiper Belt.

Whatever the finer details of Chiron's origin may be, it appears that Chiron is a celestial visitor—perhaps temporary, but definitely timely.

(Note: For astrological purposes, we will refer to Chiron as a "planet," as is the astrological custom.)

Chiron's orbit is quite eccentric when considered from a planetary perspective. Not so from a cometary viewpoint. Its orbit, which has a period of between 49 and 51 years, is tipped steeply in relation to the plane of the ecliptic: 6.9° to be exact. Its orbit is also very elliptical. If zero is a circle and 1.0 is a line, then Chiron's orbit has an ellipticity of 0.3786. The next nearest to this are Pluto at 0.2482 and Mercury at 0.2056.

From an astrological point of view, Chiron's ellipticity means that it does not spend an equal amount of time in each sign of the zodiac. Chiron's shortest transit of a sign occurs in Libra—about 1.75 years. The longest transit of a sign occurs in Aries—about 8.25 years. The ramifications of this unequal transit of the zodiac signs will be explored shortly, as will the ramifications of eccentricity and ellipticity of planetary orbits in general.

To confuse matters even more, Chiron's orbit, primarily between Saturn and Uranus, sometimes wanders inside the orbit of Saturn.

All of the preceding is significant when one considers the soul's journey of awakening as a passage from the innermost planets to the outermost.

Overall, Chiron appears to be somewhat of a rogue in the general scheme of the solar system. For this reason, some early astrologers gave Chiron the keyword *maverick.*

---

3. Astronomical Units. One AU is a measurement of distance corresponding to the mean distance between the Sun and the Earth.

4. See NASA's website: http://nssdc.gsfc.nasa.gov/planetary/chiron.html.

5. For more information on the Centaurs, refer to the work of Zane B. Stein at his website, *Chiron & Friends:* http://www.geocities.com/SoHo/7969/chiron.htm.

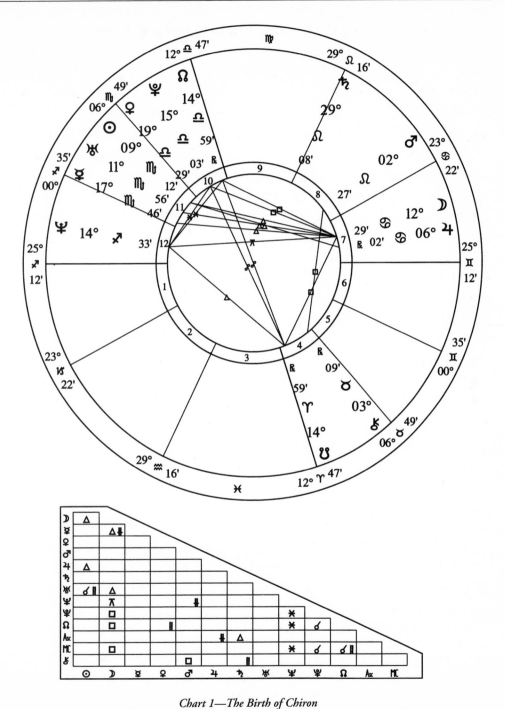

Chart 1—The Birth of Chiron
November 1, 1977 / 9:56 AM PST +8:00 / Pasadena, CA, USA
34°N05', 118°W09' / Geocentric Tropical Zodiac / Koch Houses / True Node

Interpreting Chiron's Planetary Characteristics

Chiron's aforementioned planetary characteristics can help us begin to draw a picture of Chiron's astrological influence. The most relevant points are (1) Chiron's highly elliptical orbit, (2) its degree of inclination from the ecliptic (declination), (3) its possible association with the Kuiper Belt and its energetic origin, and (4) its erratic orbit between Jupiter/Saturn, and Uranus/Neptune. Let's look at each of these in turn.

(1) Chiron's highly elliptical orbit means that it spends more time at one end of the zodiac than the other. It spends the least time in Libra and the most time in Aries. The cycle of its apparent acceleration and slowing will be discussed later in terms of the generational cycles of healing and spirituality that correspond to this movement (chapter 5, "Life Cycles"). Suffice it to say, due to its elliptical orbit, Chiron tends to exaggerate and express Arian characteristics while minimizing and repressing Libran characteristics.

We will take the view of Arian and Libran characteristics according to the zodiac of the Mysteries, mentioned in chapter 1. This view asserts that Aries represents the height of material consciousness, individuality, fragmentedness, disconnection, and aloneness. Aries is associated with the Moon and our dualistic *lower* nature. Libra, according to this same view, represents the ultimate balance of consciousness, where we are awakened to our unity and divinity. Libra is associated with the Sun and our potentially unified *higher* nature.

Thus, from the point of view of the Mysteries, Chiron exaggerates and expresses separation, isolation, aloneness, fragmentation, duality, lopsidedness, individualization, abandonment, deprivation, rejection, and diffusion of consciousness (the material/emotional, Moon-centered perspective—we will explore the connection between Chiron and the Moon later). Conversely, Chiron minimizes and represses connectedness, togetherness, wholeness, balance, unity, oneness with everything, belonging, nurturing, being wanted, being loved, and the focusing of consciousness (the spiritual, Sun-centered perspective).

Chiron's elliptical orbit also means that it spends more time *farther* from the Sun than *closer* to the Sun. This, again, translates into a feeling of woundedness—a feeling of being denied "full time in the Sun." The place and importance of the Sun in the planetary healing journey and the relation of this to Chiron will be discussed shortly.

In summary, Chiron, from the apparent view, exaggerates and expresses woundedness and minimizes and represses healing. Having said this, it is important to note that woundedness and healing are *perceptions*. A truer formulation would be that Chiron accentuates the *perception of woundedness* and understates the *perception of healing* in our lives.

Herein lies the essence of our earthly journey. To a greater or lesser degree, we come into life with a growing sense of being separate, cut-off, isolated, alone, fragmented, without meaning, without direction, in chaos, forsaken, abandoned, and/or without love. Such feelings grow during the first part of our lives, primarily (but not exclusively) from birth to about age thirty-six. This is the "descending," incarnational journey (of the smaller cosmogonic cycle of our present lifetimes). How we express or repress these feelings in our lives depends on who we are (in essence), where we come from (meaning past lives), why we are here (our calling), and where we are going (our destiny). The specific nature of our individual woundedness can be seen in the sign, house, aspects, and travel of Chiron in the natal chart.

Our woundedness engenders an innate drive toward connectedness, togetherness, wholeness, unity, oneness with everything, belonging, nurturing, being wanted, being loved, finding meaning, finding direction, finding harmony, finding balance, finding inner peace, and finding love. This drive expresses itself increasingly in our lives, primarily (but not exclusively) from the age of thirty-six to seventy-two and beyond. This is the "ascending," "ex-carnational" journey (of the smaller cosmogonic cycle of our present lifetimes).

The specific ways in which we strive for these things—broadly called *healing,* according to our paradigm—can also be seen in the sign, house, aspects, and travel of Chiron in the natal chart.

There are two caveats to the preceding. First, we must remember that any single planet is but a part of a larger astrological picture that represents a hologram of our lives and us; the chart reading process seeks to integrate each planet into that larger picture. Second, different people react differently and to different degrees to the same planetary influences; the mechanisms that make this so—the differing conditions of *opacity, translucence,* and *transparency* to planetary influences—will be discussed later.

(2) Chiron's degree of inclination from the ecliptic (declination) makes it somewhat of a rogue in the solar system, and gives it an unusual perspective, aligning it with Uranus and Pluto in many ways.

Astrological studies of both ellipticity and angular inclination of planetary orbits show that these features exaggerate a planet's astrological influence. This, combined with the size of the orbit, gives a starting point for an appraisal of comparative planetary influences.

Let's consider the solar system a unified Being of higher consciousness. The planets are its major *personas,* revolving around a central *essence,* i.e., the Sun. From this perspective, ellipticity, angular inclination, and orbital size determine the degree of *polarization* of the consciousness of the planetary personas. Greater ellipticity, angular inclination, and orbital size result in greater extremes of expression, greater nonconformity of viewpoints, and greater influence overall, compared to the other planets. *From this perspective, comets such as Chiron represent some of the solar system's most extreme emotional expressions.*

Moreover, Chiron's degree of angular inclination (as well as the aforementioned orbital ellipticity) suggests that it is somewhat of a loner. At the same time, it receives a different perspective from its conformist planetary siblings who keep to the more socially acceptable tracts of the solar ecliptic. There is much time for deep and solitary introspection.

(3) Chiron's possible association with the Kuiper Belt is also an interesting point. To understand why, we must understand the origins of planetary bodies and their orbits; we must understand the *Seven Rays*.[6]

Recent astrophysical discoveries concur with ancient metaphysical knowledge concerning the origins of solar systems. The origin of our solar system is a "cone" of light originating from the galactic center,[7] which is diffracted/diffused by seven constellations as it "descends" into the Seven Rays of creation. Each of the seven sacred planets and seven non-sacred planets of esoteric astrology[8] is associated with one of these Rays.

The diffraction, deflection, and/or reflection of each Ray on its "descending" journey accounts for the orbital characteristics of each planet. The more diffraction, deflection, and/or reflection of a Ray there is, the more extreme and nonconformist are the orbits of its associated planets. In addition, subsequent astrophysical calamities—such as planetary collisions—can affect a planet's orbital characteristics (psychologically corresponding to traumatic experiences).

Apart from the Seven Rays and their associated planets, our solar system also hosts planets and other celestial bodies, such as some comets, *that have their origin not directly from the galactic center.* Some of these planets and bodies are *secondary reflections* of the original cone of light of our own solar system. Still others come from Rays that have been deflected, reflected, or diffracted *from other Rays of other solar systems apart from ours.* The latter represent the interactions of consciousness between star systems.

---

6. Refer to the book *Esoteric Astrology* by Alice Bailey (available in its entirety on-line at http://laluni.helloyou.ws/netnews/bk/astrology/toc.html). In addition, refer to the work of Dr. John Demartini of the Concourse of Wisdom School of Philosophy and Healing, Houston, TX.

7. During the quasar stage of a galaxy, which is half of a larger quasar/black hole cycle.

8. There are seven non-sacred planets according to Dr. John Demartini, but *five* non-sacred planets according to Alice Bailey.

Such bodies of "foreign" celestial consciousness enjoy the benefit of "seeing" our solar system from an outsider's perspective. Although on the one hand they are extreme emotional expressions, on the other hand they are like impartial observers and/or challenging interactions. The benefits of considering the views of such interstellar-originating immigrants, such as Chiron and Pluto may be, are then obvious.

(4) Chiron's erratic orbit, although primarily tracing a path between Uranus and Saturn, periodically "waves a hand'" at Jupiter and Neptune. (Chiron periodically crosses Saturn's orbit, and it periodically encroaches upon Uranus's inner orbit.) This is indicative of the wide scope of ideology and experience that is available to Chiron. If we consider the affairs of these other planets, we will begin to see that Chiron represents a kind of bridge between them—a bridge between levels of consciousness.

The bridge from Saturn to Uranus is a bridge from the crystallized (and often dead and outmoded) structures of the establishment or the status quo and new and revelatory ways of looking at things. Saturn represents the protective boundary of consensus reality. It relies upon tangibles and so-called facts. It is the material perspective.

Uranus, on the other hand, challenges us to see beyond our narrow and blinkered ideas, beliefs, and attachments. It challenges us to attain a higher and broader perspective on our lives and on the world at large—to see how each piece of the puzzle has a place and a purpose, beyond our naïve judgments of right and wrong, good and evil, and positive and negative.

The challenges of Chiron's interaction with Jupiter are (1) to move beyond exaggerated and infantile action and reaction, and to strive for a more mature attitude toward responsibility and hard work in relation to our healing and evolution of consciousness; (2) to uncover the Inner Child aspects of ourselves, which have been covered, repressed, forgotten, ignored, and/or otherwise negatively condemned by our woundedness; (3) to awaken to, acknowledge, and embrace our innate knowledge and wisdom; and (4) to balance our perceptions of positives and negatives—i.e., our dualistic illusions—thus revealing the perfection of our lives.

The challenges of Chiron's interaction with Neptune are (1) to move beyond the necessity for obtuse and contrary reactions to challenges and confrontation in favor of seeing the unity of seemingly opposite viewpoints (this is compassion, in its truest sense); 2) to resolve fundamentalist and simplistic thinking and apparent paradoxes into unified and all-encompassing, heartfelt understanding; and (3) to move beyond the tendency and need for definition and dualistic ideation, and to merge into the unified and silent space of truth and love. (Each of these three points is simply a different facet of the same challenge: to move from polarized emotions and thoughts into unconditional love.)

In a sense, Chiron's message would be sufficient if it only served to illuminate and bring the issues of Saturn, Uranus, Jupiter, and Neptune into a more unified understanding. As it happens, it does this and more. The resolution/synthesis/unification of all these issues brings a new level of consciousness—a broader and more inclusive understanding, not only of the themes and ideas associated with the outer planets, but of those of the inner planets, too.

Chiron's Place in the Solar System

According to ancient knowledge and supported by the latest astrophysical discoveries and theories, the creation of the solar system—the *descent,* the Fall, the *involution* of consciousness, the *wounding*—consists of light/consciousness journeying from the galactic core to our local stellar neighborhood, "fanning" out and resolving itself into the primeval planets. Then, from each of the planets, the light/consciousness is focused toward an *ascending* confluence that we call the Sun. Having risen to the Sun, the light/consciousness then ascends through the remaining planets, encompassing each on its journey, all the way back to the boundary of the solar system (magnetopause). This is the *ascension,* the Return to Grace, the *evolution* of consciousness, the *healing*. From here, the light continues its ascent, ultimately rejoining with the galactic core consciousness.

The "descending" portal from the spiritual realms (outer planets) to the material realms (inner planets) is Saturn. Conversely, the "ascending" portal from the material realms back toward the spiritual realms is facilitated by the Sun.

In short, we must resolve our Saturn issues (encapsulating all the issues of the inner planets) in order to pass through the Sun portal and thus return to higher consciousness (the outer planets and beyond). Chiron, being the gateway beyond Saturn, is the key—the bridge to higher consciousness (broadly called healing).

Further understanding can be gained by recalling that mythical Chiron was fostered by Apollo, the Sun/light god. Recall, also, Chiron's eventual return to galactic space (in the constellation of Sagittarius, i.e., toward the galactic core)—space/consciousness *beyond* the mythical Saturn (Kronos) and ruled by mythical Uranus, the Sky Father.

The Historical Picture Leading Up to Chiron's Birth

We can gain further insight into Chiron's own nature and into why its discovery and influences are so important for the evolution of the consciousness of humanity by looking at the historical picture leading up to Chiron's discovery alongside the unprecedented conflagration of outer-planet aspects during this time. Unfortunately, this goes beyond the scope of this book, but this information and research are available online at http://www.martinlass.com/library.htm#issues.

Chiron's Birth

We can also gain further insight into Chiron and its influences by studying its "natal" chart—i.e., the chart for when it was discovered. (See Chart 1—The Birth of Chiron, at the beginning of this chapter.) Again, this goes beyond the scope of this book, but a chart delineation of Chiron's birth is available online at http://www.martinlass.com/chironbirth.mhtml.

CHAPTER FOUR

Friends, Associations & Rulers

Let's distill the essence of what we have discussed so far and add yet other issues and themes to our tapestry by exploring some of Chiron's zodiac friends and associations, and some candidate signs for its rulership.

Saturn as Master Trainer

Saturn prepares the way for an introduction to Chiron. Without Saturn's strict training and discipline, the path to Chiron is either closed or precarious and uncertain. The placement of Saturn in the natal chart, its aspects thereof, and its transiting relationships in our lives determine the possibilities and opportunities for approaching Chiron at any given time in our lives. Whether we take up the opportunities and explore the possibilities is up to us.

The relationship of Saturn to Chiron—placement, aspect, and transit—in the natal chart, in transit to the natal chart, and in real-time aspect at any given time will also determine these same opportunities and possibilities.

The question arises, then . . . is it possible that a person may not have favorable opportunities and possibilities of approaching Chiron due to the nature of his or her natal chart and the subsequent lifetime transits (or lack thereof) of Saturn and Chiron? To answer this, we must remember that the picture of planetary influences in relation to our lives is a holographic picture, i.e., the planets mirror our consciousness, and our consciousness is mirrored in the planets; we could say that our consciousness before incarnation *attracts* us to a particular point in time and space that corresponds to our issues and thus we are born. Furthermore, what we might normally classify as "unfavorable" aspects and transits, when looked at from a higher perspective, offer the same opportunities and possibilities as any others. The challenge is to see the *forms* these opportunities and possibilities take, which, in and of itself, is an integral part of our healing and evolutionary journey; it is all about the awakening of higher consciousness. The differences from one chart to the next lie merely in the *forms* that the inherent opportunities and possibilities take. This is what astrology seeks to reveal.

The healing journey begins with Saturn because Saturn is the ruler of forms. It is an interesting paradox, then, that Saturn provides the tools—the practical steppingstones—we require to move beyond the illusion of forms. However, in order to derive the maximum benefit from Saturn, the required steps must be taken consciously and intentionally. If Chiron is the portal to the outer planets, then Saturn is the gatekeeper.

Saturn's requirements in this respect are responsibility, seriousness, discipline, intention, resolve, attention, focus, persistence, steadfastness, and effort. Remembering that these are the foundation stones of the healing journey represented by Chiron, let's summarize each stone, so to speak.

Responsibility (for Our Lives) and the End of Blame

- We each play a part in creating the circumstances and events of our lives.
- Forgiveness is a steppingstone on this path.
- Beyond forgiveness, we learn to love our lives and love others just as they are.
- The outside world is a perfect reflection of our consciousness.
- We get back what we put out—no more, no less.

Seriousness (Regarding Our Healing and Evolution of Our Consciousness)

- Requirement to cease running away from, avoiding, making light of, and/or ignoring the whisperings of our spiritual hearts.

- Requirement to take stock of our lives and ourselves—past, present, and future.

- Requirement of self-study.

Discipline

- Anything worth pursuing is worth pursuing in a disciplined way.

- Sporadic efforts bring sporadic results; consistent efforts over time bring long-term and permanent results.

- Requirement to apply practical skills and methods to spiritual pursuits.

- Saturn impels us to become more disciplined about our spiritual paths when restrictions, limitations, meaninglessness, missingness, boredom, ill health, and/or adversity force us to reassess our priorities.

Intention to Pursue Healing and Evolution of Consciousness

- Nothing conscious happens without intention.

- Without intention, we are subject to the intentions of others.

Resolve

- Lack of intention can result in challenging and adverse circumstances and events.

- Confronted by such circumstances and events, we are impelled to make a resolve concerning our healing and evolution of consciousness.

Attention

- Attention is one of the major keys for healing and evolution of consciousness.

- Without consciously directed attention, we are slaves to our lower nature—slaves to life, to others, and to every passing emotion or thought.

- Attention is the muscle we must develop in order to master our lives.

- Lack of conscious attention brings chaotic consciousness and, ultimately, a breakdown of physiology.
- Without the development of conscious attention, we cannot approach our wounds and issues, through which the gifts of our lives are revealed.
- Focused attention is the key to *presence,* which is the key to transcending the illusions of the lower mind—the key to healing and evolution of consciousness.

Focus

- Focus arises from the conscious use of attention (applied with intention) toward a specific goal or purpose.
- The understanding of such a goal or purpose comes with responsibility, seriousness, discipline, attention, and resolve toward self-study.
- Focus represents relatively unified and awakened consciousness acknowledging its goal or purpose of healing and evolution of consciousness.

Persistence

- Only through persistence can a true and permanent change of being (awakening) occur.
- Persistence means seeing challenges, adversities, and setbacks as the opportunities and milestones of healing and evolution of consciousness.
- The fuel for persistence comes from acknowledging our heart's deepest wish: the wish for healing and evolution of consciousness.

Steadfastness

- Steadfastness is the act of holding the knowing in our spiritual hearts in the forefront of our consciousness, in the face of all outside circumstances, and despite the protestations of our lower nature.
- Ultimately, the knowing in our spiritual hearts is love. Steadfastness is the steady and continued acknowledgment of love.

Effort

- Effort is Saturn's currency.

- Without plain hard work, nothing of value can be achieved.

- Wounding is effortless (reactions), taking us ever further into duality, whereas healing is effortful (actions), bringing us ever closer to unity, truth, and love.

- Effort challenges our lower-natured illusions; it shines light into the darkness; it brings the wound into view, helping us grow, heal, and evolve.

To repeat, Saturn is the gatekeeper to the outer planets. We must apply Saturn's aforementioned keys in order to access our wounds and issues. Once accessed, Chiron will assist our healing and evolution of consciousness, allowing us to further access the outer planets.

And yet, having said this, the wound itself—the domain of Chiron—ever drives us toward our destiny, our higher purpose, and our divine design. At a certain point, Chiron inevitably drives us up against Saturn. We reach an impasse of consciousness, more often than not reflected in an impasse in our external lives (often reflected in Saturn transits). At this point, we are impelled to reassess our relationship to Saturnian issues and themes in our lives and to get serious about our journey of healing and evolution of consciousness.

The Moon and Chiron

The Moon is the emotional expression of our dualistic lower nature, formed in childhood as a response to our lopsided perceptions and reactions to the world around us (which have their basis in the nature of the senses, nervous system, and brain). *As such, the Moon is inherently the expression-vehicle for our woundedness. It is Chiron's face seen through our lower nature, so to speak.*

Our lower emotional expressions (Moon) ultimately have their origins in our woundedness (Chiron). Conversely, our woundedness is *expressed* in the mirror of our Moon-ruled lower nature. As we can see, the two planets are integrally linked.

The Moon represents, to a large degree, the routes of "escape" and avoidance we take when things get too difficult to deal with in our lives—when our wounds and issues become too painful and/or confronting.

This brings us to an important point: every apparent escape route or avoidance tactic *has inherent within it all the elements—factors, circumstances, and environment—required for the healing journey.* This applies equally to all Moon placements.

On the one hand, the Moon represents a kind of governor, regulating the degree of awakening and truth we are capable of dealing with at any given time; the Moon protects us and wraps us up in cotton wool.

On the other hand, the Moon takes us, by virtue of our attracting and repelling "charges" —the personas/emotions/perspectives of the lower nature—into situations, circumstances, and environments where our wounds and issues will invariably be illuminated, thus encouraging healing and resolution.

Said another way, *the healing path is already contained within the wound.* If Chiron *drives* us by virtue of our wounds and issues (i.e., our voids and values), then the Moon, through our lower emotional "charges," *steers* us along that path.

As our wounds are healed and our issues resolved, the expression of the Moon changes, reflecting the evolution of our lower nature; we align to a higher octave of the Moon's expression. Moreover, as we heal, we gradually transcend the Moon; said another way, we become the masters of the Moon—the masters of our emotional nature. As masters of our emotional nature, we are then free to make use of the palette of emotional colors in the pursuit of our life's path/purpose/calling/destiny.

Said yet another way, as we master our emotional (lower) nature, initially the realm of the Moon, our emotional nature increasingly enters the realm of the Sun—i.e., it becomes more unified, coherent, conscious, intentional, and self-determined. From being unconsciously *reactive* and Moon-ruled, our emotional nature becomes Sun-ruled and consciously *active.* Emotions—being but conditional fragments of unconditional love—are synthesized/merged/transformed into love. In this way, our healing journey takes us to our divinely designed life's purpose and the outward expression and manifestation of this. This brings us to another point . . .

The other aspect of the Moon that is connected to Chiron is the Moon's nodes. On the one hand, the North Node represents the direction of our lives—our destiny, purpose, goal, aim, major lesson, and so forth, as well as our gifts, talents, and service to the planet. On the other hand, the South Node tells us where we have come from and what gifts, talents, lessons, issues, wounds, and so forth that we bring with us into this lifetime. Because our wounds, indicated by Chiron, drive us *toward* our life's path/purpose/calling/destiny and *toward* the expression and manifestation of our divine design (by virtue of our voids and values), thus Chiron is connected to the Moon's nodes.

Again, Chiron drives and the Moon steers. Chiron is the *experience* of our woundedness, the Moon itself is the *expression* of our woundedness, and the Moon's nodes outline the past (South Node) and future (North Node) of our healing/evolutionary journey.

The Virgo/Pisces Polarity

The polarity of the zodiac signs of Virgo and Pisces holds many keys to understanding Chiron and its issues and themes inasmuch as these signs epitomize both wounding and healing.

Perhaps the most important theme of Virgo and Pisces in relation to Chiron is the law of the One and the Many (the cosmogonic cycle), aforementioned. Traditionally speaking, Virgo represents the height of fragmentation, separateness, and discreteness—the mass of innumerable disconnected data in need of synthesis. On the other hand, the positive aspect of Virgo entails this very synthesis, without leaving out any seemingly small or insignificant details. Attention to detail, as a pursuit, is practical, pragmatic, and down-to-earth, not to mention it being a factor in healthy cynicism. Such are the earthy foundation stones required if we are to sail in the heavens.

Pisces, traditionally speaking, represents the *loss* of fragmentation, separateness, and discreteness, i.e., the merging into a singular and undifferentiated mass unconsciousness. The positive side of Pisces is the *conscious* merging back into oneness, wholeness, truth, and unconditional love. This is the result of the healing journey.

The law of the One and the Many says that, on all scales from the microcosm to macrocosm, the universe is comprised of cycles of oneness becoming manyness and then returning to oneness. Our journey from spirit into matter (the wounding, Pisces to Virgo) and the return to spirit (the healing, Virgo to Pisces) is a manifestation of this law.

Virgo separates and defines—the act of dualistic perception, without which the world as we know it would not exist. Differentiation is one of Virgo's keywords. This separating and differentiating process fragments our consciousness and is the essence of the wounding.

At the same time, however, the world—the creation—is built upon this duality. For any act of creation, the greater the detail envisioned, the more firm and long-lasting its manifestation.

The difference between the two manifestations—differentiation as a symptom of wounding and differentiation required for creation—lies in our states of consciousness and in our respective places in the cosmogonic cycle. On the one hand, differentiation as wounding happens on the descending journey; we are *unawakened* or *innocent angels.* Our descent into creation offers us the opportunity to *awaken* our consciousness through the mirror of duality. On the other hand, differentiation required for creation happens on the ascending journey; we are *awakened* or *experienced angels,* now assisting in the co-creation of the world.

At the other end of the polarity, Pisces *merges* and dispenses with definition. It recognizes that truth has no words, no definitions, and no names. However, the two sides of the Piscean paradox are represented by the *unconscious* and *conscious* aspects of merging. The unconscious side is *pre-awakening*—our consciousness as *innocent* angels. The conscious side is *awakened* merging—our consciousness as *experienced* angels. This latter case is the essence of the healing.

The wounding, seen through Virgo, is mirror-reflected in Pisces. Through Virgo, the wounding is experienced as fragmentation, differentiation, and consciousness-isolating specialization. Through Pisces, the wounding is experienced as a penchant for feeling like a victim to outside circumstances. The wish for a return to oneness in the face of the fragmentation of our consciousness often leads us into self-pity, into "poor me" reactions, and into feelings of powerlessness. The theme of surrendering to a higher power is also associated with this Pisces reflection.

On the other hand, the theme of surrendering to a higher power—the healing journey—is mirror-reflected in the Virgo theme of responsibility and attention to small matters. If we forget the small things and the details, we leave behind the very things that comprise the totality of the unified consciousness we seek. Therefore, one of Virgo's higher octave themes is *inclusion,* i.e., including increasingly more into our conscious awareness. All things are connected; *how* they are connected is the Virgo question. This question unconsciously drives the healer to explore all possible connections between body systems and between body, mind, and soul. This is the path of *synthesis*—of connecting the dots. Again, this is the healing journey.

Virgo consciousness seeks to "get it right"—to master a thing or process to the "nth" degree. All things must be in balance. This requires focus, attention, concentration, and intention. It requires that we are awake to each and every detail. Like Saturn, the sign of Virgo is the training ground for self-mastery and for us as potential co-creators. When we "get it right," we can then merge (Pisces) back into oneness *without losing ourselves.* The eternal paradox of the One and the Many remains within us, but as *awakened* or *experienced* beings of light.

Lastly, the polarity of Virgo and Pisces represents the Earth-focused cynic and the Heaven-focused faithful adherent, respectively. The Earth-focused cynic denies that anything exists outside what can be touched, seen, smelled, heard, or tasted. In our denial, we cut ourselves off from an awareness of our inherent divinity. We remain in a state of fragmentation that is filled with dualistic illusions.

Conversely, the Heaven-focused faithful adherent denies the efficacy and reality of all things of the visible world. In our denial, we cut ourselves off from the possibility and potential of true awakening to our divine nature. We remain in an undifferentiated sleep state that is filled with fantasy and dream images. In this state, we are unable to fulfill our ultimate role as budding co-creators. The complementary opposites of Virgo and Pisces epitomize the nature of our woundedness.

Having said this, we *require* both these zodiac personas for balanced consciousness to be born. The cynic keeps us practical and earthed and guards against blind faith and susceptibility. The faithful adherent continually challenges the cynic within us—challenges the illusions of the dualistic material world.

Ultimately, we will awaken to the truth that we are spirit *and* matter, One *and* Many. One side cannot exist without the other. Our focus (perception) on one side of the equation, to the exclusion of the other side, epitomizes our woundedness. *Realizing that we are both One and Many is part of the healing journey.* Here, the illusory paradox of the Virgo/Pisces polarity dissolves and a higher understanding is revealed. Nothing has changed . . . the One has not become the Many. Neither has the Many become the One. We have merely awakened to our true nature, which is inherently both One and Many, simultaneously.

The 6th/12th-House Polarity

The polarity of the 6th and 12th houses also expresses Chironic themes and issues. Perhaps the most important theme is that of the paradox of the *inner* and the *outer.* The 6th house essentially remains inwardly focused. It is the final stop of the inwardly focused lower hemisphere of the natural zodiac. The 12th house essentially remains outwardly focused. It is the final stop of the outwardly focused upper hemisphere of the natural zodiac. At the 6th house, we sit at the threshold of the acknowledgment of the *other*—the outside world— that lies just beyond the anaretic degree to the 7th house. (The anaretic degree is the final degree of a house or sign before it transitions into the next house or sign.) At the 12th house, we sit on the threshold of acknowledgment of our individuality when we pass beyond the anaretic degree to the 1st house.

Yet, paradoxically, in the 6th house, we are concerned with the manifest world around us, and, in the 12th house, we are concerned with the world within us, beyond the senses. In the 6th house, we see the outside world and ultimately recognize it as a reflection of ourselves. In the 12th house, we see our inner world and ultimately recognize it as a reflection of the outside world. Neither inner nor outer makes sense without the other. Which is real? Inner or outer? Neither, on their own. Taken together, we finally begin to taste the truth that lies beyond our illusory reality.

The 6th house is the house of the *tangible,* and the 12th, the house of the *intangible.* The parallels to the Virgo/Pisces polarity are obvious, as these are the natural signs of their respective natural houses.

How does all this relate to Chironic themes? Chiron, as we have seen, represents the borderline, the potential bridge between consciousness turned upon itself, in denial of a greater reality (the *other*), and consciousness turned outward, seeking contact and connection to a greater reality, as represented by the outer planets and beyond. At this threshold, we are as children, suddenly realizing that the world is not just for us. We realize that there are other consciousnesses around us, interacting with us.

This act of perception is, paradoxically, an integral part of the wounding *and* the healing. As the wounding, the act of perception is a process of separation, differentiation, definition, and consciousness-isolating specialization. As part of the healing journey, the act of perception is an acknowledgment of higher consciousness, ever including more within our concentric sphere of awareness.

The paradox of the One and the Many is similarly encapsulated in the 6th/12th-house polarity. From the 12th to the 1st house, the One becomes the Many again (individuality as a manifestation of the Many). From the 6th to the 7th house, the Many (fragmented individuality) becomes the One again (realization of the connectedness to others in an inseparable, symbiotic relationship).

The two hemispheres of the natural zodiac—lower and upper, culminating in the 6th and 12th houses, respectively—are but two halves of a greater truth. Like yin and yang, each complements the other *and contains elements of the other*. The seeds of fragmentation are contained in the upper hemisphere with a separation of consciousness into *self* and *other*. The seeds of unity are contained in the lower hemisphere with the realization that the universe is contained *within us*. Resolving the paradox is the Chironic journey of healing.

On a more practical note, the 6th house, traditionally being the house of work, methodology, healing, and service, provides the solid basis for the *inclusion* and *synthesis* required for ultimate awakening to our inherent oneness and divinity. The 12th house, traditionally being the house of the psyche, the unconsciousness, the isolated, the repressed, the domination of the unseen collective, and so forth, provides the material and environment that inspires soul-searching. Such soul-searching will inevitably awaken us to our *individual* value, purpose, and place in the larger plan. Again, both halves of the equation are necessary for the healing journey as outlined by Chiron.

The Anaretic Degree

So, what about the anaretic degree itself? Moreover, what is its relation to Chiron?

Traditionally, the anaretic degree, being the final degree in a given zodiac sign or house, represents the point where transcendence and evolution *must* take place; otherwise, recapitulation—cyclic repetition—will occur. In this way, the anaretic degree is related to the point where one octave becomes a new octave; it is also related to Pluto.

Issues and themes are brought to a head in this degree, demanding attention and resolution. A quantum leap of consciousness is required to push us through into the next concentric sphere of consciousness. The anaretic degree shines a light on all unresolved, undissolved, and unhealed aspects of the issues at hand. It brings our repressed issues into sharp relief. *In Chiron terms, the anaretic degree represents the alchemical retort in which all elements are made visible, allowing healing to take place.*

The discovery of Chiron was preceded in the 1950s and the 1960s by a virtual anaretic degree: the melting-pot turmoil of these years. Having pushed through this degree, we are now blessed with the emergence of the new paradigms we are exploring in this book.

The Transition from Virgo to Libra

We have spoken about the transition from Virgo to Libra and from the 6th to the 7th house in terms that are more traditional. Let's now look at it from the perspective of the aforementioned zodiac of the Mysteries. When we consider this transition, we must take into account the issues we have previously discussed: the symbolism of the lower and upper hemispheres, the self and the other, the anaretic degree, the Virgo penchant for attention to detail, and inclusion as a principle. When we do, we can begin to glimpse the original meanings of Virgo and Libra, according to the Mysteries.

Virgo, according to the zodiac of the Mysteries, represents the final step before potential enlightenment. It is the step where we finally "get it right." It is where we finally *include* everything, without leaving any detail behind. It is where we finally see the connections between all seemingly disconnected things. It is where we have attained mastery over the physical reflections of our spiritual being and where we have attained mastery over the dualistic illusions of our lower nature. In short, we have finally achieved a relatively *balanced* consciousness.

Libra, therefore, represents the point of balanced consciousness, freed from dualistic illusions. It represents the fire of awakened and focused consciousness—the consciousness of the Sun, according to the Mysteries.

The transition from Virgo to Libra represents the final step in the healing journey via the anaretic degree. If this final step is not achieved, we play out the cycle repeatedly (possibly, as incarnations) until we "get it right" and evolve to the next octave.

According to the Mysteries, the healing journey is a journey from earth to water to air to fire. In the zodiac of the Mysteries, Virgo brings together earth, water, and air into fire. Libra is a fire sign. Thus, these signs represent the final steps to healing—to Libra-ruled Sun consciousness (the Sun being the portal to the spiritual realms of ether, space, and time), beyond the dualities of the material realms (see table 1).

Obsessive-Compulsive Disorders

We can understand some of the requirements of the Virgoan healing journey by looking at what the current consensus calls "obsessive-compulsive disorder," or OCD. Interestingly,

Density	Zodiac Sign	Planets
Earth (solid)		Moon gate and inner planets
Water (liquid)		Moon gate and inner planets
Air (gas)	Virgo (brings together earth, water, and air into fire)	Chiron (catalyst for Moon and inner-planet issues)
Fire (plasma)	Libra	Sun portal to the outer planets[1]
Ether		Outer planets
Space		Outer planets
Time		Outer planets/magnetopause

Table 1—The Healing Journey (Astronomical and Metaphysical) According to the Mysteries

the elements of OCD are part of the process of healing. Moreover, we all have these elements. It does not mean we are crazy; it simply means we are all on a healing journey.

In short, when our focus keeps returning to the same issue—repeating actions, thoughts, and feelings, driven by guilt or fear—we are being given a golden opportunity. We are being given a wake-up call, by which we can finally get to the bottom of a given issue in which we may be "stuck." Such OCD-type behaviors perfectly mirror our states of consciousness.

Again, true to Virgo's highest themes, we are being encouraged to *remember* everything, to *include* everything, to *connect* everything, and to put ourselves into the picture of what we are observing or studying. Such efforts, seen from the perspective of the current consensus, could be defined as OCD or, perhaps less brutally, as anal retention or perfectionism.

---

1. According to esoteric astrology (Alice Bailey et al), the Sun represents a kind of guard-station between the material and the spiritual realms. Those wishing to pass through this station are required to pass certain tests. For example, in Egyptian mythology, Thoth, the deity of Truth, weighed the hearts of the newly dead to see if they merited entry into the Sun realms. In esoteric astrology, such guard-stations are referred to as "ring-pass-nots." The Sun is a local ring-pass-not, whereas the solar magnetopause is a non-local (meaning beyond time and space as we know it) ring-pass-not.

Despite such negative tags, there are positive aspects to OCD-type behaviors.[2] *In fact, the force of evolution requires a seemingly obsessive focus on our wounds and issues.*

In the beginning, our OCD-type behaviors are driven primarily by fears and guilts. The *gift* of our fears and guilts, like the gift of pain, is that they *point us* to our wounds and issues. As we resolve these issues and heal our wounds, our focus gradually shifts from these to our higher purpose in life. The more we see, feel, acknowledge, and embrace this higher purpose—our divine design—the more seemingly obsessive we become. However, we are now driven more by love than by fear or guilt.

In this way, one could say that *focus on our divine design eventually becomes our most all-encompassing OCD-type behavior.*

Seen from this perspective, was OCD ever really a disorder? OCD-type behavior simply reflects our need for healing. Simultaneously, it drives us *toward* that healing. Lastly, in its higher-octave expression, it reflects our acceptance of healing in the form of the conscious embracing of our divine design.

OCDs do not change, neither are they ever cured or fixed . . . they just change form. Clinically diagnosed OCDs are simply "styles" of OCDs that are currently considered disorders. By ascribing such clinical labels, we are diverting attention away from ourselves and are effectively saying, "I'm okay, you're not." In truth, we all have OCD-type behaviors, and they serve every one of us on our paths of healing and evolution of consciousness. In the same way that a master musician practices music repetitively until mastery is achieved, so we must repeat our lessons of life until we master them. When mastered, as an act of love and gratitude, we celebrate our life by "obsessively" pursuing our divine design. Perhaps we can remember this the next time we meet an irritatingly perfectionistic or hypercritical Virgo!

The Journey from Aries to Pisces

In the natural zodiac, the cycle from Aries to Pisces, through each of the signs in turn, is the perfect metaphor for the healing journey. Aries represents the individual—separate, disconnected, and fragmented from the whole. It represents the most material, most dualized point in our journey. It is the place of our greatest woundedness. Chiron takes the most time through Aries and thus exaggerates Arian issues the most.

---

2. It is important to understand that, from Chiron's perspective, there is no such thing as a solely negative character trait. All traits—in fact, all things in the world—have equal negatives and positives. However, the positives are often hidden and/or repressed. Such is the nature of our wounding.

From one perspective, Aries is the starting point in the cycle. From here, healing becomes possible after the long journey into the duality of the material world. Aries represents the very beginning of the return journey. Pisces will be our final destination in this healing cycle—oneness, wholeness, and unconditional love.

Chiron will be our companion all the way. Chiron exemplifies the woundedness that keeps us stuck in the issues of any given zodiac sign, at the same time offering a path of healing from sign to sign. To move from one zodiac sign into the next requires that we resolve, synthesize, and transcend the issues of the sign we are in. In a sense, in order to do this, we must invoke the themes and issues of the opposite zodiac sign, as we saw in the previous section. Chiron comes in here, helping us see the flip sides of wounds and issues of a particular sign that we might be stuck in. Moreover, the transition from one sign to the next is an ongoing process of *including more* and of *expanding our personal horizon of consciousness,* until we have encompassed and unified it all in the sign of Pisces.

Sign to sign, Chiron mirrors the wounds and issues. Sign to sign, Chiron is the catalyst. Sign to sign, Chiron offers a pathway of healing.

The Lower and Upper Hemispheres

We have said that the lower and upper hemispheres of the natural zodiac represent the polarity of self and other, respectively. The separation of the world into self and other is a necessary requirement in the awakening and enlightenment process; *the wounding is necessary for the healing.* In the final analysis, nothing changes except our conscious awareness. Wounding and healing are eternal.

The self—the lower hemisphere—is cut off from the outside, neither acknowledging it nor being aware of it. It represents the world we know, the world we have come to understand, and the world we may have even come to love. In a sense, this is the place of *unconscious* oneness, where the dualistic idea of an "outside" does not yet exist.

Conversely, the other—the upper hemisphere—draws a boundary line between the inner world and the outer world, between the known and the unknown, and between the loved and the yet-to-be-loved. Such distinctions and differentiations serve to illuminate our true nature in the mirror of dualistic reality. Unconscious oneness (self) precedes fragmentation of consciousness (wounding, the other). Fragmentation of consciousness (wounding, the other) precedes conscious oneness (healing, self and other merged).

Chiron and Neptune

The descending journey into duality/materiality, via Chiron, is the wounding; here, unconditional love (Neptune) becomes conditional love (Venus). The return journey—the healing journey via Chiron—entails the synthesis of our polarized personas into greater unity, truth, and love. This is the path from Venus (lower-natured conditional love) to Neptune (higher-natured unconditional love), which is paved by Chiron and the healing journey.

In a sense, Chiron, with probable origins in the Kuiper Belt *outside* the orbit of Neptune, but itself orbiting *within* the orbit of Neptune, give us a preemptive taste of the consciousness of Neptune and beyond—the consciousness of unconditional love.

For these reasons, Chiron and Neptune are closely aligned in the horoscope. Working with Saturn (attention, persistence, work) and Uranus (the big picture), Chiron encourages us to see all sides of given issues—the visible/expressed and the hidden/repressed. When the two sides of our perceptions meet, illusions dissolve, questions cease, and the mind becomes quiet. In this wordless state, we experience truth, oneness, and love directly. This is the domain of Neptune.

In the horoscope, the interpretation of Neptune and its influences and meaning has long been problematic—a mystery. When taken together with Chiron and the healing path Chiron offers, Neptune's place and role become clearer.

The Sagittarius Connection

Although there is a connection between the planet Chiron and the sign of Sagittarius by virtue of the centaur symbol, it doesn't necessarily follow that this connection goes deeper than this. Early astrologers jumped at this obvious connection and quickly pronounced Chiron a ruler of Sagittarius. However, the Sagittarian ideal is *truth,* symbolized by the greater truth, oneness, and love of the galactic core (located in the constellation of Sagittarius, from our perspective).

True enough, we are told that Chiron was immortalized in the constellation of Sagittarius. However, this represented the *culmination* of his healing journey, *not* the journey itself. Chiron's themes, on the other hand, have more to do with the journey. Chiron represents the *pathway* to Sagittarian ideals. For this reason, I would be reluctant to assign rulership of Sagittarius to Chiron. We'll discuss the rulership question shortly.

The Sagittarius/Gemini Polarity

If anything, it is in the Sagittarius/Gemini polarity that Chironic issues and themes become apparent. Like the Virgo/Pisces polarity, the study of the Sagittarius/Gemini polarity can illuminate Chiron's themes of wounding and healing. The dualities are presented in table 2.

According to Chiron, beyond all these dualities and encompassing them sits the journey of wounding and healing. In the healing, the two sides of the Sagittarius/Gemini polarity—*knowledge* and *being*—merge into love, and the greater plan lying behind our existence emerges.

Gemini	Sagittarius
The *particular*—scattered pieces of information and experience with few or no unifying factors.	The *general*—the overarching picture without reference to details.
A form of the Many.	A form of the One.
Concerned with *knowledge*. Knowledge without wisdom/being is empty.	Concerned with *wisdom* and *being*. Wisdom/being without knowledge is impotent.
Concerned with intellectual *understanding*. Intellectual understanding without experience is empty.	Concerned with *experience*. Experience without understanding is impotent.
Concerned with *communicating* and *expressing*. Communicating/expressing without knowing is empty.	Concerned with *knowing*. Knowing without communicating/expressing is impotent.
The Knowledge of the Many, of the dualistic and material world.	Before healing, the Wisdom/Being of undifferentiated oneness, but *innocent* or *unawakened.*
The wounding journey from *innocent* and *unawakened* consciousness into duality.	The healing journey from the dualistic world to *experienced* and *awakened* consciousness.

Table 2—Gemini/Sagittarius Polarities

Complementary Opposites in the Zodiac

This brings us to an important realization. We have explored the Virgo/Pisces polarity and the Gemini/Sagittarius polarity in some detail and found that each polarity reflects the cosmogonic cycle of wounding and healing—Chiron's themes. Not only this, but each polarity offers us understanding that can help us heal and move beyond the apparent polarities.

Not surprisingly, if we examine each of the remaining zodiac pairs/polarities—Aries/Libra, Taurus/Scorpio, Cancer/Capricorn, and Leo/Aquarius—we will find Chiron sitting in the middle of each, offering a path of resolution, healing, and evolution of consciousness. (An article about the zodiac pairs can be found at http://www.martinlass.com/paradox.htm.)

Let's summarize our understanding of the zodiac pairs/polarities:

All zodiac pairs/polarities reflect the cosmogonic cycle of wounding and healing and offer a unique path of awakening to our true nature and of returning to love.

The wounding journey consists of unity becoming duality—the world split into innumerable complementary opposites, such as pain and pleasure, positive and negative, good and evil, black and white, hot and cold, light and dark, and so forth.

As we have said, the zodiac is a mandala of consciousness. On the surface of the zodiac, we see the dualistic world: the complementary opposites of Aries/Libra, Taurus/Scorpio, Gemini/Sagittarius, Cancer/Capricorn, Leo/Aquarius, and Virgo/Pisces, mirroring every conceivable human persona/emotion/polarity.

The healing journey consists of the reunification of all dualities—all polarities, all complementary opposites, and . . . *all zodiac pairs.* Chiron is present during the wounding—it mirrors the wound—and is the catalyst and pathway to healing. In this way, Chiron represents the pathway to the reunification of all zodiac opposites. The synthesis of each pair is truth, oneness, and love. The synthesis of the entire zodiac would mean transcendence of all wounds and issues in the solar system and our evolution into the stellar realms between the solar system and the galactic core.

From this perspective, the zodiac is one of the most powerful tools we have been given for a return to our divine/stellar origins.

Chiron and the Opposition Aspect

Oppositions represent the lowest and most polarized state of consciousness, whereas conjunctions—particularly occultations—represent the most unified. Said another way, oppositions represent woundedness—the result of the descent of light/consciousness into the material creation.

The subsequent ascent or healing journey is a metaphoric and metaphysical journey through the planetary aspects—from the opposition, through the square, the quincunx, the sextile, the trine, to the conjunction, parallel, and occultation. (The minor aspects fall in between these.) Because Chiron expresses our deepest wounds, its relationship to extreme aspects such as the opposition becomes apparent.

Here is how it works . . . In the natal chart, we tend to exaggerate one side of a planetary opposition and minimize the other. This does not remain the same over time, however. We tend to swing back and forth between the poles, first exaggerating one side and minimizing the other, now exaggerating the other side and minimizing the first. The opposition represents seemingly opposite, contradictory, conflicting, and disconnected issues, both sides of which are seeking resolution and synthesis.

Here is where Chiron comes in, offering us a way of transcending the seeming paradox. We do this by finding the hidden flip sides to the issues expressed in the opposition. For example, where an opposition appears to be creating conflict in our lives, how is that conflict serving us—helping us—to come to a higher understanding? How is it illuminating our dark and disowned parts and the issues and wounds in us that seek resolution and healing?

Realizing that all things serve our healing and evolution of consciousness is part of the healing. The resolution of the opposition takes us to Uranus—to a higher, more encompassing logic. (This is another reason why the Chiron-Uranus oppositions between 1952 and 1989 were so important.)

Using Chiron's understanding of oppositions and its tools of healing, we can resolve/heal any opposition (or any other aspect, for that matter), *even if Chiron itself is not involved in the particular aspect.* It is all a matter of finding the balancing sides to our otherwise polarized perspectives (as reflected in our charts).

Oppositions, like the zodiac pairs, ultimately represent lessons of love. The Chiron Paradigm says that all things serve us on the path back to love. Seeing how this is so is part of the journey.

The Rulership Question

Initially, Chiron's rulership sign was considered Sagittarius. The reasons for this, aforementioned, were the symbol itself—the centaur—and the myth of Chiron, where he was immortalized as a star in the constellation of Sagittarius. Although these connections are worthy of consideration, all my experience working with Chiron has shown me little connection between Chiron and Sagittarius in a practical sense. As an ideal—i.e., truth, wisdom, the big picture, galactic consciousness, and so forth—Sagittarius certainly represents the culmination of the healing journey. However, it does not address the steps and details along the way, which Chiron so perfectly epitomizes.

The details of the healing journey and the practical application of healing methods thereof rightly belong to the sign of Virgo. The association of Chiron with Virgo is easily demonstrated in the innumerable case histories I have done. Our previous discussions about Chiron and its relationship to Virgo represent the distillation of these case histories.

Yet, the healing theme of Chiron is not the whole picture; there is also the wounding. The *wounding* aspect of Chiron has more association with, and connection to, the sign of Pisces and the 12th house. It is here where we express our sense of hurt—our feelings of being wounded, victimized, wrongly done by, and abandoned by the universe. And as we have seen, the Virgo/Pisces polarity reflects the themes and issues of both wounding and healing.

However, the *journey* into the wound has more association with, and connection to, the sign of Scorpio and with Chiron's Kuiper brother, Pluto. This is the journey into the underworld, into the darkness, before the light is revealed.

Then, there is the Libra connection. The healing journey aspect of Chiron leads us inevitably and inexorably toward a Libran balance of consciousness, particularly from the perspective of the Mysteries, aforementioned. However, like Sagittarius, Libra represents the *result* and *goal* of the healing journey. Similarly, the sign of Aries represents the *culminating point* of the wounding, not the wounding per se. In addition, I have not found sufficient practical evidence in my case histories to suggest that the rulership of Libra be assigned to Chiron.

Overall, it would seem that Chiron rules *not* a given sign or signs specifically, but rather rules the *processes* that occur *between* signs. Chiron is a bridge, a catalyst, an intermediary, an intercessor, a way station, a go-between, a ferryman, a linking factor, and an alchemical force. In the preceding material, we have explored the many places where Chiron resides, and each one represents a *linking factor* or a *potential journey* between two "points."

Moreover, as we have explored, Chiron, as a *comet,* represents an extreme emotional expression of the solar system. It represents a reflection of a need within the consciousness of the solar system for a new perspective, an expanded horizon, a quantum leap of consciousness. From the point of view that Chiron may be a temporary visitor, it again represents a connecting agent, a catalyst, an alchemical ingredient, a process, and/or a journey.

From the psychological point of view, emotional outbursts (such as Chiron may represent in the greater solar picture) draw attention to issues and themes that are begging for attention, resolution, dissolution, and healing. Chiron, being discovered at this time in history, reflects issues and themes that are just under the surface of our evolving collective consciousness. Simultaneously, Chiron represents the catalyst to impel the emergence of these themes and issues, giving us the opportunity to learn from them, deal with them, and finally heal them.

If I had to ascribe Chiron's rulership to one sign, I would have to say Virgo. Although Mercury is traditionally the ruler of Virgo, it leaves a lot to be desired in terms of representing the complete scope of Virgo. Mercury more rightly rules Gemini.

Moreover, Chiron's issues and themes cross the borders of Virgo substantially into many other signs, as we have seen. I believe that a more complete planetary ruler of the sign of Virgo has yet to be found. On the other hand, perhaps we need to move beyond the paradigm that attaches a planet, as ruler, to one or two particular signs. In the meantime, Virgo will certainly suffice, particularly at this time in history when old paradigms of healing are giving way to new ones. In this case, Mercury certainly deserves to be at least the secondary ruler of Virgo.

Chiron and Relationship

This book would not be complete without a short exploration of Chiron and its place in relationships. Relationship is generally associated with Venus, Libra, and the 7th house. Although it seems somewhat removed from our discussions so far, there is sound logic for presuming that Chiron plays not a small part in determining our relationships and in the psychology thereof.

Zane B. Stein suggested the linkage in his earliest work on Chiron.[3] The Magi Society[4] has also done extensive study in this area, and they affirm that Chiron—in aspect (particularly declination aspects), progression, and transit, particularly to Venus—is a major player in this area. Although we will not explore the finer details of their study, we will set out the essence of the connection between Chiron and relationship.

We have asserted that Chiron represents our deepest and most primal wounds and issues. Furthermore, we have suggested that our wounds (what we try to run from and/or avoid) determine our values (what we strive for and seek). In addition, our wounds and issues can certainly resonate with those of others, creating emotional attractions and/or repulsions.

Given the preceding, we tend to be attracted to others for a number of different reasons; possibilities include empathy, sympathy, admiration, a common ideal, and/or a common way of looking at the world. We may be unconsciously attracted to particular people because we wish to rescue them, wrap them up in cotton wool, soothe their wounds, and/or protect them from harm: "You're drowning . . . I'll save you." Conversely, we may be attracted to someone because they offer us these same things: "I'm drowning . . . save me." Lastly, we may be attracted to someone with whom we feel a kinship due to similar wounds and issues: "We're in the same boat."

We have also asserted that our woundedness takes us on a journey to circumstances, situations, and environments that offer us the greatest potential for healing and evolution of consciousness. *This includes attracting us to, or repelling us from, specific people.* Through relationship, we are given the opportunity to see the hidden, repressed, and denied aspects of ourselves (our wounds and issues) in the mirror of the other. (In the worst case, though, we deny and disown these aspects, projecting them upon our partners and creating conflict.)

Then, there is the Libran connection. In short, we seek relationship (Libra of the modern zodiac) because we innately wish to return to oneness and love (Libra of the Mysteries). No better is this expressed than in our innate longing to find our true soul mate. This innate longing is nothing more or less than an expression of our woundedness. Chiron's role becomes clear: (1) it points to our wounds and issues, as mirrored in our every relationship, and (2) it offers a healing path within the context of relationship.

---

3. Zane B. Stein, *Essence and Application: A View from Chiron.* Originally published in 1985. The revised, 1995 edition is available to order on his website at http://www.geocities.com/SoHo/7969/page6.htm.

4. See http://www.magiastrology.com.

In the chart, Chiron's role in relationship can be seen most clearly in its interaction with Venus. In fact, a study of long-lasting relationships reveals a higher-than-average statistical predominance of Chiron-Venus aspects (both in longitude and in declination). These aspects show up in people's synastry, in their composite (midpoint) charts, and in the transits at the time of their meeting. The important aspects between Chiron and Venus are trines, conjunctions, parallels, contraparallels, and occultations.

If the Moon represents the outer face of Chiron in the area of our lower emotional nature, then Venus represents the outer face of Chiron in the area of relationship, attraction, romance, and earthly love (as distinct from unconditional love). Taken together, Venus and Chiron in our natal and progressed charts, in synastry, in composite (midpoint) charts, and in transit will tend to reflect (1) who we will be naturally attracted to; (2) who will be a long-lasting partner for us; (3) when, where, and how we will meet, react to, get along with, and interact with potential or current partners; and (4) what the respective benefits, blessings, lessons, and gifts of the relationship are likely to be.

The further exploration of Chiron in relation to Venus and relationship is the subject of a future study, beyond the scope of this present work.

CHAPTER FIVE

Life Cycles

. . . life exists at the edge of chaos,
moving from chaos into order and back again
in a perpetual exploration of emergent order.
—Brian Goodwin, biologist.[1]

Cycles of Spirituality and Healing

Due to its elliptical orbit, Chiron's influence waxes and wanes over time. This waxing and waning traces cycles of greater and lesser intensity/involvement in spiritual and psychological matters, specifically pertaining to the themes of wounding and healing. If we combine this with the ever changing tapestry of aspects with other planets, we get rich and complex patterns of rising and falling impetus to pursue spiritual matters (meaning healing and resolution of our wounds and issues).

The point of delving into the details of the larger cycle of Chiron, historically and psychologically, is to give our personal wounds and issues a larger context—one of the keys to

---

1. Brian Goodwin, *How the Leopard Changed Its Spots: The Evolution of Complexity* (New York: Charles Scribner's Sons, 1994), p. 182.

healing, according to the Chiron Paradigm. For professional as well as amateur astrologers, this will certainly enhance our astrology chart reading skills.

The most basic pattern is created from Chiron's transits to its natal positions in peoples' charts (Chiron-Chiron transits). (See Graph 1—The Chiron Cycle, in the appendix.) The important life transits, in chronological order, are:

- Chiron sextile natal Chiron

- Chiron square natal Chiron

- Chiron trine natal Chiron

- Chiron quincunx natal Chiron

- Chiron opposition natal Chiron (half-Return)

- Chiron quincunx (2nd) natal Chiron

- Chiron trine (2nd) natal Chiron

- Chiron square (2nd) natal Chiron

- Chiron sextile (2nd) natal Chiron

- Chiron Return

Some of these transits are more important and influential than others. We will be discussing these transits as a cycle in each of our lives, shortly. However, let's first look at Graph 2—Year-by-Year Ratio of Chiron-Chiron Transits in the General Population, in the appendix.

Here, we see the way in which the density (in time) of collective Chiron-Chiron transits waxes and wanes over time. The reason for this lies in Chiron's elliptical orbit, where Chiron spends significantly more time at apogee (Chiron's farthest point from the Earth) than at perigee (Chiron's closest point to the Earth). The waxing and waning of Chiron's influence is more dramatic even than Pluto's (Chiron's ellipticity being 0.3786 compared to Pluto's 0.2482). The net result is that the outward manifestation of wounding and healing issues—the impulse toward spirituality—is more intense during some years than during others.

The points of greatest intensity occur when Chiron is in Libra (1945, 1996, and 2047) and of least intensity when it is in Aries (1970–71 and 2021–22). This may seem counter to our previous assertions inasmuch as we said that Aries represents the most wounded time of our journey of consciousness. If we think about it, though, the times of our greatest darkness *birth* the impulse to move toward the light, i.e., to move toward healing. During Arian times, Chronically speaking, we are the most impelled to seek meaning and connection in our lives, as these appear to be missing. Consequently, we see an escalation over the ensuing twenty-five years of interest in, and pursuit of, spiritual and healing matters.

The peak of intensity occurs during Libran times. Chronically speaking, this represents the most awakened time. It is a time full of planetary connections (transits-to-transits and transits-to-radix) and, consequently, consciousness of these matters. Although it is not an easy time, it is, in retrospect, a most rewarding time in terms of healing and evolution of consciousness.

During these peaks (with Chiron closer to the Sun), the brilliance of the light assaults us. Either we *react* to our *unpreparedness* by backing away from the light and again seeking the solace and solitude of the Arian realms, or we *act* from our *preparedness* by embracing the light and moving closer to Sun consciousness.

In short, *when we are in darkness, we seek the light, and when we are in the light, if too bright, we seek the darkness.* This is the self-regulating mechanism of our evolution of consciousness. Moreover, it is the driving force behind the cosmogonic cycles of the cosmos, including our cycles of incarnation.

Historically, the collective peaks of intensity of Chiron-Chiron transits in the twentieth century occurred in 1945 and 1996.

In a sense, the light became too bright in the late 1930s and early 1940s. Saturn squaring Chiron between 1935 and 1952 compounded this effect; it made dealing with our wounds and unresolved issues a painful and tedious task, and we were not necessarily ready for this. One of the manifestations of our reaction to the extreme illumination of our woundedness was World War II. The *solar maximum* of 1946 further compounded the situation.

Our efforts to retreat from the light and from our exposed wounds and unresolved issues can be seen in the post-war years. During these years, we focused more on our material comfort and on building social, economic, and political structures to support our material comfort. It was a time of economic growth and family values—the so-called Baby Boomer times.

The 1996 peak of intensity represented the saturation point of the New Age movement; people had had enough of a "good thing," and they were getting sick of hearing the same ideas dished up in the same way. The New Age movement is destined to become increasingly materialistic and economically oriented. This must occur if it is to survive. *It will become part of the new establishment. It will become the new expression of Saturn.*

The last *trough* of intensity was in 1970–71, at the end of the 1960s. In a sense, the 1960s represented the force that turned the cycle back toward the light. Since World War II, we had become increasingly attached to our material world and less connected to spiritual concerns. As our sense of disconnection from spirit grew, we began to express it outwardly. The result was the 1960s. The growth of the New Age and ecology movements from the early 1970s onward mirrored the collective intensifying of personal Chiron-Chiron transits until 1996.

The next trough occurs in 2021–22. As we approach this trough, it will become increasingly necessary to slough off the dead forms of what was originally the New Age movement—to break down the now-stagnant patterns of this now-Saturnian expression. From here, a new cycle of healing and evolution of consciousness will begin. It will embrace the same themes as in the 1960s and as in the beginnings of the twentieth-century New Age, *but in different forms,* more appropriate to the times. The next peak of activity after these new beginnings will occur around 2047.

In the meantime, we are moving into a time of technological acceleration. We are moving into a time of accelerated mastery of the material world through science, technology, and, most importantly, communications.

Having said all this, it is necessary to realize that Chiron's aspects to other planets, in particular the outer planets, adds to, or subtracts from, the basic Chiron cycle. The intensity of the 1945 peak was accentuated by the Saturn-Chiron squares during this time, by the 1941 Chiron-Pluto conjunction, and by the 1946 solar maximum. The intensity of the 1960s, during a trough time, was accentuated by the intense aspects of Chiron to Pluto, Uranus, and Saturn, not to mention the ongoing oppositions of Uranus to Chiron over a period of an unprecedented thirty-seven years.

Similarly, the Libra-to-Aries retreat of Chiron in this present cycle (from 1996) was accentuated by the Chiron-Pluto conjunction of late 1999.

These other planetary aspects to Chiron are part of the rich tapestry of the Chiron cycle, forming the colors, hues, and tints of the basic Chiron cycle, as well as determining the intensity of any given part of the cycle.

Perihelion, Perigee, and Aphelion

We also need to be aware of the times when Chiron is closer or farther away from the Earth and the Sun. This is particularly relevant in Chiron's case due to its highly elliptical cometary orbit, as it necessarily affects the intensity of its influence upon us. The *perihelion* of Chiron is the point at which Chiron is the closest to the Sun in its orbit.[2] The *perihelion opposition,* or *perigee,* of Chiron to the Earth is Chiron's closest point to the Earth. The *aphelion* of Chiron is Chiron's point of greatest distance from the Sun.[3]

Obviously, the closer to the Earth a planetary body is, the greater its influence upon us. Moreover, the closer a *cometary* body like Chiron is to the Sun, the more *active* it becomes, as frozen material on its surface volatilizes into the gases that surround the comet like a halo.

Chiron's last perihelion occurred during the 1996 peak of the Chiron-Chiron transit cycle—on February 14, 1996, at 14°04' Libra. Its last perigee occurred on April 1, 1996, at 11°07' Libra.

The fact that the perihelion and perigee correspond to the fastest-moving part of Chiron's cycle/orbit and that they occur in Libra emphasizes the importance of the signs of Libra (perihelion sign) and Aries (aphelion sign). We have explored this previously.

Taking the preceding into consideration, it follows that it is vitally important where Chiron was in its cycle when we were born, and that this must be considered in the chart reading process. If Chiron was at or near perigee, perihelion, or apogee, this has certain ramifications.

In addition, it is also important to consider the *direction* of Chiron's travel—toward or away from the Sun and/or Earth (not to mention Chiron's retrogrades). From mid-Aries through to mid-Libra, Chiron is approaching us; this represents growth from self-centered-ness and isolation to acknowledging and embracing the *other,* aforementioned. From mid-Libra to mid-Aries, Chiron is receding from us; this represents the widening of conscious-ness to include more of the universe; but, paradoxically, this can make us feel increasingly isolated, impersonal, disconnected, and alone.

Another upshot of Chiron's movement toward and away from the Sun is that this same movement takes it closer to Saturn on the approach side and closer to Uranus upon the re-ceding side.

---

2. Approximately 8.46 AU from the Sun.
3. Approximately 18.94 AU from the Sun.

As Chiron approaches the Sun, it also approaches Saturn's orbit. As it does, our wounds become increasingly illuminated and, therefore, difficult to deal with, and we tend to move toward more conservative Saturnian values. In other words, we tend to seek solace and safety in the known, in the material, in the tangible, and in "safe" structures. We saw this tendency in the conservatism of the 1940s.

Conversely, as Chiron moves away from the Sun, it also approaches Uranus's orbit. As it does, our wounds become more distant, and our sense of disconnection and aloneness increases (particularly as Chiron moves through Aquarius). Our sense of connection to the Earth recedes, and we tend to move more toward revolutionary values and anarchistic ideals. In short, we react to our sense of isolation by shaking the place up, trying anything and everything to free our consciousness from its restraints and apparent exile. We saw this tendency in the radical nature of the 1960s.

The upshot of all this is that it is important to consider which part of the cycle we were born in—was Chiron approaching or receding?—as this will tell us a lot about our perspectives on our wounds and issues.

Interestingly, those born up to seven years or so *before* perigee/perihelion or apogee (i.e., before their first Saturn–natal Saturn square) are blessed to experience Chiron in both directions in their early life. This gives them an improved chance of finding a balance between the polarized elements of their lives.

Now let's widen our exploration of Chiron's eccentric orbit and discuss the Chiron cycle.

The Chiron Cycle

The Chiron cycle is the cycle and its subcycles derived from Chiron's elliptical orbit and its resultant uneven transit through the signs of the zodiac. These two factors contribute to the fact that each of us, depending on when we were born, experiences Chiron's transits to our natal Chiron at different times in our lives. We outlined these major lifetime transits in the first section in this chapter. Before we examine each of these transits in detail, though, let's look at the cycle as a whole. (See Graph 1—The Chiron Cycle, in the appendix.)

Graph 1 outlines the Chiron cycle for those born between 1930 and the end of 1999. It traces the age at which each of these major transits occurs in a given lifetime, depending on the birth year. As we can see, the only transit that occurs at roughly the same age, regardless of the birth year, is the Chiron Return around the age of 50–51. Graph 2, explored previously, was derived from this first graph.

We might also notice that those born around 1945 and again around 1996 have the greatest spread in the intervening times between these major transits. The first major transit occurs as early as five years old for some born between 1941 and 1944 and between 1991 and 1994.

On the other hand, those born around 1970–71 have the least time between transits. Moreover, for most people born between 1953 and 1969, the 1st square does not occur until after the age of twenty.

These two extremes must necessarily have significance not only for the individuals born in these years but also for the *generations* born in these years. From one point of view, the later we experience the first major Chiron-Chiron transit—the 1st square—the more we tend to feel a sense of disconnectedness, isolation, fragmentedness, woundedness, and aloneness. This is particularly so, considering we have come all the way through puberty into adulthood without having had Chiron's aid, without which our healing path is on hold, so to speak.

Furthermore, as it turns out, those of us born with a late 1st square are part of the latter stage of the outward sweep of Chiron toward its Arian aphelion. This intensifies the feeling of abandonment by the universe and the feeling of being left in the darkness of our own wounds. These feelings are aptly reflected in Chiron in Aquarius (feeling of being cut off from others and the greater cosmos) and Chiron in Pisces (feeling of being abandoned by the universe/God).

From this is birthed a longing for connection, a need for healing, and a quest to find a way of returning to unity and wholeness. Those born during these years birthed the New Age movement and all its associated offshoots—offshoots such as alternative medicine, ecology, a return to the ways and beliefs of indigenous races, and the resurgence of interest in spiritual matters. Moreover, these people aided in the discovery of Chiron and contributed to the manifestation of Chiron's messages and musings, even if they themselves were personally unaware of Chiron.

On the other side of the coin, those born between 1970 and 1996 will have an ever *decreasing* interest in the so-called New Age movement, its offshoots, and Chironic matters. The generation of my children, for example, all born in the 1980s, is not the least bit interested in in-depth pursuit of spiritual and/or healing matters, despite the fact that I can see the workings of Chiron in their lives. They simply are not consciously aware of these workings, nor are they interested in finding out about them.

This is not to say that these years did not produce some spiritual people; they certainly did. These people just operate and express their spirituality in more practical and materially oriented ways. It is just that the specific issues of wounding and healing are not high on their agendas. They are, in a sense, unable to understand why my generation is so concerned with these matters and why we spend so much time trying to understand them.

In addition, this generation has the "answers" ready-made for them by my generation and so does not feel the need to question these areas of life. The dark side of this coin, though, is that this generation will have only ready-made "answers" for their own children and not self-experienced truths. Their children (my grandchildren) will feel unfulfilled by this and will tend to seek their own answers to their spiritual questions—perhaps guided by their strange and hippie-like grandparents! And so the cycle repeats . . .

In short, *those born between 1971 and 1996 represent the balance to the views, ideals, and concerns of those born between 1945 and 1970.* These are the two halves of the same cycle. People in the latter range of years have tended toward spiritual matters, whereas people in the former range of years are tending toward material matters.

Having said this, though, *at every point in time, all stages of the cycle are represented within society.* The apparent difference lies in where we are collectively focused at any given time. At certain times, we collectively focus on and *express* one pole while *repressing* the other pole; at other times, it is exactly the reverse. The Chiron cycle can show us which side of the spirit/matter duality will be expressed and which will be repressed at any given point in time.

At the beginning of this new century, we are moving away from the peak of an expression of the spiritual side of our lives (1996) and toward an expression of the material side (2021–22).

In addition to the preceding, there are larger cycles of which the Chiron cycle is but a subcycle, and we must consider these if we are to account for the differences between one Chiron cycle and the next. Uranus, Neptune, and Pluto all represent such larger cycles, but pertaining to themes and issues somewhat different from Chiron's.

The most striking larger cycle that pertains to Chiron is the larger cycle of expression and repression of the spiritual/material paradox. If we put the beginning of this larger cycle at around the Age of Enlightenment (alternately and more informally called the Age of Reason), around the time of Newton, then we are now not much more than halfway through this cycle.

The Age of Enlightenment/Reason was a return to the scientific, mechanistic, material view of the world. In the 1900s, we saw the beginning of a return to the mystical, animistic, spiritual view of the world. In addition, this return was amplified by the approaching peak of a 500-year solar cycle. Therefore, we conjecture that the *expression* of the latter view will continue for some hundreds of years into the future before being subdued once more by the former view.

Moreover, the impending precessional transition from the Piscean Age to the Aquarian Age (2100s) will amplify the swing back toward a more mystical, animistic, spiritual view of the world by adding collective values, universal ideals, and collective bonding to the equation and by revealing the connections between science and religion/spirituality.

Within these major cycles, the shorter Chiron cycle will cause an ebbing and flowing of emphasis on, and outward expression of, the mystical, animistic, spiritual view of the world *within* the larger cycles for the next several hundred years.

In the last thirty years, we have certainly seen evidence of a swing *away* from New Age ideals. Interestingly, the current outward-journeying phase of the Chiron cycle is also seeing a backlash against pseudo-religious/spiritual assertions of connections and correlations between theoretical physics—itself the "spiritual" end of the material sciences—and metaphysics and spirituality. During this phase of the cycle, instead of conjecturing about "God particles" and/or about how quantum physics "explains" consciousness, we will find ourselves increasingly demanding concrete proof and looking for practical applications of the strange and counter-intuitive theories of quantum physics.

However, having said this, the Chiron Paradigm seeks a broader view that transcends the material/spiritual paradox. It seeks to show how science and religion/spirituality are essentially saying the same thing. In the final analysis, the Chiron Paradigm asserts that materiality and spirituality are two sides of the same coin of light, consciousness, and love.

The final thing that contributes to differences between one Chiron cycle and the next is the intensity/number (or lack thereof) of major aspects between Chiron and the other outer planets. The intensity/number of such aspects between 1952 and 1989 was a case in point, as it encompassed the tumultuous 1960s. Details of this outer-planetary drama and its historical significance can be found at http://www.martinlass.com/library.htm#issues.

Phases of the Chiron Cycle

Let's now look at each of the major Chiron-Chiron transits. Taken together, these transits trace the ebbing and flowing of our impulse to either delve into our wounds and unre-solved issues or not. It traces times when our wounds and issues are thrust to the fore, de-manding acknowledgment and demanding that we attend to them. Whether we feel able to deal with these wounds and issues depends upon our preparedness, our willingness, and our *translucence* to planetary influences. (We will discuss this last point later.)

Natal Position

Although not strictly speaking a transit, the natal placement of Chiron determines the sen-sitive point in the natal chart with respect to later transits. It represents what we feel is most missing, unbalanced, unjust, and/or most in need of correction, fixing, or getting rid of in our lives. This, in turn, determines what we seek in life, who we relate to or not, the paths we walk, things that we will attract or repel, and the destiny we will meet. In short, the natal placement outlines our specific wounds/voids that determine our values. In addition, it encapsulates the healing path and the gifts in our wounds.

In a sense, Chiron's natal placement drives our life's path/purpose/calling/destiny, the nature and details of which are seen in the Moon's nodes.

The natal position of Chiron is the backdrop against which the drama of subsequent Chiron-Chiron transits will take place.

The 1st Sextile

The 1st Chiron-Chiron sextile manifests in a relatively unconscious way. The period in which it can occur ranges from three to about sixteen years old. In short, it represents the appearance in our lives of opportunities and connections to healing/evolutionary possibili-ties. Although we are primarily unconscious to the nature of our woundedness and to the possibilities that this transit brings, it is as if a window has been opened upon our wound-edness—one that offers a potential path of healing.

It may be a person who comes into our lives. It may be the discovery of an interest, perhaps representing a future career path. It may be a place of solace discovered. It is often accompanied by an awakening of creativity, which reflects, unconsciously, our inner secrets. If it occurs later—say, in the early teens—it can be an awakening to the world, its mysteries, its joys, and its sorrows. This was certainly the case for me at the age of fifteen to sixteen.

Due to the early nature of this transit for some, it can be difficult to pinpoint the exact events and circumstances to which it corresponds. What we can say, though, with relative certainty, is that the later it occurs, the more a sense of woundedness mounts within us, impelling us to seek a healing and/or spiritual path.

In many ways, the 1st Chiron-Chiron sextile sets the path of healing and evolution of consciousness that we will subsequently follow (albeit unconsciously until the Chiron-Chiron opposition). During this transit, our values, arising from our wounds/voids, will be expressed, manifested, and cemented. This is a time of outward expression/manifestation of our divine design, although this expression is still embryonic and may be difficult to see at the time.

The 1st Square

The 1st Chiron-Chiron square represents the time in our lives when we are first made *conscious* of our specific woundedness. This transit can occur as early as age five and as late as twenty-three. Although we are made conscious of our woundedness during this time, we are, for the most part, unable to deal with it, grasp its deeper meaning, or soothe its effect upon us. It is, in a sense, a reaffirmation and deeper etching of our original wounds. These wounds drive us on the evolutionary path toward our ultimate healing and toward the expression and manifestation of our divine design. The deeper the wounds (voids), the greater the gifts (values). Core wounds create core values.

During this time, our woundedness surfaces (the nature of which is set out by Chiron's sign and house placements at our birth and its aspects to other planets). That which we feel to be missing in our lives is brought into painful awareness. We may be missing a sense of connectedness or a feeling of love. We may have a deep need for security. We may have lost our faith or trust. We may have a deep need for companionship, and so on and so forth.

Whatever the case may be, the 1st Chiron-Chiron square represents an *impasse* of healing, at the same time as an illumination of our inner woundedness, a glimpse at our inner fragmentation, and, at times, a glimpse at our dark side. Akin to Saturn, this square impels us to make an inner resolve, although we generally cannot carry out our resolve until the transit has passed. The resolve is invariably in the nature of a healing wish, whatever the form may take, even if the native does not equate this inner resolve with healing at all.

The 1st Trine

The 1st Chiron-Chiron trine represents a time when we are highly likely to meet opportunities for healing and evolution of consciousness to a degree not previously encountered. We may meet teachers, mentors, or companions—spiritual or otherwise. We may encounter healers, whatever the modality. We may simply be inspired at the time to pursue healing and/or spiritual matters. During this time, answers seem to be forthcoming and pathways open, allowing us to resolve some of our issues and heal some of our woundedness. Such healing/resolution can be either externally driven or internally pursued.

It can also be a time when we begin to sense with greater clarity what we may be here to do. That is, we may begin to sense our divine design. We probably will not yet be able to put this into words, though; this generally comes much later, closer to the 2nd Chiron-Chiron trine.

This transit can occur as early as age seven. Obviously, the earlier the transit occurs, the more likely the healing/resolution is to be externally driven rather than internally pursued.

The exact nature of the opportunities this transit brings will be mirrored in the other planets transiting natal Chiron during this time (and the aspects these make to transiting Chiron), as well as in transiting Chiron's sign and house.

The 1st Quincunx

This transit can occur as early as age ten. It represents a time of questions, reassessment, new perspectives, and the assimilation of events, circumstances, and outcomes of the previous trine transit. It can be a perplexing and somewhat unsettling time, but a time that impels us to gain greater clarity—to come to a new level of consciousness concerning the wounds and unresolved issues that plague us. It can be a time of shedding old skins, and, in this way, it is akin to Pluto in its effect, albeit far less intense.

During this time, it is as though we are working our way through an obstacle course, complete with puzzles we must solve and decisions we must make about our next steps.

In addition, during this time, we may recognize allies in those people, things, events, and situations that we previously viewed as our enemies. In other words, we may begin to see the blessings in the crises and the gifts in the wounds; this would represent a new level of consciousness pertaining to these things.

The Opposition

Aside from the Chiron Return, the Chiron-Chiron opposition (or half-Return) is by far the most important and influential of the transits of the Chiron cycle. It can occur as early as age thirteen and as late as thirty-seven.

This transiting opposition represents the fulcrum point of our (potential) journey of healing and evolution of consciousness. (I say "potential" because we always have a choice to take up the challenge of healing and evolution of consciousness or not.) There are about ten years on either side of this transit when we *must* consciously awaken to our woundedness, whatever form it takes, and take positive steps toward our healing and evolution of consciousness. If we do, we begin to glimpse, to a greater or lesser degree, the answers to the four basic questions of existence—the questions being, *Where do we come from? Where are we going? Who are we?* and *Why are we here?* In short, our divine design becomes clearer.

The opposition transit is a time of intense illumination of our wounds and issues. Unlike the square transits, however, we are certainly able to take positive steps toward healing/resolution during this time. It is perhaps the most acute and most active time of our conscious journey. We could liken it to the birth pangs of spirit.

Anything standing in the way of our integration, our awakening, and the activation of our divine design can and does surface, sometimes in dramatic and cathartic ways. The opposition is akin to Uranus inasmuch as it shines a bright light into the darkness of our unawakened consciousness. It impels us to seek a higher understanding and synthesis of the otherwise dualistic illusions and lopsided perceptions of our lower nature. Beyond our contradictions, paradoxes, and conflicts, there is a hidden unity, concordance, and metadox (union of opposites).

The healing journey is about awakening to a larger picture. It is about seeing the connections in, and sensing the perfection and "rightness" of, those things, people, and events that we previously condemned, disowned, failed to acknowledge, blamed, or otherwise judged negatively. In short, it is a process of seeing the blessings in the crises and of discovering the gifts in the wounds.

If we do not attend to our woundedness or seek resolution of our issues during the ten or so years on either side of the fulcrum point of this transit, we enter a "mid-life crisis." During this crisis, the meanings of our lives become more distant and seemingly unattainable.

This mid-life crisis is linked with the Uranus–natal Uranus opposition (Uranus half-Return), occurring roughly between the ages of thirty-eight and forty-four. It represents a time when the work we have done or not done toward our potential healing and evolution of consciousness is paid or not paid. If we have done the work, Uranus can connect us to a higher state of consciousness, linking us with the affairs and consciousness of the outer planets. The balancing and integration of our consciousness, corresponding to the alignment of our chakras, makes it possible for this Uranian activation to take place. Chiron's role in the chakra energy system of the body/mind is to clear the channels, allowing the outer planets' influences and "messages" to be heard and digested.

If, on the other hand, we have not done the work of healing and evolution of consciousness before this Uranian transit, we may experience a withdrawal from this potential contact with the outer planets—the so-called mid-life crisis. More on this in a moment . . .

So we can see the importance of the Chiron half-Return as a prelude to the Uranus half-Return—the importance of attending to our wounds and issues during this time.

The 2nd Quincunx

The 2nd Chiron-Chiron quincunx, similar to the 1st, represents a time of assimilation, reassessment, and redefinition of the issues brought up by the previous opposition transit. It is a time when we are impelled to try to make sense of our journey of healing and evolution of consciousness up to the present and to come to a more integrated understanding of it all.

Conclusions we may have come to during the preceding Chiron-Chiron opposition may now seem incomplete or not completely satisfactory. Something still seems to be out of place, but we cannot tell what it is. We are simply being encouraged by this quincunx transit to come to a higher understanding of all that we have been through. We are being encouraged to see *more* of the big picture, to connect *more* of the dots.

During this time, the odd pieces that do not appear to fit the big picture will plague us, frustrate us, irritate us, unsettle us, and generally intrude upon our peace of mind. We may feel, at times, like an office assistant trying to file a backlog of paperwork in a disorganized filing cabinet.

Nonetheless, this time can be very fruitful if we pursue each disparate piece of the puzzle with a view to understanding its unique place as well as its part in the larger scheme. Ultimately, everything in our lives is connected to this larger scheme. The healing journey consists of discovering how each thing fits and interrelates with all others.

The 2nd Trine

The 2nd Chiron-Chiron trine, similar to the 1st, is a time when our vibratory frequency is aligned to people, places, things, and circumstances that offer great possibilities for our potential healing and evolution of consciousness. During this second trine, though, we are more likely to recognize these opportunities and possibilities more quickly and to consciously pursue them. We are clearer about our path and about ourselves (presuming we have done sufficient "work" on ourselves up until this time).

During this transit, it is highly probable that we will meet guides, teachers, mentors, and other people offering us opportunities for healing and resolution of our wounds and issues—opportunities to evolve.

In a sense, this transit represents an affirmation of our path and of our life's purpose. It is a time when many things will come together in our understanding, naturally and consciously. It can be a time of deep healing, resolution, and connection. This transit, like the trine aspect in general, resonates with Neptune and, as such, awakens us to the possibility and actual experience of unconditional love (being the ultimate result of all healing).

Interestingly, this transit can occur before, after, or during the Uranus half-Return, aforementioned. The two transits are very similar inasmuch as they both bring together the results of all previous work we have done on our healing and evolution of consciousness. The Uranus transit, however, tends to be more upsetting—more dramatic and *revolutionary*. The 2nd Chiron trine is more harmonious and less confronting, although still *revelatory* in its effect.

If this Chiron transit *precedes* the Uranus half-Return, it acts as a prelude, i.e., a taste of things to come. If the two transits take place *simultaneously,* one adds to the other, and the overall effect is amplified. If the Chiron transit occurs *after* the Uranus transit, then it acts as a postlude, affirming and finalizing the effects of the Uranus transit—whether these effects are positive or negative.

The 2nd Square

The 2nd Chiron-Chiron square, like the preceding trine, can occur before, during, or after the Uranus half-Return. This timing will determine the specific nature of its effect.

In general, this transiting square tends to bring to the fore our unhealed and/or unresolved wounds and issues. Our ability and/or willingness to deal with these during this time are generally limited again. In this way, this transiting square, like the first Chiron-Chiron square, is aligned with the energy of Saturn. However, the degree of limitation will depend on the nature of accompanying transits and aspects, such as the aforementioned Uranus half-Return.

If we have done little in the way of attending to our healing and evolution of consciousness, this square will bring up all kinds of regrets, resentments, painful memories, and core wounds. An inexplicable sense of loss and a feeling of the meaninglessness of our lives often accompany it. We may feel that if we could but turn back time, things might be different. Again, this represents a kind of mid-life crisis. Chiron's answer to this is to learn to love things just as they are and to endeavor to see the benefits, blessings, lessons, and gifts in them, despite the pain and suffering they seemed to have caused at the time.

If, on the other hand, we have attended to our healing and evolution of consciousness, this transit will still bring up regrets and painful memories. However, we will experience increased ability and willingness to deal with these things as they come up. It is as though we are being given a chance to go deeper into the healing process, to finalize any loose ends, and to resolve any regrets, painful memories, and continuing issues.

If this transiting square occurs *after* the Uranus opposition, we are generally better equipped to deal with whatever comes up, providing we have done sufficient work in the past. If this square occurs *before* the Uranus opposition, it is generally more difficult and represents a time when we are being given a chance to clean up our act, in preparation for the activating effect of the Uranus transit. If this Chiron square occurs *simultaneously* with the Uranus opposition, then the depth, intensity, and acuteness of the healing journey are multiplied, but so too is the potential healing result.

The 2nd Sextile

The 2nd Chiron-Chiron sextile, like the 1st sextile, represents opportunities for, connections to, and possibilities for, healing and evolution of consciousness. Unlike the 1st sextile, though, we are more conscious and can better recognize these potential pathways.

It is a time, too, when there can be an increase in creativity, creativity being simultaneously one of the *keys* to healing and one of the *results* of healing. There can be fruitful meetings, events, and journeys during this time—an exchange of healing energies between us and people, places, and things. This transit, like the sextile aspect in general, is akin to Mercury in its influence.

As with all sextile aspects, though, we must activate it, consciously and intentionally, by our wish for, and efforts toward, our healing and evolution of consciousness. (This applies less to the 1st Chiron-Chiron sextile, though, as we are generally too young to make such conscious and intentional efforts.)

The Chiron Return

The Chiron Return—when Chiron has completed a full cycle of the zodiac and returned to its natal position in our charts—represents the culmination of the cycle of healing and evolution of consciousness up to the age of 50–51.

Its effect will lie somewhere between two extremes, depending on our overall level of attention to, and conscious work on, the healing and evolution of consciousness in our lives to date. In all cases, our original wounds and their attendant issues will surface again. Whether we respond with love or with fear, guilt, remorse, anger, and/or resentment will depend on our previous work.

If we have not attended to our wounds and issues during our lives and have not worked toward healing and higher consciousness, ultimately aspiring to unconditional love, we will be thrust back into the thicket of our woundedness. In this case, our core wounds and issues will surface again, demanding attention, healing, and resolution. In a sense, we are required to repeat a grade of school.

However, the likelihood of truly beginning in-depth work on our subsequent healing and evolution of consciousness definitely diminishes with time. This is due to our age, to the general level of crystallization of our personality, and to associated emotional habits, masks, protective mechanisms, and ingrained escape tactics. This is not to say that it is impossible. It simply becomes more difficult over time and we become less inclined to bother with it.

In this case, the Chiron Return can be, paradoxically, a time we hardly notice due to the success of our long-standing patterns of avoidance and evasion. Conversely, it can be a time of monumental regret. The Chiron Return can open the Pandora's box of our core wounds and long-standing unresolved issues. Unable to deal with or answer the tortured callings that arise from our fragmented consciousness, we go into crisis or, alternatively, even deeper into retreat. Only in the final moments of death, maybe many years later, will we have an opportunity to feel healing and sense the truth of the love around us and in us. It is only then that the stranglehold of our personality mechanisms finally relaxes with the weakening of our physical vehicle. I venture to suggest that, if you are reading this book and have gotten this far into it, you will not have to fear the aforementioned scenario!

If, however, we have attended—to a greater or lesser degree—to our wounds and issues during our lives, the best we can look forward to is a deep sense of completion and peace during this transit. Although our core wounds and issues will arise again during this time, our previous work will help us to appreciate and finally love these wounds/voids and to recognize that they have given us our core values and, ultimately, our divine design. In short, we would not be the people we are today without having gone through what we have gone through. This can be a time of great gratitude for our lives and for what we have been given for our healing and evolution of consciousness.

It will also be a time when we can move into another octave of our journey. The cycle repeats, but on another, finer energetic level. We are given an opportunity to move to deeper levels of healing and higher levels of consciousness, forever expanding to the limits of the solar system and, simultaneously, approaching the focused consciousness of the Sun. Increasingly, love is our guide, rather than fear and guilt.

In truth, the effect of the Chiron Return lies somewhere between these aforementioned extremes. Some issues—those we have fully worked through—we will transcend, moving into a new energetic level of healing and into a new cycle. Others we will have to recapitulate in the next Chiron cycle, striving for more understanding, higher consciousness pertaining to the issues themselves, and deeper healing of old wounds. Still other issues will be deeper wounds, only recently uncovered by the previous cycle and representing our fresh lessons.

The Uranus half-Return and the Chiron Return work hand in hand to align us with, and connect us to, the outer planets Uranus, Neptune, and Pluto. It can be a spiritual coming of age, if we are ready. If we are not, then the destructive/recycling forces of Pluto will accelerate our decay, seeking to spade us in, so to speak, in preparation for our physical death and for our rebirth into a new cycle, i.e., into a new incarnation.

CHAPTER SIX

Interpreting Chiron in the Natal Chart

Opacity, Translucence, and Transparency to Planetary Influences

Before discussing Chiron in the chart—in the signs, in the houses, and in aspect—it is necessary to preface this with a discussion on the varying effects of planetary influences upon us.

As previously mentioned, the degree to which we are aware of, and are personally influenced by, the planets varies from person to person and from lifetime to lifetime. This is one of the reasons why, even in controlled studies, unquestionable proof of astrology has been so elusive. Another reason is that studies of this kind—and, in fact, astrologers themselves—tend to focus on zodiac signs and houses rather than on the aspects (longitude *and* declination) between the planets. This, however, is another topic. The other reason studies of this kind remain inconclusive and/or ambiguous is that they do not consider the changing cultural consciousness of humanity over time and its reflection in the changing *interpretation* of the zodiac signs and houses themselves. Astrology is not just a science, not just an art, but is also a cultural expression.

In any case, one of the reasons that the personal awareness and effect of planetary influences varies from person to person is that each of us may be at a different stage/level of our evolution of consciousness in this lifetime. In addition, we may each be in a different phase of the larger cycle of our incarnations.

When we are extremely unawakened—early on in our evolutionary journey through the solar system—planetary influences do not tend to affect us in a personal way; this is also true when we are early in a new *cycle* of incarnations. Instead, we fall almost entirely under the mass influence of the planets; we are carried, so to speak, by the overall movement of the consciousness of humanity—by the collective consciousness of Gaia.

In this case, free will is for all intents and purposes almost nonexistent, despite our illusions to the contrary. We are buffeted this way and that without our intervention or ability to resist. As the great Russian/Armenian teacher and visionary G. I. Gurdjieff said of the "ordinary" man, we are but *automatons,* reacting to external and internal influences, unaware that we are but machines with no free will.[1]

There is little sense in trying to read the personal horoscope of a person in this stage of their evolution. They will not understand what you are saying, nor will you, as a reader, be able to correlate the areas and events of their lives with the planetary positions. One of the signs of such an unreadable horoscope lies in a distinct lack of major aspects. This mirrors a lack of focused consciousness—the sign of the earlier stages of a person's evolution or of a new cycle of incarnations. This first-case scenario is what we are calling being *opaque* to planetary influences.

The second-case scenario we are calling *translucence* to planetary influences. This is perhaps the most common case, although the degree of translucence varies from person to person in a spread throughout humanity that covers all degrees. By translucence, we mean that planetary influences have an effect on our lives *personally* as well as collectively. We are, to a greater or lesser degree, *aware* of these changes of energy and the effects they have on the different areas of our lives. We may not be aware of astrology, as such, but we are certainly aware of the changing energetic landscapes of our lives.

At this stage of evolution, an astrological reading becomes both possible and meaningful. At this stage, we can speak about the real influences of Chiron and about the nature of our woundedness and unresolved issues. Before this, our words fall on deaf ears. Even the

---

1. P. D. Ouspensky, *In Search of the Miraculous.* See bibliography.

level of *interest* in these themes is dependent upon our stage of healing and evolution of consciousness and/or upon our phase in the current cycle of our incarnations (not forgetting the importance of the part of the Chiron cycle in which we were born).

Books such as this are written primarily for those who fall, for the most part, into the *translucent* category.

The third and final stage in our journey of healing and evolution of consciousness corresponds to being *transparent* to planetary influences. In this case, having worked entirely through our issues, learned our lessons, and healed our wounds, the influences of the planets no longer affect us either personally or collectively. They simply pass through us, neither affected themselves nor affecting us. *In this case, our consciousness is simultaneously focused at the Sun and at the solar magnetopause.*[2]

At this third and final stage, an astrological reading, such as we prepare these days, again becomes meaningless and irrelevant. A reading for this stage of our evolution would require a new astrology, based upon the Sun and the surrounding stars—i.e., a *stellar* astrology.

In truth, we each have areas of our psyche that are opaque, some that are translucent, and some that are transparent. If we average these areas, we get a combined energetic *frequency* that is our unique signature and mirrors our overall stage of healing and evolution of consciousness.

If we were entirely opaque, we would also not be alive. Conversely, if we were entirely transparent, we would not be here on Earth; we would be in another realm of existence, beyond this one. The astrology reading process, and indeed astrology itself in its current form, is the most useful when we are *primarily* translucent to planetary influences. During this stage, we are, to a greater or lesser degree, at least aware that we are here for some reason other than to eat, defecate, breathe, sleep, and reproduce—even if we do not know the reason yet. We are on a relatively conscious search for meaning, for connection, for a larger context, and for contact with other consciousness. To a greater or lesser degree, we have in our consciousness the four age-old spiritual questions: Where have we come from? Where are we going? Who are we? and Why are we here?

The search for the answers to these questions *is* the healing journey, hence its connection to Chiron.

---

2. This seeming paradox is resolved by understanding Einsteinian relativity, its relation to consciousness, and the illusory nature of time and space. However, this goes beyond the scope of this book. Refer to the work of Dr. John Demartini of the Concourse of Wisdom School of Philosophy and Healing, Houston, TX.

Fate versus Destiny

Leading on from the previous section, we now offer a definition of the difference between *fate* and *destiny* in our lives.

Fate is the action, on a collective scale, of planetary influences upon those parts of our consciousness that are opaque, i.e., relatively unawakened. Concerning these unawakened and unresolved issues and wounds, we fall under mass influence. We are led along by the mass movements of the consciousness of the whole planet—by the consciousness of Gaia. In short, our polarized personas/emotions send us this way and that, and all the while, we are thinking we have free will. In truth, it is merely fate at work. We are steered unconsciously (by our Moon-ruled polarized personas/emotions) to where we have the greatest possibility of seeing the nature of our issues.

Destiny, on the other hand, is the action, on a personal scale, of *stellar* influences upon those parts of us that are relatively translucent or transparent, i.e., relatively awakened in consciousness. This corresponds to the inner state that is able to hear and consciously act upon the messages of the soul, as heard in the spiritual heart. It corresponds to Sun-consciousness. We are aware, to a greater or lesser degree, of our divine design in relation to these parts of us and can consciously act toward its fulfillment; further, we consciously choose to do so. We are guided, not by the planetary influences we have called fate, but by the higher consciousness of the Sun and the stars themselves. We have *certainty* and *resolve* and, as such, are the *masters* of the world around us, rather than being a slave to it. The world cannot stop a person who is in alignment with his or her destiny. Destiny shapes the world.

Chiron's Place and Emphasis in the Chart

Chiron, in the natal chart, represents the place of our greatest voids, of our deepest wounds. It mirrors that which we feel is the most missing, most unbalanced, most unjust, most inequitable, and/or most in need of fixing, changing, or getting rid of in our lives. It represents the areas of our consciousness where we are the most fragmented, scattered, disconnected, isolated, alone, and/or hurt.

On the other side of the coin, Chiron also sets out the potential path of our healing, of the resolution of our issues, and of our greatest final service. It defines the *nature* of our service to others and to the planet, which we have called our divine design. The details and *forms* of its *manifestation,* however, will be mirrored more in the North Node, the Sun, the Midheaven, and the Ascendant, combined with their attendant aspects. This is an important distinction.

A sparsely aspected Chiron indicates a relatively low awareness of the nature and manifestation of a person's specific woundedness and their healing path. This does not mean to say that the person is unevolved. It simply means that their focus in life is not specifically in the area of healing per se. Such people will learn the same lessons and walk the same healing journey, but they will do so unconsciously, without the benefit (some would say burden!) of conscious knowledge of their healing and spiritual path.

Conversely, when Chiron makes multiple aspects in a natal chart, it generally, but not exclusively, indicates a high awareness of the nature and manifestation of the native's specific woundedness and their healing path. The questions of existence, aforementioned, are more likely to be in the forefront of their consciousness.

Whether our charts are sparsely or thickly populated with Chiron aspects, Chiron represents the driving force of evolution, causing us to seek values that are the antithesis of our voids/woundedness. So much psychology could be explained if psychologists understood Chiron and its perspectives.

The power of Chiron must not be underestimated. It is akin to Pluto in its intensity and in its power to drive us. Unlike Pluto, Chiron's influence and effect may appear hidden at first, but when the key is found, Chiron opens up the rest of the natal chart in a way that was previously impossible. When we understand Chiron's place and the way it manifests in a person's life, so many of the other features of their chart naturally fall into place, revealing a bigger picture.

Working with Chiron in the Chart

It is important to remember at all times that the natal chart is an integrated and dynamic picture. To take one feature out of context and proceed to draw conclusions from it without reference to the whole will bring unsatisfactory results. The job of the astrologer is to integrate all the features and reveal the larger plan behind all the pieces—a larger plan that unifies the chart into a grand tapestry. The evolved astrologer seeks to reveal the larger plan that is already there rather than trying to make the pieces fit into their own preconceived ideas about life and about the person they are reading for.

To work successfully with Chiron in the chart, we must attend to both sides of its message equally—the wounds *and* the gifts, the wounding process *and* the healing path. We must also put these into the context of the other major features of the chart. In particular, we must consider the nodes of the Moon, representing the life's path and direction. We must consider the Sun, representing the higher self and its potential expression and manifestation. In addition, we must consider the Moon itself, representing the lower self, its wiles, and its emotional mechanisms; we must consider the Moon's role as the exterior face of our woundedness.

The astrologer must also have a conception of the dualistic/polarized nature of the psyche, as expressed through the planets, the opposing signs of the zodiac, and the angular aspects. We must consider the planets' light and dark sides, their higher and lower natures, their positive and negative manifestations, and, ultimately, the higher synthesis of all sides. Otherwise, the reading process becomes lopsided and colored by the reader's own polarized personas/emotions. This is a tall order, no doubt, but an ideal we can approach by steps.

As astrologers, we must not forget that the clients' issues are *our* issues. As we work through these issues during the reading, so we can help the client work through them. As we aim to help others, so we are helped. If we are open and humble, we will get as much out of the reading as the person we read for.

When working with Chiron in the chart, it is first necessary to *touch* the wounds and issues, even if very softly. From here, we can then begin to work with these, begin to illuminate the paths and possibilities for healing, and begin to balance our perspectives on these wounds and issues.

Before this, though, we must try to understand a person's overall life's path/purpose/calling/destiny. For this, we look to the Moon's nodes.[3] The nodes can tell us what we have come into life with—our lessons, our gifts, our issues, and so forth. It can then tell us what direction our life is pointed in—our potential, the general nature of our life's purpose, and the area of life in which this purpose will be played out.

Having thus determined the life's path, we then look to the Sun to see in what ways and in which areas we will *express* this life's path.

We might then look for any aspects that the nodes and Sun make to other planets; this will be the *context* in which the nodes and Sun operate in our lives.

---

3. Martin Schulman's book on karmic astrology and the Moon's nodes, *Karmic Astrology,* is an excellent reference if we remain cautiously aware that his bias is primarily toward the negative side of the total picture.

We can then look at Chiron and see how we will be driven along the life's path; what are the wounds/voids that determine the values we seek? Looking at the Moon and relating it to Chiron, we will be able to see how our wounds will express themselves through our lower nature. We will see the evolution of protective patterns and escape mechanisms that help us deal with our wounds and issues at an acceptable and bearable rate.

Then, we might look at the aspects that Chiron makes to the nodes, the Sun, the Moon, the Midheaven, and the Ascendant and try to determine how these features of the chart interrelate; this will be the context in which Chiron operates in our lives.

From here, we may then deal with the others planets, each in turn. We may look at their issues separately, in relation to planets other than Chiron, and then in relation to Chiron.

Working in this way, a bigger picture gradually begins to emerge, and the pieces begin to fall into place. Gradually, we will see how our wounds drive us perfectly toward the fulfillment of our life's path/purpose/calling/destiny. From a higher perspective, the wounds, the healing journey, and the gift of the divine design are one. In a well-read chart, there will be no superfluous pieces, no loose ends. Such a complete synthesis is the aim of the dedicated reader. The chart as a whole will make sense, each feature a part of the overall tapestry. When we see our life spread out before us and we see and feel the perfection of this larger plan, we connect with the *guiding hand* that lies around us and within us at every moment, waiting for us to awaken.

Such a revelation of our lives, made possible by this type of astrological reading, is, in itself, a healing gift. Astrology and healing are natural partners.

We will give a detailed example chart delineation in chapter 13.

CHAPTER SEVEN

Chiron in the Signs

When looking at Chiron in the signs, we must remember that the signs give the essential nature of Chiron as opposed to the real-life context in which this nature manifests (environment, nurture), the latter being seen in the house placement. However, it is important always to consider the sign placement alongside the house placement, never in isolation.

Chiron in Aries

The Wound

A profound lack or loss of self-worth. A core feeling of worthlessness, unworthiness, and even undeservingness of life itself. Self-denial. A feeling of not being wanted, needed, or useful. A feeling of being uncentered, unfocused, and/or lacking solidity.

The Search

The search for *self,* for identity.

The Wound's Expression

Tendencies toward putting others first, seeking to please others, sacrificing self, sabotaging self, giving away power to others, failing to stand up for self, being afraid to take a stand, and/or meandering through life, influenced by the slightest change of atmosphere or energy.

Alternately, as a reaction, tendencies toward futile grandstanding, bravado, aggressive reactions to what we perceive as others' putdowns, misplaced stoicism, championing the causes of others in order to feel valuable and worthy, and/or stubborn resistance to asking others for help despite our desperate plight.

Escaping the Wound

Tendencies toward living vicariously through others, compulsively needing to help others (altruism overruling all egoism, positive and negative), trying to rescue others who also lack self-worth, retreating from conflict, confrontation, and challenge, and/or avoiding circumstances and situations where taking a stand or expressing an opinion is required.

The Healing Path

The people we try to please, whom we sacrifice ourselves to, help, rescue, or live vicariously through, will ever mirror our true worth, ever encourage us to discover, acknowledge, embrace, and ultimately love ourselves and our unique gifts. Simultaneously, the part of us that will never be put down—the spirit—will ultimately fight back against our self-deprecation and against its reflection in the outside world—i.e., against others putting us down. When enough is enough, we will stand up and affirm our true worth. We are not designed to be doormats.

Where are we unique, special, and gifted (in forms that we may not be acknowledging)? No person on the planet is superfluous or identical to another. Each of us serves a special and unique purpose/service or we would not be here.

The Gift

The discovery, acknowledgment, embracing, and loving of our special and unique divine design. The realization of the indestructibility of spirit, despite the transience of forms. The acknowledgment of the divine within us. The growth of *presence* and spiritual solidity; and the sharing of this by our mere *presence,* true self-love, and positive ego. The ability to remain firmly but gently in our own space, despite the opinions and actions of others.

Chiron in Taurus

The Wound

A deep insecurity. A core fear of losing safety, security, abundance, and/or love; the underlying conviction that these were taken away, were lost, were or are in deficit, and/or were or are missing. A loss of trust. A deficit of values.

The Search

The search for security, safety, trust, and love, often mirrored through material values. The search for universal values.

The Wound's Expression

Tendencies toward trying to grasp, hold on to, cling to, covet, and/or hoard security, safety, abundance, and love, whether it is with respect to people, things, or core ideals. Tendencies toward being materially and/or emotionally demanding, clinging, and/or self-centered. Tendencies toward aligning self with transient values; alternately, devaluing self and life. Whatever form, though, it is all a quest for love.

Escaping the Wound

Tendencies toward (1) clinging to material things and to emotionally safe and secure environments, (2) avoidance of risks, and/or (3) immersion in comfort and "good living," though cautious with money.

The Healing Path

Ultimately, we will realize that the safety, security, values, and love we seek are not to be found in the material world. They can only be found in the spiritual heart—in the wellspring of spirit and in the love that invisibly pervades all things.

In the meantime, our efforts to find and keep material safety, security, values, and love will gradually become decreasingly able to answer our needs. As Emerson said, *nothing of the senses can ever satisfy.* Abundance in the material world is but a reflection of the true abundance—that of the spiritual heart, of spirit, and of love. Love is the ultimate value.

The Gift

Understanding the connection between the material and spiritual worlds. Learning how to manage and increase the abundance of the material world. Financial prudence, investing skill, management ability with material resources, steady persistence with these gifts, and a long-term perspective.

Ultimately, the gift is discovering, acknowledging, embracing, and loving the true well-spring of safety, security, abundance, and values, i.e., the spiritual heart, spirit, and love. The material world is the playground of spirit, the schoolroom of the higher *self,* and the mirror of the soul, ever enticing us to awaken.

The gift is a return to the trust that love will always *be* there, always *is* there, and was *never* missing. It is the realization that when we lose, we simultaneously gain—the universal law of conservation and compensation; also, that we cannot lose spirit (spirit being love), be-cause spirit is eternal, omnipresent, and indestructible; we are spirit (love) and spirit (love) is us.

Chiron in Gemini

The Wound

A deep-seated feeling of being unable to communicate with others, verbally inept, unable to fit in socially, unintelligent, and/or unable to see the connections between one thing and the next. The hidden feeling of being uneducated or stupid compared to others. The feel-ing of not being "up with the times."

The Search

The search for understanding, awareness, integration, education, and/or rapport with others.

The Wound's Expression

Tendency toward putting others with intelligence, with social, communication, and writ-ing skills, with higher education, and/or with scientific minds, on a pedestal; conversely, putting them down. Tendency toward depreciating, denigrating, and/or hiding our own skills, intelligence, and talents, particularly in early life. Can find it difficult to believe in self and own ideas, manifesting as an extreme drive to become what we admire in others or, conversely, to reject/belittle others' talents, intelligence, and gifts. Self-deprecation can also manifest as a need to gather allies against a world that we perceive as unsupportive and/or denigrating of our apparent lack of intelligence or understanding—i.e., the formation of secret and/or subversive peer and/or social groups. Tendency toward gossip. Obsessive need to gather knowledge and understanding to allay an inner fear of disintegration of self.

Escaping the Wound

See the previous section. In addition, tendency toward hiding our talents, intelligence, and skills, so as not to be put on the spot or compared with others. The development of a fortress of protection—an area of life expression and skill in which no one can criticize us. Avoidance of social situations. Reclusive behavior. Inner communication with other entities—imagined or real—sometimes manifesting as an outward announcement of personal contact with "higher" powers (as in channeling and mediumship).

The Healing Path

Remembering that what we think is missing in our lives is what we unconsciously strive to obtain, the healing path is awakening to, recognizing, embracing, and finally loving the specific *form* of our intelligence and communicative expression. Time spent in the recesses of the mind (due to avoidance of social contact, avoidance of confrontational intellectual exchange, and the feeling of being inferior to others in this respect) later bears useful fruit—the fruit of unique, coherent, intuitively intelligent self-expression and communicative methods that offer unique perspectives to the world. Healing questions include: *Where is my unique expression? Where is my innate intelligence and intuition? Where is there a deep understanding growing in me? Where is there an advanced form of communication growing in me?*

Those whom we put up on a pedestal or, conversely, put down in a pit, mirror those aspects of ourselves that we have yet to recognize, acknowledge, embrace, and love. The healing path is recognizing the unique forms that our gifts, talents, and intelligence take.

The Gift

Unique, deeply thought-out, coherent, and intuitively intelligent understanding. The ability to share this with others in unique ways. A valuable and unique perspective on the affairs of the world around us, personally and/or globally. A drive to explore subjects of interest with unparalleled intensity and in the utmost detail. Rapport and communication with other realms of life—terrestrial and/or celestial, seen and/or unseen.

Chiron in Cancer

The Wound

The core belief and feeling that love was lost, was never there to begin with, and/or will never be found in the future. The belief/feeling that the world is not supportive, nurturing, caring, mothering, and/or loving; alternatively, that although love exists, it is either forever unrequited or we are not deserving of it. The core belief that we are unlovable and/or have been abandoned.

The Search

The search for our roots, for reunification with the "mother," and/or for the cosmic bosom —the wellspring of creation, the source of love. Ultimately, the search for the love within.

The Wound's Expression

An underlying feeling, more often unconscious, of emptiness, loneliness, and emotional pain. A tendency to sabotage relationships, to withdraw love, to withdraw *from* love, and/or to wish for relationships with unattainable partners. Conversely, a tendency to smother others in love, caring, nurturing, support, and so on. The wish to wrap others in cotton wool, soothe their pain, and look after them, all the while feeling a gnawing emptiness inside. The tendency to try to rescue those we see as unloved, uncared for, or abandoned, sometimes manifesting as matchmaking and/or collusion or interference in others' relationships. Love of animals, small children, nature, and/or ecology. Pursuit of softness, gentleness, and peace, although our inner world is often hard, harsh, and/or at war with itself. Alternately, going to any length to obtain the love of others: lying, cheating, deluding self and others, sacrificing self and innermost desires, boasting and putting on pretenses, giving all of self to others, and/or looking after others.

Escaping the Wound

Tendency toward investing emotional energy—love, caring, nurturing, support—in others; toward rallying and campaigning against perceived abandonment, neglect, deprivation, and lack of care, love, and support; toward supporting social welfare schemes; toward avoiding close personal relationships for fear of abandonment; and toward drowning our sorrows and feelings of emptiness in various external pursuits, addictions, and/or self-imposed isolation/seclusion.

The Healing Path

Those whom we seek to love, care for, nurture, support, and wrap in cotton wool each mirror aspects of ourselves in need of love, caring, nurturing, and support; however, we do not allow ourselves to receive these things. Healing questions include: *What did we do or not do in our lives that makes us feel as though we are unworthy and/or undeserving of love, caring, nurturing, and support? Why do we deny ourselves this? What is the source of our guilt?*

The love that we miss lies *within* us, cut off by our own self-judgments, which are mirrored in our judgments against others as well in others' judgments of us. The healing path will take us on a journey that will ultimately awaken us to the reality of love within us and around us. Ultimately, by trying to aid others in their search for these things, we will see that they already exist in these peoples' lives, but are simply unrecognized in form and unacknowledged in existence; this is mirrored by our own lack of recognition and acknowledgement of the love around us and within us. As we learn to love ourselves—the essence of all healing—we simultaneously become aware of the love around us that is and was always there.

The Gift

The discovery, recognition, and acknowledgment that love is and was always there, in us and around us, that there is *nothing but love,* that *we* are loved, and that no part of us is unlovable. The ability to *receive* love as well as give it. The ability to recognize the *forms* love takes in our lives and in the lives of others. The discovery that support, caring, and nurturing exist everywhere and for everybody, but in forms that we may not have previously recognized—i.e., that a *guiding hand* exists and is active in all our lives.

Chiron in Leo

The Wound

The feeling that we cannot express ourselves, that our self-expression, life-spark, and/or creativity have been or are being squashed, and/or that our self-worth is damaged or missing. The feeling of not being a part of the celebration of life. The feelings of being uncreative, unimaginative, uninspired, unappreciated, unrecognized for our specialness or particular station in life, not given our proper due or respect, and/or disliked or not sufficiently adored.

The Search

The search for our value beyond ego and personality. The search for spontaneity, for our Inner Light, for our God-spark. The search for the freedom to sing our song without fear or guilt.

The Wound's Expression

Seeking to express and create, but tending initially to hide the results. Trying to join in the flow of life, but feeling inadequate and afraid, leading to attempts to create "reasons"— achievements, accolades, artistic creations, public image, etcetera—why we are deserving of joining in. Fear of being in public, being seen, being on stage, being on show, or being put on the spot. Feeling unworthy of being the center of attention.

Conversely, trying to stand up and be seen, recognized, appreciated, lauded, respected, and/or loved. Attempting to gain appreciation, recognition, accolade, respect, and the public eye—to steal the center stage—despite feeling unworthy inside.

Alternatively, putting others' talents and creative expressions on show—particularly children's—supporting and looking after them, and/or living vicariously through their achievements, recognition, and accolades. The love of children and of their freedom of expression and creativity.

Escaping the Wound

Tendency toward avoiding being in public, being on show, and/or being the center of attention. Reluctance to accept accolade, compliments, recognition, and so forth. General self-depreciation of our own creative talents and our modes of self-expression. Hiding the results of artistic and creative output. Putting others' talents and creative expressions on show—particularly children's—supporting and looking after them, and/or living vicariously through their achievements, recognition, and accolades.

Alternately, an obsession with being seen "on stage" and/or in the public eye—anything for attention, accolade, and adulation.

The Healing Path

Ultimately, the pain of seeing others succeed in areas where we innately know we should succeed will drive us to the outward acknowledgment and expression of our inner worth—our creativity and our self-expression. Our innate creative urge and wish to shine will win out in the end, whether in this lifetime or another.

Alternatively, those whom we assist with their success/self-expression will constantly mirror our own innate urge to shine—our innate urge to burst forth and celebrate our own existence—thus impelling us to do likewise.

Conversely, by trying to build up our own public image, by attempting to gain appreciation, recognition, accolade, respect, and/or the public eye, and/or by trying to steal the center stage, we gradually learn where our true light shines. The mirrors of approval, disapproval, support, and reprimand will teach us where our unique creativity and self-expression lie. In this way, we will eventually celebrate who we are, *exactly as we are,* in gratitude and love for the universe that created us. Such gratitude and love are the true seeds of our wish to create—of our wish to give something back to the universe.

The Gift

Permission to shine—to sing our song, so to speak. The acknowledgment of the divine creative principle that lies at the heart of our creation; then, the freedom and ability to give back to the universe through our own creations, self-expression, and celebration of life. To be able to stand before others, unashamedly being who we are, thus inspiring others to acknowledge *their* unique divine designs and the gifts of *their* lives.

Chiron in Virgo

The Wound

A deep feeling of being incomplete, fragmented, scattered, disconnected, and/or impure. The feeling that something is "wrong" with us, physically, emotional, mentally, and/or spiritually—something that needs "fixing," changing, getting rid of, and/or healing. An inexplicable and nagging sense of dissatisfaction with the way things are.

The Search

The search for wholeness, connection, and soul-satisfaction. The search for integrity, subtlety, purity, and exactitude. The need to "get it right." The search for healing, taken in the broadest sense.

The Wound's Expression

Dissatisfaction with ourselves and with others in our lives. Tendency to try to fix, correct, change, control, and/or get rid of things that, or people whom, we perceive to be not good enough. A generally critical nature, particularly in regard to our line of work and our more serious pursuits. Tendency toward a scattered, disorganized manner of living or, conversely, having a highly perfectionist nature that makes it uncomfortable for others to be around us; both extremes of this polarity can create illness/disease as a mirror of our polarized state of consciousness. Tendency to seek, simultaneously and paradoxically, having ourselves validated by others and yet having them affirm to us that there is something "wrong" with us. Tendency toward hypochondria. Can be zealously and/or fanatically health-conscious.

Escaping the Wound

Tendency toward criticizing others, blaming others, and/or trying to fix, correct, change, or get rid of others. Can be highly judgmental. Tendency toward perfectionist/compulsive focus on details as a means of trying to escape from the inability to integrate our understanding and our picture of the world. Can be obsessive-compulsive. Sometimes, ceasing to try to understand things and just blindly, by rote, going through the prescribed steps of living.

Alternately, just letting everything go, living in total disorganized chaos, and blaming the world at large for being imperfect. In this case, tendency toward bohemian, hedonistic, and/or promiscuous living.

The Healing Path

The healing path consists of gradually putting together the pieces of our lives into an integrated picture. The more pieces we collect and integrate, the more the picture is revealed to us. By seeking to help, heal, fix, correct, and/or change others and ourselves, we learn the art of integration and healing, whether we call it this or not; Virgo is the sign in which Chiron is most comfortable.

By seeking integration and, ultimately, wholeness, we gradually reveal the inherent unity and integrity *that already exists*. The healing process itself consists of raising our consciousness to see the bigger picture, the plan, the perfection, the balance, and the harmony that already exist. Such is the journey from Virgo to the sign of balance, Libra, according to the zodiac of the Mysteries. It is seeing how even our illusory perceptions of imbalance and incompleteness serve us on our journey of healing and evolution of consciousness and ultimately lead us to our divine design.

The Gift

The unveiling of the divine plan—the perfection, balance, and harmony of life. The development of methods of integration, "wholing," and healing. Learning to love things and people just as they are. Learning to love ourselves just as we are. The gift of gratitude for life and for our divine design. A deep sense of inner peace in the acknowledgment that "all's right with the world." Healing. Oneness. The return to love.

In addition, the ability to integrate masses of seemingly unconnected information/data into a coherent picture/creation. The development of the skills and arts required for our ultimate service: becoming co-creators. Creation requires the utmost attention to detail, the utmost focus, the utmost ability to juggle all the required pieces, and, lastly, the sense of the overall plan and the acknowledgment of its loving source (spirit).

Chiron in Libra

The Wound

The core wound of feeling alone, incomplete, and/or separate. The feeling that there is something or someone missing in our lives. This placement, more than any other, reflects our longing for our soul mate. Additionally, the acute awareness/feeling/perception of imbalance in ourselves and in the world around us (remembering that, ultimately, imbalance is the illusion of our wounded lower nature).

The Search

The search for the pieces of ourselves in the mirror of others, for companionship, for contact and connection, and for our soul mate. The search for balance, harmony, beauty, grace, proportion, and perfection.

The Wound's Expression

Tendencies toward fearing being alone, sacrificing self and inner direction for the sake of being with others, staying with others despite innately knowing that our path is to leave, and/or keeping others around us in our lives. We are constantly seeking balance, harmony, beauty, and peace while, to a complementarily opposite degree, we experience inner turmoil, disharmony, conflict, and struggle. Tendency to be deeply disturbed by interpersonal conflicts. This placement can express as creativity and artistic flair in an effort to create the harmony, balance, beauty, and wholeness that we seek. It can also manifest as energy loss, chronic fatigue, and/or over-expression burnout.

Escaping the Wound

Tendencies toward burying ourselves in relationships, and/or sacrificing our inner direction and calling for the sake of finding, keeping, being with, and staying with others. Inclination to seek contact with other realms of life—i.e., nature, art, nature spirits, angels, psychic guides, and those on the "other side." Putting on masks and making up stories about self in order to attract others. Living a double life—the face we wear for others and the face we wear in solitude. Can be a tendency toward trying to sabotage/upset the balance of things around us as a reaction to our personal sense of imbalance; afterward, we beat ourselves up for doing this.

The Healing Path

Every person with whom we have a relationship, whether up close and personal or more at a distance, is a reflection of ourselves. More importantly, each person reflects aspects of our true soul mate—the other "half" that we feel is missing. Most importantly, however, each of the aspects of our true soul mate, seen through others with whom we are in relationship, *is an aspect of ourselves that we have yet to discover, recognize, acknowledge, embrace, and finally love unconditionally.* What we sense we are missing is actually within us already, awaiting our discovery. The divine mirror we have been given is the reflection that others offer us. The paradox is that, when we have become consciously whole and healed, we have no more need of a soul mate, and yet this is when we are truly ready to be with them.

We feel alone because we are cut off from ourselves, cut off from our divine origins, cut off from oneness/God/universe/love.

Each piece of ourselves that we discover, through its reflection in another, increases our sense of wholeness, completeness, and, hence, contact with life and love; we feel increasingly balanced, harmonious, and at peace. "I am you and you are me." Forms differ, but essence is the same.

By seeking to discover/uncover the balance, beauty, grace, proportion, and perfection of things and people we see around us, we are simultaneously revealing our own inner balance and perfection. The reverse is equally true. Balance already exists; we simply do not see it at first, this being the nature of our woundedness.

The Gift

The realization that all we need is within us already; we are complete and perfect as we are—we just did not see it at first. The gift of realizing the magnificence and magnitude of the love inherent in the design of material life inasmuch as it offers us an unparalleled mirror through which we can awaken to our divine nature, our light, and our divine design. The mirror of others—the tool of duality—allows us to awaken to aspects of ourselves to which we were previously oblivious—aspects that we were denying, judging, not acknowledging, and/or not loving. Such is the healing journey.

Discovering the harmony, balance, proportion, beauty, and true perfection of all of life—the outer world of the *other* as well as the inner world of *self*. (In the end, they are one and the same.)

In addition, contact with all life, on all levels, and in all realms. The more whole and healed we become, the more we see that separation and aloneness were illusions, and the more we feel the real presence of others in our spiritual hearts, beyond time, space, and even death. Love goes beyond all dimensions and dissolves all boundaries.

Chiron in Scorpio

The Wound

The core feeling of being disconnected from, or abandoned by, spirit, manifesting in a deep-seated fear of loss and/or death. The feeling that the world is against us, that others seek to bring us down, that others may be plotting against us, and/or that others manipulate us and/or undermine us.

A deep doubt concerning our own immortality—i.e., questioning whether this visible life is all there is. The fear of total annihilation.

The Search

The search for transformation and evolution of consciousness. The search for spirit, for the immortal, and for the unchangeable within us. The search for *trust* in spirit.

The Wound's Expression

Tendency toward building immense walls of protection, internal and/or external. Tendency toward clinging to others and to the sense of security they may offer, and working secretly to keep it so by whatever means required. The fear of loss, death, and/or annihilation tends to make us highly and jealously protective of the people and things in our lives; alternately, it may make us vindictive, destructive, maligning, and backstabbing.

The tendency toward striving to make some kind of immortal contribution to life and the world in order to counteract the fear of our own impermanence and/or annihilation. The tendency toward striving to understand the essence of life itself, to touch life, and ultimately to touch spirit. Conversely, there can be a preoccupation with death and dying.

Lastly, there can be self-destructiveness and/or suicidal tendencies as an unconscious striving to be free from our attachment to the material plane and/or as a self-fulfilling prophecy of annihilation.

Escaping the Wound

Tendency toward making light of, or making entertainment out of, death, dying, and/or destruction. Tendency toward obsessing over death and dying. May tend to seek a bohemian or hedonistic lifestyle. Tendency toward clinging to partners and possessions with jealous ferocity. May tend to explore psychic phenomena and evidence of life after death. Possible workaholic tendencies. Potential for destructiveness toward others and their possessions. Tendency toward seeing relationships in terms of conflict and/or war, and/or viewing the world and others as the enemy.

The Healing Path

The deep fear of death will ultimately drive us to seek the origins of life, to seek the intangible spark that lies within all tangible life, and to seek the immortal and the indestructible.

In seeking this in the external world, we are looking into a mirror that reflects back to us our own immortal nature.

The wounds of loss and death will ultimately cause us to introspect deeply. We will eventually see that those aspects of things we have lost and people who have died still exist around us and in us. They still exist, but in new forms, unrecognized at first. Their essence always remains and is accessible to us in states of gratitude and love; they are always in our spiritual hearts. We will eventually see that those aspects of *ourselves* that we feel we have lost or have died within us also still exist, again just in different forms.

Here, the healing journey is seeing that the world of forms is a transient illusion, behind which lies the truth of the immortal *actuality*—the truth of spirit, oneness, and love. Furthermore, the healing journey consists of awakening to the service that this transient illusion offers us: it is a mirror in which we can eventually see our true and immortal nature and awaken to our divine design.

The healing journey will teach us that by trying to hold on to the forms of things and people we are in fear of losing, we actually *contribute* to their loss and death. When we smother the forms, we prevent them from breathing. However, when we see, embrace, and love the essence within and are no longer attached to the forms, the forms can change, but we are never in a state of loss or missingness. Love brings all essences together in the spiritual heart.

I am reminded of a poem by William Blake (who had Chiron in Scorpio):

> *He who binds to himself a joy*
> *Doth the winged life destroy,*
> *But he who kisses the joy as it flies*
> *Lives in Eternity's sun rise.*[1]

The Gift

The discovery, recognition, acknowledgment, embracing, and loving of spirit. The transcendence of the dualistic illusions of material forms. The releasing of people and things to live freely in that playful illusion, knowing in our spiritual hearts that we can never lose or miss their essence, their presence, or their love. The realization that all transient aspects of people or things that we lose, or who die, are still around us and/or within us, their forms different, but their essence the same.

---

1. David V. Erdman, ed., *The Complete Poetry and Prose of William Blake* (New York: Anchor Books, 1988).

The awakening of the immortal part of ourselves. The realization of the indestructibility of spirit and that, in the death of every form, there is a simultaneous and entirely balancing birth. The gift of giving something immortal to others and to the world at large. The reaffirmation of the divine—of God/universe/oneness/love.

The gifts of intensity and depth of inquiry. The passion for life, knowledge, and understanding.

Chiron in Sagittarius

The Wound

A deep-seated feeling of meaninglessness, pointlessness, loss, or absence of inspiration. The core wound that says that there is no bigger picture, no *guiding hand,* no higher realms of existence. Existentialist. Can be a fear of open spaces and/or of having no boundaries. A feeling of being dwarfed by the immensity of life and the world. The feeling that we are not wise, but that wisdom is in the hands of others. The fear that we cannot know or will never find the answers to life's most important questions. The feeling and/or fear that others are taking or may take the air out of the balloon of our idealism, vision, and optimism.

The Search

The search for meaning, for the larger plan, for the Master Designer. The search for the higher *self.*

The Wound's Expression

Tending to fear inquiry into "deeper" matters. Tendency toward reliance on others for answers to important questions of existence, putting others on a pedestal in the process. Nonetheless, despite the fear, there can be an insatiable appetite for gathering others' knowledge and understanding. However, there may be a fear of questioning what is given to us—safer to take things at face value. Thus, an inclination to become involved in religious and spiritual groups that dictate a prescribed belief structure.

The tendency to seek a safe and known environment while avoiding challenging situations and opportunities. Conversely, an obsessive need to experience all paradigms and environments firsthand, even if it means discarding previous beliefs and rational constraints; connected with this, a possible foolhardy disregard for personal safety.

Escaping the Wound

Tendency toward burying ourselves in the rituals and structures of daily life, in organized religions, and/or in other such peer/support/factional/sectarian groups. Can be reclusive. Tendency to fear and/or avoid change. Can become dogmatic, overzealous, and/or uncompromising in beliefs and attitudes. Can be reticent and unsure of self in matters that lie beyond everyday life. Can put others on a pedestal, demeaning our own capacity for knowledge and wisdom.

The Healing Path

By gathering the knowledge, understanding, and wisdom of others, we ultimately discover a common thread, and answers begin to emerge. More importantly, by doing this, we begin to see and acknowledge our own innate wisdom and understanding through the outer reflection.

By gradually becoming too comfortable with, and too entrenched in, the known, pat answers, and predigested viewpoints, we ultimately long for the unknown; this is evolution's innate drive. Impelled by our longing, we gradually become more willing to approach the boundaries of our current consciousness and knowledge; we start asking questions. Somewhere inside, we *know* that there *is* meaning to life, that there *is* a bigger picture, and that we are an integral part of it all.

In the end, knowledge is simply a commodity; true understanding and wisdom come from the marriage of knowledge with *being*—with our essence. Knowledge is simply a mirror we use to awaken us to what we already know in our spiritual hearts—to awaken us to our divinity, our light, and our perfection.

The Gift

The discovery, recognition, acknowledgment, embracing, and loving of our own innate wisdom and understanding. Inner knowing. Inner certainty. Gnostic awakening. The realization that meaning lies within us, that the divine lies within us.

The quest for adventure; to be pushed against the boundaries of the known; to have our answers lead us to more questions. The joy of discovery. The awakening to the miracle of existence, the magnificence of the universe, the adventure of life, and the truth of spirit.

Chiron in Capricorn

The Wound

The wound of feeling unrecognized, unappreciated, unnoticed, unacknowledged, unheard, and/or "passed over." The feeling that there is no structure in life—that it is disorganized, chaotic, and too ephemeral. A deep-seated fear of loss or absence of concrete and tangible realities. A fear of losing control or being out of control. A fear that we cannot or will not find or know our place—our vocation and function—in the larger plan.

The Search

The search for order, control, vocation, and/or mastery. Richard Nolle says, "The desire to conquer time."[2]

The Wound's Expression

Tendency toward seeking recognition, appreciation, accolade, respect, and/or status. Tendency toward seeking to be heard (can manifest as speaking loudly, ignoring others, and/or interrupting others); alternately, hiding our worthiness to be recognized, appreciated, respected, and so forth, and/or keeping silent while others are being heard. Tendencies toward seeking to create structure and organization in our lives and the lives of those around us, avoidance of anything we cannot touch, smell, see, hear, or taste, and/or compulsively needing to be in control of every aspect of our lives and, sometimes, of others' lives.

Lastly, with this placement, we may trip from vocation to vocation, trying our best to find our place, to feel useful, to feel appreciated, and to be recognized for our station. We are like a jigsaw piece trying to find its place in the puzzle.

Escaping the Wound

Tendency toward trying to attain recognition, acceptance, accolade, and so forth, by associating ourselves with others whom we feel have these things; i.e., infatuating and "chasing" people of power, fame, and money. Tendencies toward becoming "anally" attentive to order, structure, and organization and/or trying to control others. Alternately, placing ourselves under the control of others and/or external organizations in order to bring order and structure to our lives—e.g., enlisting for military service. Tendency toward talking constantly or, alternately, hiding in the shadow of others.

---

2. Richard Nolle, *Chiron: The New Planet in Your Horoscope: The Key to Your Quest* (Tempe, AZ: American Federation of Astrologers, 1983).

The Healing Path

The need for recognition, appreciation, acceptance, respect, status, and accolade gives us an insatiable drive to excel in the eyes of others. This gives us a motivating force to fulfill our goals. Ultimately, the things for which we receive the most recognition, appreciation, acceptance, respect, status, and accolade *will be in alignment with our divine design.*

What we truly seek is to love ourselves—to recognize, appreciate, accept, and respect ourselves—*as we are,* exactly as we have been divinely designed to be.

Furthermore, if others are not listening to us, it is because *we* are not listening to us—not listening to our inner voice (conscience) and/or our inner inspiration. The more we learn to listen to our inner voice/inspiration—the voice of our soul/spirit—the more others will listen, hearing the truth and wisdom we have to offer.

The chaos that we feel and fear is *within* us and is a measure of our fragmented consciousness. We innately seek to bring order to our consciousness, and we begin by trying, unconsciously or consciously, to bring order, control, and organization to the outside world. In the process, we are learning to create and maintain our creations.

The need for control, order, and organization ultimately stems from the innate knowledge that we are destined to become co-creators. To create and sustain a creation requires the utmost control. It requires the clarity of mind that comes from ordered thinking and disciplined application and organization of all available resources.

The Gift

The recognition, acknowledgment, and appreciation of who we are, exactly as we are, exactly as we have been divinely designed to be.

The recognition, acknowledgment, and appreciation of the wisdom of our inner voice/inspiration; and the gift of sharing our wisdom and understanding with others.

The development of the abilities to organize, create order, manage ourselves, and manage things and other people. The discovery of our vocation, in line with our divine design—our life's path/purpose/calling/destiny. Training as a potential (and inevitable) co-creator. An appreciation of the nature and gift of the material world as a training ground for co-creators.

The inner peace of orderly consciousness.

Chiron in Aquarius

The Wound

The core wound of feeling like an alien or outsider—of feeling isolated, cut-off, abandoned, separate, alone, distant, and removed from the rest of humanity. Feeling as though home is very far away. Feeling different from others, as though there is something wrong with us. Feeling like a stranger in a strange land. The inability to see our place in the world. Feeling separate from the collective consciousness. Feeling exiled from society.

The Search

The search for connectedness, contact, belongingness, and grounding. The search for our place in the larger picture—in society, in the global community, and in the cosmos.

The Wound's Expression

The feeling of utter aloneness and yet, paradoxically, the tendency to seek solitude. Feeling like an outsider in social circumstances. Feeling alone in a crowd. Tendency to stand apart from others, yet seeking to be among others. Paradoxically, the feeling of relief when finally truly alone. The tendency toward seeking contact with higher consciousness—i.e., seeking a more objective view, a broader perspective, a more universal paradigm. Trying to put the pieces together into a bigger picture.

Tendency toward being deliberately obtuse, contrary, reactionary, eccentric, and so forth, in order to put distance between others and us. Tendency toward secretly or overtly lauding our "differentness" from others as a kind of mark of superiority, all the while feeling inferior inside.

Escaping the Wound

As above (last paragraph). Alternately, tendency toward trying to be constantly among others; conversely, tending to be reclusive. Tendency toward avoiding close personal relationships, remaining friendly but being cool toward, and distant from, others. Can find ourselves attending to universal and humanitarian causes as a way of trying to feel connected to a bigger picture and to feel as though we belong.

The Healing Path

By being in a position of feeling like an outsider looking in at the world and people around us, we are impelled to figure out why we feel so different and so cut-off. Our position gives us the possibility of increasing our objective knowledge and of seeing a bigger picture of life.

Here, the healing journey is the process of putting each thing we observe in the world, including ourselves, into a larger context and seeing how it fits into, and is an integral part of, the whole. This, in turn, is an outer reflection of our inner predicament and of the potential healing process. Each external piece we link with the whole is a piece of ourselves put back into the larger context. Gradually, we feel more a part of the whole, more integrated, and more connected to the whole. We begin to see our place in the world. We begin to feel as though we belong. Our sense of contact with others and with the cosmos at large grows.

Ultimately, we will grow to love our aloneness as well as our connectedness, realizing that the former gives us the space and impulse in which to make further connections and in which to see an ever larger picture of life. A healing question might be, *In what ways are our differences in* form *(from others) actually similarities in* essence?

The Gift

The gift of objectivity, of seeing the bigger picture, of being able to stand back and glimpse the view from "on high." The gift of connection—of reconnecting with the universe and humanity. The gift of aloneness in which we can, paradoxically, be in silent communion with the universe.

Here, the wound ultimately drives us toward seeing, acknowledging, and embracing the higher divine logic (mirrored in Uranus) upon which all creation is based. From this point of view, no part is separate, disconnected, or alien to the bigger picture; all the pieces fit into the jigsaw puzzle of life, and no pieces are left in the box when the puzzle is finished. When this is witnessed in all its magnificence, love and gratitude are the only possible responses. Seeing the magnificence of the divine plan is, in itself, the ultimate healing.

Chiron in Pisces

The Wound

A loss of faith and/or trust in the divine/God/All/oneness/truth. A deep-seated sense of betrayal, victimization, and/or disenfranchisement by life and/or God/universe. A loss of faith
in the power and omnipresence of love. The fear of being hurt—physically, emotionally,
mentally, and/or spiritually. A core belief in the injustice, inequity, unfairness, merciless-
ness, and victimizing nature of the universe. A feeling of being forsaken by God (whoever
our God or gods may be), mirrored in the Christian story of the Crucifixion.

The Search

The search for oneness, for the divine, for love, for timelessness and spacelessness, and for
God (whoever our God or gods may be). The search for the balancing factors in injustices,
inequities, victimization, disenfranchisement, and painful events and circumstances.

The Wound's Expression

Tendency toward shutting our inner doors to the universe, to the divine, to God, and suffering silently within ourselves (private hurt), yet, paradoxically, seeking to merge, to return
to oneness, and to become whole again. Tendency toward developing a hard shell and a
pragmatic and sometimes cynical exterior manner with others. (This is the most common
expression). Conversely, can be overly sensitive, gushing, and teary. Can be susceptible or
gullible to outer influences that appear to offer love or union with something divine and/or
mystical.

Can be a fear of opening up to others, yet needing close personal contact; this can lead
to clouded judgment when choosing partners. (Yet, paradoxically, each partner will offer another reflection of what we need to see about ourselves.) Sometimes, our suspiciousness, fear
of opening to others, fear of being hurt, and lack of trust will sabotage our relationships.

Nonetheless, tendency toward being highly sensitive inside—even overly so. Can feel
like a victim of the injustices, inequities, and suffering of the world; this can cause us to
champion underdogs and lost causes, to try to rescue the disenfranchised and the
wounded, to sympathize with perceived victims, and/or to try to soothe others' pain and
suffering.

Can manifest as agnosticism or even atheism.

Often expresses self through artistic and creative output.

Escaping the Wound

Tendencies toward retreating into our shell, not showing our sensitive nature, making light of serious subjects in a humorous, cynical, and sometimes sarcastic way, and/or avoiding spiritual, psychological, or philosophical questions in favor of getting on with practical, pragmatic, and tangible activities. Tendency toward avoiding intimacy in close personal relationships.

Alternately, tendency toward allowing ourselves to be influenced, captivated, brainwashed, controlled, overtaken, and assimilated by people, groups, or organizations professing (honestly or dishonestly) to have divine connections and/or higher ideals. Can tend to give our spiritual power to others.

Tendency toward blaming the world for injustice, unfairness, inequity, victimization, and hurt to self and others. Trying to rescue others. Championing lost causes, underdogs, and apparent victims.

The Healing Path

The universe will never stop knocking at our door. Our sense of betrayal, injustice, inequity, unfairness, victimization, and so on will constantly draw us into situations that will challenge us to see a more balanced picture. These feelings will challenge us to see the justice behind the seeming injustices, to see the fairness behind the seeming unfairnesses, and to return to a sense of trust that the universe is actually looking after us all.

Feeling as though we did not deserve to be treated a certain way or subjected to certain events and circumstances causes us to seek retribution, redress, justice, and/or revenge. In this process, we will gradually see a larger picture and begin to understand the higher logic behind these things. The final issue is neither redress nor compensation, but realizing that there was never anything to forgive; all was perfect as it was—a part of the divine plan.

The path to oneness is only attained when we can see that all things serve us in our lives—that all things serve our healing and evolution of consciousness. All things are divine acts of love. The more we see and acknowledge the hidden purpose behind seemingly "wrong" events and circumstances, the more we are inclined to open the doors that we shut so tightly in the beginning. The more we can do this, the more we regain trust in a *guiding hand,* trust in a universal plan, trust in a God, and trust in the omnipresence of love.

Paradoxically, we regain trust by trusting and faith by having faith. Real trust and faith, though, are based upon observed facts; they are based upon a balanced perception that sees all sides of any given situation. Balanced perception sees the justice in the injustice, the fairness in the unfairness, the equity in the inequity, the blessings in the crisis, the cloud's silver lining, and the lessons, gifts, and service inherent in every manifestation of creation.

The Gift

The return to trust and faith in spirit/God/the divine/the universe. The revealing of the love of the creator. A return to oneness, wholeness, and completeness. The opening of the spiritual heart to giving and receiving love freely. Being able to look anywhere in our lives and in the lives of others and see nothing except the action and presence of love.

CHAPTER EIGHT

Chiron in the Houses

When looking at Chiron in the houses, we must remember that the houses give the *context* in which the essential nature of Chiron (seen in the natal sign placement) expresses itself. The sign placement is *nature,* whereas the house placement is *environment* and *nurture*—the stage upon which the play is enacted. So, it is important always to consider the house placement alongside the sign placement, never in isolation.

For these reasons, and to shine a guiding light on the chart integration process, I have offered two examples of sign/house integrations for each house definition.

Chiron in the 1st House

Our woundedness is most likely to be played out through our sense of self, sense of identity, and sense of self-worth. The manifestations of the wounding will very often be physical in nature and expressed through the body and through our physical self-image. See also Chiron in Aries, in chapter 7.

Example 1. Chiron in Leo in the 1st house could be a wound where we felt that our creativity, ego, will, and joy of life were repressed and/or damaged by physical abuse and/or restriction or by psychological damage to our sense of self.

Example 2. Chiron in Aquarius in the 1st house could be a wound where we felt isolated, cut-off, abandoned, and as an outsider to the world by the fact that we were physically ignored as a child, ostracized for being different or strange, and/or separated bodily from our parents—e.g., adopted, orphaned, homeless, and so forth.

Chiron in the 2nd House

Our woundedness is most likely to be played out through the issues of emotional and material security, safety, comfort, values, and well-being. See also Chiron in Taurus, in chapter 7.

Example 1. Chiron in Sagittarius in the 2nd house could be the wound of a sense of meaninglessness and lack of wisdom due to being brought up in an environment where all physical needs and comforts were provided (born into a rich family, for example), but devoid of inner or spiritual guidance. Conversely, being brought up in dire material adversity, the seeming injustice of it all and the frightening immensity of the world seen from the streets, might give expression to the wound of feeling as though there is no guiding force in life, no overall balancing and just plan, and, ultimately, no God.

Example 2. Chiron in Pisces in the 2nd house could be a wound of feeling betrayed or victimized by the world, expressed through feeling denied or cheated of emotional and/or material security (such as an inheritance), safety, and/or comfort.

Chiron in the 3rd House

Our woundedness is most likely to be played out in the arena of knowledge, the mind, communications, media, and siblings. See also Chiron in Gemini, chapter 7.

Example 1. Chiron in Cancer in the 3rd house may manifest as a wound of feeling unloved, uncared for, and/or not nurtured or looked after by virtue of feeling ignored, not communicated with as a fellow human, shunned by siblings, and/or not being given credit for intellectual ability.

Example 2. Chiron in Taurus in the 3rd house could be the wound of feeling deeply insecure, deprived, and/or handicapped (lack of abundance) in the area of the intellect due to growing up in a rural/working-class environment. Perhaps a deep mistrust of intellect. Perhaps a feeling of a lack of communication of love and trust.

Chiron in the 4th House

Our woundedness is likely to be played out in the arena of the home environment, through parents and children, through community participation (or lack thereof), and/or through nature and the environment. Wounds and unresolved issues pertaining to our roots are also illuminated here. See also Chiron in Cancer, in chapter 7.

Example 1. Chiron in Libra in the 4th house could be the wound of feeling alone, incomplete, and/or separate in the home environment. Something seems missing in the relationships between parents and children; home life fails to fill our void, our need for contact, and/or our need for companionship/friendship (e.g., as in a "boot camp" family setup).

Example 2. Chiron in Aries in the 4th house might be the wound of feeling a deep inadequacy and low self-worth in the wake of seemingly brighter siblings or parents with huge public profiles. Alternatively, it could be a feeling of being powerless to do anything about the plight of the third world or about ecological crises; we may feel as though we are all a scourge upon the Earth's surface, causing us to hate humanity (which is the mirror reflection of hatred of self.)

Chiron in the 5th House

Our woundedness is most likely to be played out in the arena of creativity, the Inner Child, sexuality, romance, self-expression, self-determination, and the ability to shine or not. See also Chiron in Leo, in chapter 7.

Example 1. Chiron in Gemini in the 5th house may express as a wound of feeling stupid or ignorant when it comes to creative matters. Alternatively, it might be a feeling of inability to communicate what is inside of us or to bring this to a wider audience.

Example 2. Chiron in Virgo in the 5th house might be the wound of feeling a deep dissatisfaction and/or self-criticism with any of our creative efforts and/or our efforts to be outwardly open and expressive. This, in turn, may be directed toward our children in the form of hypercriticism and nitpicking, causing them to fear expressing themselves or showing their own creativity.

Chiron in the 6th House

Our woundedness is played out primarily through the workplace, work methodology, and service to the community. It can also be played out through issues of medicine, health, and disease. See also Chiron in Virgo, in chapter 7.

Example 1. Chiron in Scorpio in the 6th house may manifest as the wound of feeling as though people in our workplace are against us, constantly plotting, and/or constantly seeking to undermine our work and work methods. Alternatively, we may feel as though our workplace is a kind of hell to which we have been banished by a cruel God, unable to leave due to fear of loss of income, lifestyle, and/or contact with others. Alternately, we might find ourselves working in a medical situation—close to those who are ill and dying—with our fear of loss and death challenged daily.

Example 2. Chiron in Capricorn in the 6th house might manifest as a wound of feeling that our contribution/service is unrecognized, unappreciated, unheard, and not respected in the workplace. Moreover, such feelings might manifest in physical or emotional illness.

Chiron in the 7th House

Our woundedness is most likely to be played out in the arena of relationships, social interactions, and social justice (or injustice). See also Chiron in Libra, in chapter 7.

Example 1. Chiron in Leo in the 7th house might manifest as the wound of feeling unable to express ourselves—not free to explore and develop our creativity and individual gifts—due to a stifling relationship that demands most of our attention and time.

Example 2. Chiron in Pisces in the 7th house might be the wound of feeling used and abused, victimized and betrayed, by those with whom we have had relationships. Alternately, it might be that the wound of feeling a deep need for contact and for merging into oneness causes us to give ourselves away totally in relationships, until we have little left for ourselves.

Chiron in the 8th House

Our woundedness is played out primarily in the area of spiritual matters, death, dying, loss, power, sexuality, money or joint finance, and/or mortality/immortality. See also Chiron in Scorpio, in chapter 7.

Example 1. Chiron in Virgo in the 8th house may manifest as the wound of feeling an incompleteness and dissatisfaction with life due to the deaths of those close to us. Alternatively, it might be that the feeling of being fragmented and incomplete expresses through a deep inquiry into the nature of life, death, and spiritual matters.

Example 2. Chiron in Capricorn in the 8th house might manifest as the wound of feeling a lack of order and control in our lives, due to the impermanence of life around us. Alternatively, it might be that our feeling of not being appreciated, recognized, and/or respected is played out through relationships with others in the business world (joint finances).

Chiron in the 9th House

Our woundedness is most likely to be played out in the arena of travel, foreign countries, philosophy, religions, ethics and morals, and/or education. Our woundedness may be played out on an international stage. This placement illuminates the crisis of disconnection from our higher *self.* See also Chiron in Sagittarius, in chapter 7.

Example 1. Chiron in Libra in the 9th house may express as the wound of feeling alone, separate, and/or cut off from relationship and contact, expressing itself through a pursuit of spiritual matters in order to fill the void—i.e., developing a relationship with unseen realms. Alternately, we may seek relationship through travel or the Internet.

Example 2. Chiron in Aries in the 9th house might manifest as the wound of feeling inadequate, low in self-worth, and/or unsure of our identity, causing us to pursue and become involved with religious or spiritual groups; alternatively, to study philosophy and/or psychology; alternatively, to generally gain higher education to give us a greater sense of worth.

Chiron in the 10th House

Our woundedness is played out in the area of career, the public arena, business in general, mastery of our earthly purpose, and/or through our need for recognition, appreciation, respect, and acknowledgment of our achievements. See also Chiron in Capricorn, in chapter 7.

Example 1. Chiron in Sagittarius in the 10th house might manifest as the pursuit of business, management, and/or public affairs as an answer to our wound of feeling that life is meaningless otherwise and holds no secrets other than what we can tangibly make of it. A sense of achievement and accolades give respite from our inner feelings of emptiness.

Example 2. Chiron in Gemini in the 10th house might express as the wound of feeling intellectually stupid, ignorant, and/or unrecognized, expressed in a career choice that is either physically and/or emotionally based but does not require too much thinking. Alternatively, it might be that our feeling of not being a good communicator or of being inept in social circumstances might be most prominently expressed in our chosen career, such as acting or politics (e.g., Woody Allen).

Chiron in the 11th House

Our woundedness will most likely manifest in the arena of groups, community, and collective expression. We will tend to be an individual expression of the collective wounds of humanity, seeking to play a unique role in the evolution of cultural consciousness. See also Chiron in Aquarius, in chapter 7.

Example 1. Chiron in Scorpio in the 11th house might manifest as the wound of feeling that others, en masse, are talking about us behind our backs, plotting or scheming against us, and/or secretly conspiring against us. Alternatively, it might be that we fear the loss of unique cultural groups in the globalization process (these groups reflecting aspects of ourselves that we are in fear of losing through the personal evolutionary process). Alternatively, it may be that we lament the loss of spirituality in the modern world and set out to make a difference by starting groups for the pursuit of spiritual matters.

Example 2. Chiron in Cancer in the 11th house might manifest as a wound of feeling unloved or unworthy of love by humanity—the feeling that the world has become all so impersonal and uncaring. Alternatively, it might be that we wish to rescue groups of others whom we perceive to be unloved and uncared for—to become a Good Samaritan of sorts, a social worker, a foreign aid worker, and/or a champion of underdogs, down-and-outs, and minorities.

Chiron in the 12th House

Our woundedness is most likely to be played out against the backdrop of our inner life, the unconsciousness, the psyche, spiritual longings, and/or mysticism. It may be played out within the walls of institutions concerned with the welfare (or incarceration) of the mind, body, and spirit. In any case, this placement indicates that we tend to hide away the wound, clinging to our woundedness as a kind of paradoxical solace. Finding an outer divinatory expression for our mystical intuitions is necessary here. See also Chiron in Pisces, in chapter 7.

Example 1. Chiron in Taurus in the 12th house may manifest as the wound of feeling insecure, unsafe, and/or neglected in love, causing us to sequester ourselves in the relative safety of the inner recesses of our inner world and/or in the cloistered walls of an institution that will give us what we need. Alternately, it could be that our feeling of having had emotional and material comfort and love taken from or denied us is expressed in living a life of material self-denial and/or of dedicating ourselves to the pursuit of spirit.

Example 2. Chiron in Aquarius in the 12th house may express as a tendency toward becoming reclusive and nonparticipatory in life, licking the wounds of feeling alienated, abandoned, cut-off, separate, different, and/or a stranger in a strange land. Alternatively, it may manifest as a search for contact and connection by pursuing explorations of the mind, the subconscious, spirit, the astral realms, the shamanic world, parapsychology, divination, the dream state, and/or religious or spiritual groups.

CHAPTER NINE

Chiron in Aspect

A Note about Parallels, Contraparallels, and Occultations

I take the view that parallels and contraparallels both have the same influence/effect as conjunctions and should be treated as such. (Note: Parallels are not necessarily more positive, nor are contraparallels necessarily more negative.) Occultations are the most powerful of the aspects, amplifying the already powerful conjunction.

To qualify as a true parallel or contraparallel, the maximum orb should be one degree. To qualify as an occultation, the parallel should have a maximum orb of one degree, *and* the conjunction should be within ten degrees for the luminaries and within five degrees for all other planets.

Chiron in Aspect to the North Node

I am in the habit of taking the *true* node positions rather than the *mean* nodes. My studies have confirmed the accuracy of making this choice, particularly with respect to the exact dates of transits to and by the nodes.

In general, Chiron aspecting the North Node will tend to indicate that our life's path and purpose are in some way more aligned with the themes of healing and evolution of consciousness than otherwise would be the case.

Conjunction, Parallel, Contraparallel, Occultation

Chiron conjunct, parallel, contraparallel, or occulting the North Node aligns our life's path/purpose/calling/destiny with the healing journey per se. This aspect confers, more than any other, a *calling* to heal—others and ourselves. We have been chosen, so to speak, to be an emissary for Chiron's messages to the planet; we are here to do Chiron's work. Moreover, Chiron represents one of our life's primary planetary guides. This aspect can also be a tacit indication of considerable work already done on healing and evolution of consciousness in past lives.

The conjunction of Chiron and the North Node is worthy of our special attention because there is a historical significance every time it occurs.

Put simply, every time this conjunction occurs, a new batch of healers of a particular "flavor" pass their final exams, graduate, and are let loose upon the world to begin their mission of assisting humanity's healing and evolution of consciousness. (Note that, in this instance, we are not referring to persons born during these conjunctions, but those of relevant age and inclination who were activated by these conjunctions. Those born during these conjunctions will, in the future, carry on the work of those activated during these times.)

For example, the conjunction of February 1969 was in Aries. During the 1960s, Chiron approached aphelion—its most distant point, always occurring in the sign of Aries—representing the most acute inner expression of our woundedness. The 1960s was the beginning of a revolution of consciousness—the beginning of a new cycle of emphasis on spiritual and healing matters.

The Chiron-North Node conjunction of 1969 in Aries represented the graduation/activation of healers who marked the beginning of the so-called New Age—the beginning of the prelude to the Age of Aquarius. These people were the advance party, so to speak, whose task it was to take new and bold steps into uncharted territory. The territory was *personal healing.*

The next conjunction of the North Node and Chiron occurred in July 1984 in Gemini, representing the graduation/activation of healers whose task it was to be *messengers* of heal-

ing. Their messages came not only from their personal experiences, but also from channeled sources—from the higher consciousnesses of spirit guides, discarnate entities, and energetic "aliens." Their overall message was simple: "You have the power and capacity to become citizens of the galaxy, as you were meant to be. You can heal yourselves, because you
are divine and limitless. It's only a matter of choosing to embrace your destiny."

The next Chiron-North Node conjunction occurred in Libra in 1996, in the year of
Chiron's perihelion and perigee—its closest point to the Sun and Earth, respectively, and its
point of greatest expression of healing. The new "graduates" were people who had lived
through and healed co-dependency, abandonment, deprivation, relationship failure, aloneness, alienation, and separation. Their task was to help others through similar issues and
wounds. Their ultimate message was that *separation is a lie*—that, in truth, we are all connected to one another, whether we see it or not. Healing is seeing this truth, embracing it,
and living it.

Their mission was to help us reestablish a balance (in our minds and hearts) between
self and *other,* knowing that relationship is a mirror that gives us the opportunity to heal
and evolve in consciousness. And it begins with us—taking responsibility in relationships
rather than continuing to ascribe blame.

The next Chiron-North Node conjunction takes place in 2008 in Aquarius. The new
"graduates" will be called upon to heal the wounds of separation, alienation, distance, isolation, and so forth, brought about by the Age of Technology. Paradoxically, technology
and communications—the Internet, email, on-line shopping, chat rooms, cable TV, satel-
lite TV, and so forth—that have made the world a smaller place have also made us feel
more alone, cut-off, impersonal, and distant from each other. Healers of the year 2008 will
most certainly be called upon to assist us in dealing with these issues.

In summary, each time Chiron conjuncts the North Node, it represents a fulcrum
point—the peak of a cycle within larger cycles such as the Chiron cycle—for the outward
expression of healing, particularly through individuals with an inner calling to assist in humanity's healing and evolution of consciousness.

The example natal chart delineation presented in chapter 13 has this aspect.

An occultation of Chiron and the North Node would be one of the marks of an extraordinary healer (e.g., Albert Schweitzer).

Opposition

Chiron opposition the North Node generally indicates that we bring healing gifts and talents into this lifetime. It can also indicate that our current lifetime issues and wounds have strong connections to past lives (and that we may still be working through them). In any case, we will tend to be acutely aware of wounds and issues related to the pursuit of our life's path/purpose/calling/destiny.

It may also be that, in this lifetime, we are taking the lessons and gifts of healing attained in past lives and building on them in practical ways in this lifetime—for ourselves and/or for others. The specifics of this path will be seen in the sign and house placements of Chiron and the North Node. Although we may not manifest a life as a healer per se, we will certainly tend to have a healing effect on those around us.

Trine

Chiron trine the North Node indicates a high degree of resonance between our life's path/purpose/calling/destiny and the themes of wounding and healing in our lives. This indicates that healing, whatever form it takes, will be an integral part of our life's journey and will be incorporated into the service we consciously or unconsciously afford others.

For example, if our chosen life's path is, say, to be a musician, our music will almost certainly have a healing element or, conversely, will express our woundedness directly.

This aspect can be a tacit indication of considerable work already done on healing and evolution of consciousness in past lives.

Square

Chiron square the North Node indicates that our life's path/purpose/calling/destiny cannot proceed without us simultaneously attending to our wounds and issues. Because this is so, our life's path will necessarily have healing elements in it, for us and for others, whether we call it healing or not. As we deal with our wounds and issues (seen in Chiron's house and sign placements), our life's path/purpose/calling/destiny will necessarily reflect the healing lessons/experiences we have been through—for our benefit and for the benefit of others.

For example, let's suppose our life's path and its expression is to learn to communicate our inner wisdom (North Node in Sagittarius/South Node in Gemini). We will be unable to do this until we attend to the wounds that prevent us from accessing our inner wisdom (wounds represented in this example by Chiron in Pisces, where we shut the door on the universe and spirit, or by Chiron in Virgo, where we are so critical of ourselves that we cannot allow the outward expression of our seeming incompleteness). By attending to these wounds, the inner wisdom that we will ultimately communicate, according to our divine design, cannot help but have elements of healing knowledge and a healing effect upon others.

Sextile

Chiron sextile the North Node indicates that the energy and help of Chiron is available to us in the pursuit of our life's path/purpose/calling/destiny. However, as with all sextile aspects, we must initiate this connection consciously and intentionally. When we do so, we can access the gifts of our past-life healing journeys (Chiron simultaneously trining the South Node). Whether we bring these elements to bear upon our chosen path and its expression through career is up to us. It is a gift to be had, though, and we would be wise to make use of it. It means, however, attending to the wounds of this present lifetime (seen in Chiron's sign and house placements).

It is quite common for people with this aspect to choose, unconsciously, a life's path that allows the healing of their wounds and issues to take place within the context of that path. An example would be a comedian who expresses, deals with, and heals his wounds and issues through comedy. Another example would be a sportsperson who expresses and diffuses his wounds and issues through vigorous physical activity. Another example would be an attorney who works through his wounds and issues through the reflection of his clients' grievances and lawsuits.

In this way, this aspect of Chiron contributes directly to the divine design of our lives (as opposed to being merely the driving force behind the design).

Quincunx

Chiron quincunx the North Node indicates that we are being challenged to develop a new level of conscious awareness concerning our life's path/purpose/calling/destiny. We are being coaxed to awaken to our life's higher meaning. Our wounds and issues will be the catalyst that impels us to seek an understanding of why we are here and what, from a higher perspective, we are meant to be doing.

The quincunx aspect is kind of like a mini-Pluto influence, encouraging transformation by coaxing us to let go of old ways of looking at things—in this case, old ways of thinking or not thinking about our life's path/purpose/calling/destiny; being less dramatic than

Pluto, though, the quincunx niggles, nags, irritates, and frustrates us into paying attention to our wounds and issues.

Chiron in Aspect to the South Node

In general, Chiron aspecting the South Node indicates that we bring themes of healing and evolution of consciousness strongly in from the past—particularly from past lives. It can indicate that our life's path/purpose/calling/destiny cannot be fulfilled without first attending to our unresolved issues and residual wounds. It can also be the mark of a person coming into this lifetime with a specific healing mission for themselves and for others.

Conjunction, Parallel, Contraparallel, Occultation
See Chiron opposition the North Node.

Opposition
See Chiron Conjunct, Parallel, Contraparallel, or Occult the North Node.

Trine
See Chiron sextile the North Node.

Square
See Chiron square the North Node.

Sextile
See Chiron trine the North Node.

Quincunx
Chiron quincunx the South Node indicates that we are being impelled to develop a new level of consciousness and understanding about the wounds and issues of our past—in particular, issues that have their ultimate origin in past lives.

When we say origin in past lives, we must be careful not to give the impression that the specific issues of this lifetime, *in their present form,* were the same in past lives; this is not necessarily so. However, the *essence* of the issues is the same, though their manifestation and form in *this* lifetime possibly quite different. We will approach this interesting and misunderstood question in a later chapter.

Chiron quincunxing the South Node indicates that we are chained to the past as long as we fail to see it in a new light. We are chained as long as we cling to the misperceptions and illusions that form the essence of our woundedness. The fulfillment of our life's path/purpose/calling/destiny, as indicated by the North Node, will hinge upon the healing and resolution of the issues of the past.

Chiron in Aspect to the Sun

In general, Chiron aspects to the Sun indicate that we are destined in some way to *express* the messages, issues, and themes of Chiron in our lives. We are, in a sense, Chiron's emissary. Crucial themes of this aspect include the challenges of coming out of the darkness into the light and of allowing or not allowing ourselves to shine.

Conjunction, Parallel, Contraparallel, Occultation

Next to Chiron conjunct, parallel, contraparallel, or occult the North Node, Chiron conjunct, parallel, contraparallel, or occult the Sun represents the most powerful expression of the themes of wounding and healing in our personal lives—particularly in the case of the occultation.

This aspect is a mark of a healer and/or spiritual teacher. Whether a person fulfills this task in a given lifetime is dependent upon many other issues and questions. In short, with this aspect, we *express* the wound, the healing, and the themes of Chiron directly in our lives. We are, in a sense, Chiron's emissary. It is difficult for us to separate ourselves from our wounds, and it is certainly impossible to separate ourselves from the healing path, once initiated.

However, the area of life (seen through the houses) and the specific path/purpose/calling/destiny of our life (seen through the nodes)—through which Chiron's messages and expression will be manifested—will vary according. Healing, taken in its broadest sense, encompasses many different areas of life, some of which we might not initially consider healing. It is simplistic, however, to associate healing only with physical healing and the medical professions, traditional or alternative.

For example, a person with the North Node in Capricorn and the Sun conjunct Chiron in Pisces in the 5th house may have a path and purpose to take responsibility for their life and for the lives of others, returning the nurturing they have been given along the way (North Node in Capricorn). They may express this through their emotional and psychic sensitivity toward others and their impulse to rescue others (Sun in Pisces). They then may play this out in the area of the arts (5th house), creating an environment and structure in which others can express themselves, such as a performing arts complex (Node in Capricorn), thereby healing their wound of fear of self-expression (Chiron's gift and message as expressed through its conjunction with natal Sun).

We can see from this one example how crucial it is to consider all features of a chart in synergy with each other.

As one would expect, this Chiron-Sun aspect has its own difficulties and challenges, because we cannot help expressing our woundedness. The healing side can and will only be expressed/manifest if and when we attend, consciously and intentionally, to our wounds and issues.

In my own personal experience, three of my spiritual teachers, all highly psychic and all healers of the highest order, have Chiron conjunct Sun, one with an occultation.

This aspect can be a tacit indication of considerable work already done on healing and evolution of consciousness in past lives.

Opposition

Chiron opposition the Sun indicates that our woundedness constantly challenges our need to self-express, our creative urge, and our ability and willingness to shine. The initial reaction is to retreat from self-expression, to close down, to become reclusive, and/or to fear being seen. The opposition aspect, however, does not let us run away; in this way, it is Uranus's bed partner inasmuch as the impulse to self-express and to create are simultaneously *fueled* and *held back* by our woundedness, thus encouraging and even impelling us to attend to our wounds and issues.

This aspect tends to confer a wounded sense of self and ego. There will tend to be a fear of expressing ourselves, of standing out in a crowd, of being seen, of not being good enough, and/or of being inferior to others (who seem to be able to get on and be who they are without fear or reservation).

This aspect can also be the mark of a healer, as well as a call to express the messages and themes of Chiron to the world at large, in whatever form. In any case, it certainly engenders the need for deep introspection.

Trine

Chiron trine the Sun indicates a high degree of resonance between our woundedness and its path of healing, and the way in which we *express* our lives. This can be an important aspect for a healer. On the one hand, we cannot help but express our wounds and issues (in whatever form is appropriate to our life's path/purpose/calling/destiny—seen in the nodes) and their subsequent expression (seen in the Sun's placement and its other aspects). Conversely, when we attend to our wounds and unresolved issues, we cannot help but express the healing (again, in whatever area of life that might be). Again, we are Chiron's emissary in some way.

This aspect can be a tacit indication of considerable work already done on healing and evolution of consciousness in past lives.

Square

Chiron square the Sun indicates that the outward *expression* of our life's path/purpose/calling/destiny (seen in the nodes) will be initially blocked, restricted, and/or held back. This square aspect is Saturn's bed partner inasmuch as the free and open expression of our lives is dependent upon attending—seriously, consciously, and intentionally—to our wounds and issues.

As we have said—and it is worth repeating—the gift of all major aspects of Chiron in our charts is to "force" us, impel us, or otherwise coax us to attend to our healing and evolution of consciousness. When, impelled by our innate needs and longings, we attend to our wounds and issues, we then become free to express our lives and ourselves; we have transcended the square.

In general, people with this aspect tend to have somewhat tumultuous inner lives. They tend to vacillate between their wish for healing and outright avoidance of their issues. Their powers of rationalization and justification are supreme. On the one hand, they try everything to wriggle away from their woundedness (and mostly quite successfully). On the other hand, they tend to *express* outwardly their wish for healing and evolution of consciousness. This paradox creates its own ferment, engendering the need for deep introspection.

With this aspect, it is not certain nor a given that the healing journey itself will subsequently become an integral part of our life's path/purpose/calling/destiny; it will depend, in part, on the other aspects of Chiron.

Sextile

Chiron sextile the Sun indicates that there is an open channel between our woundedness, its healing potential, and the *expression* of our life's path/purpose/calling/destiny (seen in the nodes). It represents opportunities and possibilities for accessing Chiron and its messages, consciously and intentionally. To make use of this, however, *we* must initiate the connection to Chiron; it awaits us, but we need to activate it. To do this, we need to attend consciously to our wounds and issues.

This aspect represents a potential color to add to our palette of life—another thread with which to express our Inner Light. It allows us to add the healing themes to the expression of our life's path/purpose/calling/destiny. If the rest of the chart indicates a specific life's path/purpose/calling/destiny of healing, then this will serve us well on this path. If not, then this aspect will nonetheless serve to help us clear the way for a free and open expression of our chosen path, whatever that might be.

Quincunx

Chiron quincunx the Sun indicates that a new level of consciousness and understanding about ourselves is being sought—one that will arise from the healing of our wounds and the resolution of our issues.

Our view of ourselves is limited by our lopsided perceptions of ourselves—by our illusory self-image (being our Chiron wounds outwardly mirrored in the Sun, Moon, and Ascendant placements). This affects the ease with which we express ourselves and with which we allow our creativity to flow. These illusions and misperceptions have served to keep us "safe" from the challenge of greater truth, but now is the time for us to move into a higher awareness and attain greater clarity about ourselves.

This aspect brings home this evolutionary need. It confronts us with niggling, nagging, irritating, unsettling, and sometime inexplicable life difficulties that ultimately arise from our lopsided perceptions of ourselves and from the resultant way in which we express ourselves.

Chiron in Aspect to the Moon

As we have previously explored, the Moon represents the exterior face of Chiron inasmuch as it displays our lower nature, i.e., our polarized emotions, charges, issues, biases, and judgments. These lower emotional expressions arise from our woundedness, as indicated by

Chiron. Furthermore, we need to remember that the wound and our life's path/purpose/ calling/destiny are intimately connected via the Moon's nodes. The wound (Chiron) drives the life's path, the Moon "steers," and the Moon's nodes point us in a particular direction in our life.

Also, as we have said, the Moon is simultaneously a safety valve and a safe haven—it protects us from an overload of truth and light—*and* it is the mechanism that leads us to our lessons and unresolved issues by virtue of our aforementioned emotional charges (attraction and repulsion). As we work through our charges, wounds, and issues, we begin to operate on a higher octave of the Moon's expression. We also become increasingly aligned to the Sun in consciousness, the Sun being the "planet" of our higher nature.

Conjunction, Parallel, Contraparallel, Occultation

From the perspective of our lower nature, Chiron conjunct, parallel, contraparallel, or occult the Moon indicates that, when things get too difficult or too painful, we tend to retreat within ourselves, taking a kind of paradoxical solace in our wounds. It can be a "feeling sorry for myself," "poor me," "look at me, I'm in pain," and/or martyrdom posture.

The sign and house placements of this aspect will give more clues as to the exact nature of the escape route and the specific nature of the wounds.

As an example, let's take Chiron conjunct the Moon in Taurus in the 7th house. Here, our feeling of being denied and/or cheated of material and/or emotional comfort, safety, and security (Chiron in Taurus) is expressed in our relationships (7th house). When things get too difficult or painful to deal with (the Moon's response to Chiron's wounds), we might seek material and emotional comfort (Moon in Taurus) in the relationship itself (7th house). However, never feeling as though our woundedness can be sufficiently soothed, we would tend to play out the *drama* of the wound in the relationship, milking it for what it's worth.

As previously indicated, this illustrates that the arena in which we seek solace, escape, and/or avoidance can equally be where we play out the healing journey.

In its most evolved expression, Chiron conjunct the Moon confers an emotional nature that, when confronted with difficulties or painful situations, seeks to escape or avoid the pain of the wound by immediately healing the wound and resolving the issues around it. This is certainly a blessing! Of course, the downside of this is never being able to truly escape or avoid our wounds.

The occultation of Chiron and the Moon is the most powerful of the Chiron-Moon aspects, more than likely indicating a person of advanced evolution—one who is able to transform and heal their wounds on the fly. Joan of Arc epitomizes this aspect (having a parallel of Chiron and the North Node, too!)—both the healing side and the aforementioned martyrdom tendency.

Alternately, in a person of lesser evolution, an occultation can manifest as emotional dysfunction and even psychopathy.

Opposition

Chiron opposition the Moon indicates the exaggerated tendency to run in the opposite direction when our wounds and issues become too difficult and/or painful to deal with.

Ironically, by running away from the wound (Chiron, in its particular sign and house), we place ourselves in the opposite environment (in this case, the sign and house of the Moon). By definition, the environment of the lower-octave Moon can never hope to fill the void we seek to fill/heal.

For example, Chiron in Scorpio ultimately seeks re-acknowledgment of spirit and transcendence of the illusions of loss and death. When we run to the Taurus Moon, we find only materiality, impermanence, and illusory safety. We run again and find more materiality, unsatisfactory physical substitutes, and the slippery, changeable world of forms. As William James once said, *nothing of the senses can ever satisfy.*

As another example, Chiron in Leo ever seeks to overcome the fear of individual self-expression and, finally, to shine. When we run to the Aquarius Moon, we find a world where individual self-expression is lost in the sea of collective expression.

Opposition issues and wounds invariably deal with seeming paradoxes, contradictions, conflicts, either/or choices, and differences of opinion and/or perspective. These can be internal and personal, and/or they can be external and involving others. This opposition, like all oppositions, continues to throw these issues and wounds back at us until we deal with them. It says we cannot run away, because the real issues are actually in us, not outside us.

Such oppositions can be extremely difficult to deal with, granted, particularly in this case where the Moon reflects our deepest emotional wounds and issues. The rewards are great, however, when we grasp these issues and wounds with both hands, so to speak. The healing process consists of grasping and embracing each side of a given issue/wound and seeing how both sides are necessary, complement each other, and complete each other—two sides of the same coin.

The rewards of such perceptual (and, in this case, emotional) integration—integration being the essence of healing—are a higher perspective, conflict resolution and reconciliation (with self and/or with others), true inner peace, and the transformation of pain and suffering into love.

On the other hand, continued avoidance can lead to extreme mood swings and hyper-reactivity to outside influences. I have noted this aspect in the charts of many psychotics, people with bipolar disorders, and violent criminals. It takes some evolution of consciousness and/or conscious work to harness the energy of this aspect.

In summary, the gift of this aspect is that it ever impels us to attend to our issues and wounds; whether we do so is, as always, up to us.

Trine

Chiron trine the Moon indicates that our lower emotional nature, being dualistic and reactive, will tend to illuminate our wounds rather than offer us the usual protection against, or escape from, these wounds. Wounds and issues will very quickly surface, giving us increased potential for healing and resolution—providing we desist from futilely trying to avoid and/or escape. Avoidance and escape will tend to lead to hypersensitivity. I have noted a statistically significant number of patients in mental institutions who have this aspect.

On the other hand, if we attend to our wounds and issues, have attended to them in past lives, and/or we have other significant Chiron aspects (which also possibly indicate past-life work in this area), this aspect can confer compassion, empathy, sensitivity (in a positive sense), and/or the ability to quickly work through emotional issues as they arise. It can also be indicative of an elevated healing ability and/or focus in our lives.

Square

Chiron square the Moon indicates that our lower emotional nature tends to block access to our wounds and issues. This is, of course, true for all of us, no matter what our Moon sign or aspects. However, in this case, the blocking effect is accentuated, providing a highly effective escape route and avoidance mechanism.

We must remember, though, that the Moon's manifestation is twofold. On the one hand, it protects us from having to deal with more truth than we are ready for; on the other hand, it leads us, by virtue of our "charges"—our polarized personas/emotions—into situations and circumstances that offer us the perfect possibility/potential for healing and resolution of our wounds and issues.

Said simply, we attract, create, or become what we judge negatively and/or resent. Conversely, we unconsciously drive away what we judge positively and/or infatuate. We can try to run from and/or avoid things, but our wounds and issues will ever follow us. In the end, the choice to attend to our wounds and issues or not is up to us, although Chiron square the Moon tends to disincline us to do so.

This aspect, if unattended to, can manifest violence; it is prolific in the charts of murders and murderers. Interestingly, the Moon was squaring Chiron when Martin Luther King Jr. was assassinated.

However, this same intense energy can be channeled equally and successfully into productive pursuits; e.g., it is prolific in the charts of sportspeople, evangelists, comedians, and popular entertainers.

In any case, if we choose to attend to our wounds and issues, the gifts of this aspect are great, and, particularly if combined with other significant Chiron aspects, the aspect can confer healing ability and healing focus in our lives.

Sextile

Chiron sextile the Moon represents a window through which we are given the possibility of seeing the connections between the outward emotional expression of our wounds and issues—our emotional reactions, protective patterns, and avoidance mechanisms—and the origins of these wounds and issues within us. However, as with all sextile aspects, we must choose to look through the window. If we do, then this aspect can confer healing ability and healing focus in our lives, particularly if there are other significant Chiron aspects.

Quincunx

With Chiron quincunx the Moon, we will never be quite happy in the blissful ignorance and muffled womb of Mother Moon's protective shield. Something will always bother us, prick our attention, nag us, unsettle us, and frustrate us. Something will constantly impel us to attend to our wounds and issues, to come to a new and higher understanding about them, and to move beyond the dualistic illusions of the lower mind.

From the point of view of our wish for healing, this simple if unsettling aspect is a blessing in our lives—neither too confronting nor too sleepy.

Chiron in Aspect to Mercury

In general, Chiron aspects to Mercury confer potential ability to communicate and express the messages of Chiron. However, due to our wounds and issues, such communication and expression will tend to be more nonverbal than verbal, and/or more emotional than intellectual.

Chiron-Mercury aspects initially bind and repress outward communication and expression. This impels/inspires deep introspection. As we heal our wounds and resolve our issues, the special *form* of our communication and expression emerges—Chiron's gift, in this case, which is often directly connected with our life's path/purpose/calling/destiny.

With Chiron-Mercury aspects, if we attend to our healing journey and/or have other significant Chiron aspects, we cannot help expressing Chiron's messages in some way. We become, in a sense, Chiron's voice.

Conjunction, Parallel, Contraparallel, Occultation

Chiron conjunct, parallel, contraparallel, or occult Mercury initially manifests as an inability to express or communicate our wounds and issues outwardly. It tends to manifest as shyness, reticence, and/or uncommunicativeness—usually from fear of others seeing us and/or of being unable to express ourselves (to our own satisfaction). This then becomes a driving force in our lives—driving us to find alternate ways of communicating and expressing ourselves.

In practical terms, the repression of communication and expression impels/inspires deep introspection. If we attend to our wounds and issues, the results of such introspection become manifest, usually later in life, as Chiron's messages—verbal or nonverbal—and are generally in line with our divine design. In this case, we are destined to speak Chiron's messages.

If we do not attend to our wounds and issues, this aspect can lead to reclusiveness, secretiveness, and/or social dysfunction.

Opposition

Chiron opposition Mercury represents a conflict between expressing and repressing ourselves. There is initially a fear of revealing our wounded nature, so we hide it, putting on a brave or cool exterior. Our wounds seek expression, though; they can only be dealt with, healed, and resolved by being brought in to the open. Consequently, we may project such expression onto others in the form of blame, judgments, and accusations.

Continued repression of our wounds and issues can lead to illness. Alternately, it can build up over time and then explode unexpectedly in anger, rage, violence, and/or abuse—verbally and/or physically. Interestingly, Chiron opposed Mercury during the riots at the Berlin Wall in 1962.

Conversely, if we attend to our wounds and issues, this aspect represents an opportunity and a catalyst to bring our wounds and issues into the open where we can then deal with them. In more evolved persons (usually indicated by other significant Chiron aspects), this aspect can confer healing ability and focus.

Trine

With Chiron trine Mercury, if we do not attend to our wounds and issues, we may find it difficult to express ourselves, preferring to remain reticent and guarded. Expressing ourselves may be painful due to the uncomfortable and unavoidable awareness of our woundedness, like a lump in the throat. People with this aspect tend to be guarded and reticent about speaking their innermost thoughts, although there is an apparent depth to them.

This aspect, therefore, like Chiron conjunct Mercury, confers the gift of deep introspection. When sufficient healing and resolution has been done, we may then be ready to express and communicate our thoughts and share our journey with others. Even in this case, though, people with this aspect tend to weigh their words carefully, only speaking in appropriate circumstances.

In this latter case, depending on the other significant aspects to Chiron, this trine can confer healing ability and give us a sense of mission.

Square

Chiron square Mercury represents perhaps the most difficult of the Chiron-Mercury aspects; self-expression and communication can be extremely difficult and sometimes extremely painful. This makes the degree and depth of our introspection all the more intense. In addition, when we attend to our wounds and issues, it makes our subsequent outward expression and communication all the more powerful and meaningful.

If we neglect our healing journey with this aspect, mental instability is possible. I have found this aspect in a statistically significant number of people in institutions and/or who have been involved in crime. Interestingly, Chiron was squaring Mercury when JFK was assassinated.

It is also interesting that many famous singers have this aspect—Barbra Streisand, Bernadette Peters, Frank Sinatra, George Michael, Paul Simon, Paula Abdul, and Patsy Cline, to name a few. It is equally interesting how many people with this aspect have had throat surgery. (Mercury rules the voice and the throat.)

The intensity of this aspect's influence, in terms of accentuating wounds and issues of self-expression and communication, is equal to its potential for healing these same issues. In addition, it increases the potential for powerful expressions of healing messages.

Sextile

Chiron sextile Mercury confers the possibility of a deep understanding of Chiron and its is-sues and themes as well as the possibility of expressing and communicating these issues and themes. However, as with any sextile aspect, we must initiate the link consciously and in-tentionally by focusing our attention on these issues and themes.

When wounds and issues are attended to, this aspect becomes a welcome addition to the aspect set of a potential healer—for the healing of self and/or others.

If we fail to attend to our wounds and issues, this aspect remains mostly benign.

Quincunx

Chiron quincunx Mercury creates a persistent impulse to seek new ways of understanding, expressing, and/or communicating our wounds and issues, and the healing of these. No better is this summed up than by the fact that this aspect is shared by Alexander Graham Bell (inventor of the telephone), Dane Rudhyar (Sabian symbols), Jacqui Katona (Aus-tralian Aboriginal land rights activist and spokesperson), Mohandas K. Gandhi, Vanessa Redgrave (actress and freedom fighter who turned the Academy Awards into a political platform in 1978), and Placido Domingo. Each found new ways and levels of expressing and communicating their own wounding and healing issues.

This aspect does not let us rest until we attend to our wounds and issues. Neither does it give other people a rest from us, because our journey often impels us to wish to challenge the status quo and/or to bring our new consciousness to a wider audience.

The challenge of this aspect is that it requires a new way/level of *thinking* about our wounds and issues and their healing path. Interestingly, the Wall Street Crash and the recording of the first Beatles single share this aspect of Chiron and Mercury.

With this aspect, failure to attend to our wounds and issues can produce an undercurrent of unrest, frustration, and irritation, with possible resultant nervous system dysfunctions.

Chiron in Aspect to Venus

Chiron aspecting Venus confers a natural empathy and concern for Chiron's issues. Initially, it tends to create a deep longing—a deep wish for contact and for connection with others. This can be mixed with the feelings that everything is futile and that we may always be separate and alone from others.

With this aspect, our relationships will invariably be interwoven with Chironic themes —themes of wounding and healing—inasmuch as Chiron aspecting Venus can tell us a lot about the ways in which we share/express our wounds, issues, and healing with others. Moreover, it will tell us how we can use the platform of relationship as a tool for our further healing and evolution of consciousness.

Note that Venus represents the lower octave of Neptune—Venus being the planet of *earthly* (conditional) love and Neptune the planet of *unconditional* love. Venus's issues and themes are the foundations upon which our return to unconditional love is based. Chiron aspecting Venus catalyzes our journey back to love—from inner planet, Venus, to outer planet, Neptune. And the journey back to love is the essence of the healing and evolution of consciousness.

Chiron-Venus aspects are a welcome addition to the charts of persons wishing to pursue healing as a life's path—for themselves and/or for others.

Conjunction, Parallel, Contraparallel, Occultation

Initially, Chiron conjunct, parallel, contraparallel, and/or occult Venus creates a deep longing for close personal relationship. We may feel acutely cut off from close personal relationship, and/or feel that no amount of love can fill the void within us.

With this aspect, we tend to feel others' pain and emotional disturbances, leading to the impulse to rescue others, to fix them, and/or to wrap them up in cotton wool, so to speak.

In addition, people with this aspect will tend to have a healing effect upon others, whether verbally, artistically, therapeutically, or otherwise. Whatever the case may be, these people will tend to have an inexplicable attractiveness that arises from the reflection in them of our own woundedness and wish for healing.

Conversely, certain other people with this aspect will tend to become "high maintenance" after a time.

As we attend to our wounds and issues, this aspect increasingly awakens us to the fact that love was and is ever around us and in us, despite what we previously believed. As we heal our wounds and resolve our issues, we are increasingly able to share our love in more evolved ways—closer to Neptune than Venus. Such higher-octave (unconditional) love does not seek to rescue others, protect them, or fix their lives; Chiron-Venus says love is already there; learning how to see the love is the lesson. Nor does unconditional love necessitate emotional dependence on others—our dependence on others or others' dependence on us; we each already have the love we need within us; again, the lesson is seeing it.

This aspect can confer healing potential and focus and is a welcome addition to the charts of those interested in pursuing healing as part of their life's path and purpose—for themselves and/or for others.

Opposition

With Chiron opposition Venus, our wounds and issues will invariably manifest through our relationship life, constantly challenging and confronting us to attend to them. We will tend to play out the drama of these wounds and issues within our relationships, inevitably attracting partners who exacerbate them. In this way, we are being given the opportunity to heal and evolve our consciousness.

If we fail to attend to our issues and wounds, our relationship life will tend to be tumultuous and intense, to say the least. Conversely, our attention and effort in these matters will bring rewards of healing and evolution that are equal in power—for both parties in any given relationship.

If we have a leaning toward healing as a life's calling, this aspect is a blessing inasmuch as oppositions illuminate the issues of the participating planets—in this case, the wounds and issues of the heart—without respite. Even if we don't have such a leaning, the opportunity to heal the heart should not be squandered.

Either way, with this aspect, it is important for us to be aware that every partner we have is a perfect mirror of everything we have yet to love about ourselves—the negatives *and* the positives.

Trine

Chiron trine Venus indicates an amplified connection between our earthly affairs of the heart and our deepest wounds and issues. Wounds and issues will naturally arise within our relationships, but the healing path is well facilitated. This does not mean it will be easy or pain-free, though; healing always entails effort, intention, and a wish for healing.

With this aspect, we must be prepared for uncommon levels of intimacy and openness; one cannot hide with this aspect. If we are willing and put in the work, this aspect—mirrored in our relationships—will bring tremendous healing and evolution of consciousness.

Conversely, if we try to avoid or try to hide our wounds and issues in relationships, we will tend to feel unfulfilled and our partners will tend to feel shut out.

When combined with other significant Chiron aspects, this aspect confers healing potential and focus and is a welcome addition to the charts of those interested in healing as a life's pursuit—healing for themselves and/or for others.

If there are trines of Venus and Chiron in the synastry and/or composite midpoint charts of two people, these people will tend to be highly and emotionally attracted to each other, and they will more than likely develop a long-lasting bond.

Square

With Chiron square Venus, our wounds and issues will tend to stand in the way of intimacy and openness in close personal relationships. Alternately, depending on the type of relationships we have, our relationships may provide a means of burying our wounds (heads and hearts) in the sand, so to speak.

In the first case, we avoid intimacy at all costs, because this means we must bare our souls and reveal our wounded nature. For this reason, this aspect can manifest as coldness, distance, hardness, and/or toughness in our outer demeanor. We may even choose to avoid relationships altogether.

In the second case, we can become like a dependent child within the relationship, burying our face in the other person's protective care, thus avoiding the subject of our inner feelings. Outside of the intimacy of this relationship, we may remain guarded, distant, and cold toward others.

In addition, this aspect may cause us to feel unloved, unnurtured, uncared for, and/or as though we are unlovable. Furthermore, we can find ourselves sabotaging our relationships (unconsciously), leaving us wondering what is "wrong" with us.

We can access the gift of this aspect by turning inward and attending to our wounds and issues, and by squarely facing the reflection of our wounds and issues in our partner(s). Relationships are a perfect mirror of all we have yet to love about ourselves. Whether we will gather the courage to look in that mirror is up to us.

When combined with other significant Chiron aspects (particularly a T-square), this aspect confers healing potential and focus and is a welcome addition to those wishing to pursue healing as a life's path—for themselves and/or for others.

Sextile

Chiron sextile Venus gives us the potential to, and possibility of, accessing our wounds and issues through the tool of relationships. As with all sextiles, however, this aspect must be activated with our conscious attention to, and focus on, our healing and evolution of consciousness. Otherwise, it remains mostly benign.

As an addition to other Chiron aspects in the chart of a potential healer, this sextile is welcome and represents a tool in our healing toolbox.

Quincunx

With Chiron quincunx Venus, we seek a new understanding and level of consciousness about our earthly affairs of the heart, and we are destined to play out our wounds and issues through our relationships.

This aspect brings up key issues of love: whether we are loved or not, whether we are lovable or not, and/or whether we are capable of giving love. These questions will tend to constantly frustrate us, irritate us, nag at us, unsettle us, and prod us to attend to the healing and resolution of our limiting wounds and issues. If nothing else, this aspect will tend to impel deep introspection.

This aspect can be equally frustrating, irritating, unsettling, and confronting for those with whom we are in relationship; it can cause us to constantly attempt, consciously or unconsciously, to fix others, to try to lift them up when they are down, to correct their "mistakes," and so forth. In this way, this aspect, like the quincunx aspect in general, is related to the sign of Virgo.

Chiron quincunx Venus, when combined with other significant aspects of Chiron, can confer healing potential and focus and is a welcome addition to the charts of those wishing to pursue healing as a life's path—for themselves and/or for others (bearing in mind that the *forms* healing can take are manifold and not limited to consensus views).

Chiron in Aspect to Mars

Mars represents the lower-octave manifestation of Pluto—the former being the planet of earthly and physical change and the latter being the planet of metaphysical and spiritual change. In general, Chiron aspecting Mars represents the physical manifestation of our woundedness and its subsequent healing path—i.e., the things we do or do *not* do, the actions we take or don't take, the intentions we have or don't have, and the decisions we make or don't make with respect to our wounds and issues.

Mars works on two octaves, the octave of the lower nature, which *reacts,* and the octave of the higher self, which *acts.*

If Mars represents a call to action or reaction, or a call for us to make an intention, a decision, or a resolve, then Chiron aspecting Mars is a call for us to act upon or react to our wounds and issues. Reactions occur if we do not attend, consciously or intentionally, to these things. If we *act,* however—from an intention, a resolve, and/or a wish for healing—then our healing and evolution of consciousness is expedited.

Conjunction, Parallel, Contraparallel, Occultation

Chiron conjunct, parallel, contraparallel, or occult Mars initially tends to create acute, even violent reactions when our wounds and issues are triggered. Even when we are calm, there tends to be an unsettled emotional undercurrent within us. We tend to be hyper-reactive unless other astrological considerations counteract this aspect. Alternately, our energy can be entirely dissipated, leading to depression.

If we do not attend to our wounds and issues, they can manifest as acute physical illness, sudden accidents, sudden emotional outbursts, and/or excess physical energy. This energy can be very powerful when channeled into our chosen life's path/purpose/calling/destiny. Our wounds and issues constitute a powerful motivating force, whether channeled into healing per se or into other pursuits.

In any case, there is an unconscious urgency that goes with this aspect, whether an urgency to escape from and/or avoid our wounds and issues or an urgency to deal with them.

In the chart of a potential healer, this aspect can confer great physical healing ability.

Opposition

Chiron opposition Mars tends to accentuate and exacerbate all the features of Chiron conjunct the Sun, aforementioned. There is a constant tug of war between our woundedness and our reactions to them. We initially seek to flee from our wounds and issues, only to find that we crash into them again.

This aspect is perhaps the most emotionally and physically hyper-reactive of all the Chiron aspects. It can engender wars, violence, and conflict when our wounds and issues are stirred up. It can also manifest as a kind of soapbox preaching—championing for human rights and so forth and/or campaigning against perceived injustice, inequality, and abuse. In addition, I have found this aspect in a statistically significant number of charts of violent criminals.

Nonetheless, if this excess energy is channeled into our life's path and purpose, it has unparalleled physical and emotional power. In this case, extreme attention, intention, decision, resolve, and persistence are required to harness this aspect.

If accompanied by other significant Chiron aspects—particularly trines and sextiles that offer a healing path for the opposition—this aspect would be a welcome addition to the chart of a potential healer.

Interestingly, Chiron opposed Mars during the Wall Street Crash of 1929.

Trine

Chiron trine Mars adds enormous energy to our lives, but is potentially smoother and more harmonized than Chiron conjunct Mars and Chiron opposition Mars. It is still hyper-reactive, but generally lacks the jagged edges. It is less violent, less primal, and we are not so inclined to run in the other direction or to blame the world for its injustices against others and us.

However, this aspect can still lead to soapbox preaching—championing for human rights and so forth and/or campaigning against perceived injustice, inequality, and abuse. If accompanied by other difficult aspects, it can also lead to violence—apparent from a statistically significant number of criminal charts with this aspect, particularly the charts of people who committed homicides.

Whether we attend to our wounds and issues or not, this aspect can be a motivating force in our lives. On the one hand, we are driven by the impulse to escape or avoid our wounds, leading us to our divine design *unconsciously*. On the other hand, we are driven by the impulse to heal and resolve our wounds and issues, leading us to our divine design *consciously*.

This aspect is a welcome addition to the chart of a potential healer.

Interestingly, Chiron was trining Mars when John Lennon was murdered; also, during the recording of the Beatles' first single.

Square

Chiron square Mars indicates that, initially, our energy and motivation can tend to be blocked due to our wounds and issues, leading to a *deficit* of energy, unlike the preceding Chiron-Mars aspects we have explored.

The frustration arising from this, compounded by feeling thwarted at every corner, can manifest as hyper-reactions, depression, or even chronic fatigue. The difficulty of seeing and making sense of our life's path/purpose/calling/destiny saps our energy reserves.

Alternately, the frustration with our wounds and issues, building up over time like a pressure cooker, can cause us eventually to explode, sometimes resulting in violence.

The healing path, if embraced, is impelled by our need to understand why we are lacking in energy and motivation, what is the meaning and purpose of our lives, and why we are seemingly thwarted in our lives. Thwarted from taking physical steps toward these answers, we are impelled to introspect—to seek a larger view of the wounds and issues that assail us. Such is the gift of this aspect. If we rise to the occasion, we will experience a gradual return of our energy levels, inspiration, and motivation.

As a part of the chart of a potential healer, particularly if involved in a T-square, this aspect confers healing power as well as depth of insight into what motivates us as human beings.

Interestingly, when Chiron was discovered in 1977, it was squaring Mars.

Sextile

Chiron sextile Mars offers the potential to use the driving force of our wounds and issues, consciously and intentionally, as motivation for our life's path/purpose/calling/destiny and/or healing and evolution of consciousness—for others and/or for us.

As with all sextile aspects, though, we must activate this potential—consciously and intentionally—with our wish for, and efforts toward, our healing and evolution of consciousness. Otherwise, this aspect remains mostly benign.

When combined with other significant Chiron aspects, this aspect is a welcome addition to the chart of a potential healer.

Quincunx

Chiron quincunx Mars indicates a frustrating, irritating, unsettling, and incessant need to know what to do next, what action to take, why things happen the way they do, and/or what causes one thing and the next. It tends to create incessant inquisitiveness and questioning. This can be irritating to others, who may perceive it as badgering. This aspect is related to the sign of Virgo inasmuch as it impels an almost obsessive need to collect and understand all the details of the questions that plague us.

In the final analysis, our wounds and issues drive our needs and questions, ever seeking healing and resolution. If we pursue the answers to these questions, consciously, intentionally, and with persistent resolve, we will gradually feel less unsettled and more at peace with ourselves and our lives.

This aspect is a welcome addition to the charts of those wishing to pursue healing as a life's path—for others and for themselves.

Interestingly, Chiron quincunxed Mars during the Cuban missile crisis, at the death of Jimi Hendrix, during the 1967 Apollo disaster, during the LA race riots in 1965, and during the Roswell UFO incident in 1947.

Chiron in Aspect to Jupiter

In general, Jupiter represents our Inner Child. It also represents our capacity to receive abundance in its many forms and to return our inner abundance to the world in the form of our divine design. On the positive side, it represents good fortune and wisdom; on the negative side, it represents excessiveness, waste, childishness, and folly.

Chiron-Jupiter aspects show us how and in what ways our wounds and issues are attached to our Inner Child issues and to the Inner Child's ability to express itself or not. The healing path reawakens us to the innocence and childlike wisdom of the Inner Child. It takes us back to the joie de vivre that we tend to lose as we grow up. It reminds us that life is an adventure, full of magic, mystery, and magnificence. (There is a difference between our early-life childish reactions, arising from our polarized perspectives, and the childlike wisdom of the Inner Child. The Inner Child innately senses the "rightness" of all that transpires in the world and in our lives, and it ever impels us, as conscious adults, to awaken to the perfection of it all.)

Our wounds and issues generally have their origins in childhood, before the Inner Child begins to retreat with the approach of puberty. For this reason, Chiron-Jupiter aspects are extremely powerful in their potential to awaken us to our wounds and to reveal our wounds' inner wisdom. In this way, Jupiter gives us our first glimpse of the *guiding hand* in our lives.

Chiron-Jupiter aspects also bring issues of freedom to the fore—physical freedom as well as spiritual, ideological, philosophical, and political freedom.

Conjunction, Parallel, Contraparallel, Occultation

Chiron conjunct, parallel, contraparallel, or occult Jupiter represents the potential marriage of *healing* and *wisdom* acquired by delving into our wounds and issues and seeing the hidden plan that lies behind them. This aspect can be the mark of a great healer and/or teacher.

With this aspect, the adventure of our lives *is* the journey of healing and evolution of consciousness, whatever form that adventure may take. That journey will tend to be larger than life and rich in content, with our gifts on display to the world as an inspiration and testament to the possibility of healing and evolution of consciousness.

Sensing the underlying plan and feeling innately that we are all destined to be free to shine, this aspect can inspire us to champion the cause of freedom in the world—freedom from oppression and freedom from ignorance. (Martin Luther King was a perfect example of this.)

Other people living around those with this aspect may find it difficult to bear, though, as the native's openness and inner certainty about touchy issues will be both challenging and confronting.

On the other side, this aspect generally accompanies issues and wounds concerning justice, fairness, equality, morals, ethics, excesses, wastage, and deficits.

This aspect can be a tacit indication of considerable work already done on healing and evolution of consciousness in past lives. Moreover, if combined with other significant Chiron aspects, it can be the mark of a person with increased healing ability and/or who is called to heal as a life's path/purpose/calling/destiny.

Interestingly, this aspect occurs in the chart of the recording of the Beatles' first hit single in September 1962. (In this chart, Chiron and Jupiter are also the base planets in an extraordinary kite pattern involving the Sun, Moon, Mars, Neptune, and Pluto). In addition, it formed part of multiple aspects of Chiron at the time of the hanging of Nazi war criminal Ernest Eichmann in May 1962. It also occurred during the Berlin Wall riots of August 1962.

Opposition

Chiron opposition Jupiter indicates that ideals that we would otherwise embrace as adults are initially at odds with our wounds and issues—particularly those wounds of early childhood or that involve our Inner Child.

The initial reaction to this aspect is to assert that there is something "wrong" with the world—that the world is responsible for others' and our wounds. We may feel that things should have been different and could be different now *if only* . . . The "if only" inspires ideas, philosophies, morals, and ethics that we feel would support, encourage, and engender a better world for all. This psychology may be played out solely within us, serving only to make our own lives a little more bearable/comprehensible, or it may be that we project our psychology/philosophy onto the outside world and promote it to a wider audience. This may take a constructive or destructive form (consider the difference between Carl G. Jung and Adolf Hitler, both of whom have this aspect.)

Overall, we are driven by the paradox of the child's semi-forgotten and wonder-filled view of the world versus the adult's more pragmatic and uninspired view (that inevitably arises from childhood wounds and issues). Moreover, there can be a tendency to exaggerate our woundedness and its attendant issues, often blowing things out of proportion.

With this aspect, if our psychological/philosophical musings remain private, we will tend to judge, rationalize, and/or justify our predicaments as a means of apparent escape from, and avoidance of, our issues and wounds. Conversely, if our psychological/philosophical musings are projected upon, and/or broadcasted to, others, we will tend to attempt to escape from and/or avoid our own lopsided perspectives by blaming others for our predicaments; moreover, we will tend to feel we "know" how to fix the world and will tend to want to tell everybody about it.

Either way, our perspectives—lopsided or not—take us into circumstances and situations where our healing journey is enacted. What was ostensibly an escape or avoidance turns out to be an opportunity for healing—for others as well as for us.

Of course, we can expedite the healing journey by attending to our wounds and issues, consciously and intentionally. As we heal, our ideas, philosophies, morals, ethics, religious and spiritual perspectives, and so forth, evolve as we do. Moreover, we are increasingly inspired to share these with others, which is why this aspect, when combined with other favorable aspects, confers great teaching ability.

The highest manifestation of Chiron opposition Jupiter comes when our evolving adult perspectives begin to realign with those of the wise Inner Child. In short, we achieve a larger view of the world and our lives, realizing that all things were and are part of a larger plan. Life was always an adventure; we simply lost sight of the fact while traveling through the darkness of our wounds and issues. However, without the journey through the darkness, we would not now see and be able to celebrate the magnificence of the larger plan of existence. Such is Jupiter's highest message.

Trine

With Chiron trine Jupiter, we are given an uncommon opportunity to access the wounds and issues of our early childhood and/or of our Inner Child. The degree to which we actually heal and resolve these things will depend upon our willingness and intention to do so and upon the other aspects in our charts—particularly other aspects of Chiron. The specific expression of our wounds and issues and/or their healing journeys will vary accordingly.

The range of this aspect's outward expressions is apparent in the differences between people such as Martin Bryant (Australian mass murderer), Kurt Cobain (former lead singer of Nirvana, who died by suicide) and Pope John Paul II (recently deceased), who all share this aspect, but express it in vastly different ways.

With this aspect, the wounds and issues of our childhood and/or Inner Child tend to reside very close to the surface, but in a more harmonious and less confronting way than with, say, Chiron opposition Jupiter. This does not necessarily make it easier for us, though. The healing journey always requires effort, intention, and a wish to heal. And there is always the possibility of emotional backlash and violence arising from childhood wounds and issues.

This aspect is a welcome addition to the chart of a potential healer, particularly if it is part of a grand trine. It provides access to early childhood wounds and Inner Child issues—required on the journey of healing and evolution of consciousness.

In addition, this aspect can be a tacit indication of considerable work already done on healing and evolution of consciousness in past lives.

Interestingly, the very first episode of *Star Trek* aired during a Chiron-trine-Jupiter aspect.

Square

Chiron square Jupiter indicates that our early childhood/Inner Child wounds and issues are initially blocked, bottled up, and/or hidden. This tends to cut us off from the joy, lightness, freedom, and sense of adventure otherwise experienced by the Inner Child. Our resultant outward demeanor may be quite serious, heavy, "adult," harsh, disciplinary, violent, reticent, shy, reserved, guarded, and/or cold, among other possibilities.

The way this aspect will manifest rests upon our willingness to delve into our wounds and issues. If we are not willing, then we are more likely to take it out on the world around us, blaming the world for our woundedness, consciously or unconsciously. This is the more likely result of this aspect, particularly if Chiron has no other major aspects. Again, emotional backlash and violence can manifest as a reaction to childhood wounds and issues.

Conversely, if we are willing to embark upon the healing journey, this aspect will take us on a journey of rediscovering the wise but childlike part of us. Our spiritual hearts seek lightness, freedom, joy, and adventure and will ever impel us toward a state of simultaneous wisdom and innocence.

Although this is perhaps the most difficult aspect of Chiron and Jupiter, it is worth the journey, as a return to love is the end result. The journey will ultimately take us back to our childhood, showing us the lessons, benefits, blessings, and gifts of those events and circumstances that we have otherwise been judging negatively. It is a process of awakening to the perfection of our lives and to the loving *guiding hand,* both of which were there from the beginning.

This aspect is a difficult but profitable addition to the charts of persons wishing to pursue healing as a specific life's path—for themselves and/or for others—particularly if it is part of a T-square or another such larger planetary pattern.

Sextile

Chiron sextile Jupiter offers a pathway between our wounds/issues and our wise but childlike Inner Child. The resultant potential for healing our childhood wounds and issues and seeing a bigger picture of our lives is great. However, as with all sextiles, we must activate this aspect with our conscious intention and wish for healing. In this case, we must be willing to delve into our childhood and balance our perceptions of its events and circumstances. If we do not attend to our wounds and issues, this aspect remains mostly benign.

This aspect is a welcome addition to the charts of those interested in healing themselves and/or others. If it is one of a set of significant Chiron aspects, it is a welcome addition to the charts of people wishing to pursue healing as a specific life's path/purpose/calling/destiny.

Quincunx

With Chiron quincunx Jupiter, we are continually impelled to attain a new level of consciousness and understanding about our childhood issues; we are continually impelled to try to access our Inner Child wisdom and to see the service in every event and circumstance of our childhood.

With this aspect, there will tend to be a constant nagging feeling that there is another way of looking at the things that we otherwise judge negatively—i.e., there are flip sides, a bigger picture, a wider perspective, and a more inclusive view to be had with respect to the events and circumstances of our early lives. These other ways of seeing things form the basis of healing and evolution of consciousness and lead on to a larger view of our present lives.

This aspect is a welcome addition to the charts of those interested in healing themselves and/or others. If it is one of a set of significant Chiron aspects, it is a welcome addition to the charts of people wishing to pursue healing as a specific life's path/purpose/calling/destiny.

Chiron in Aspect to Saturn

In general, Saturn represents restrictions, limitations, repressions, and blockages. On the other side, it represents responsibility, seriousness, discipline, perseverance, real work, and steady progress. Despite its seemingly stern and bleak perspectives, Saturn maintains a twinkle in the eye—a secret smile—knowing that by impelling us to take stock of our lives and get serious about our healing and evolution of consciousness, we will ultimately find freedom.

When Chiron makes aspects to Saturn, we are impelled to take stock of our lives—to ponder who we are, where we have been, why we are here, and where we are going. We are encouraged and impelled by our restrictions, limitations, repressions, and blockages to begin serious work toward our healing and evolution of consciousness. Such is the gift behind our difficult and often painful wounds and issues. Saturn and Chiron work naturally together toward our ultimate freedom—the freedom of awakened consciousness—and the mastery of our lives.

Conjunction, Parallel, Contraparallel, Occultation

Chiron conjunct, parallel, contraparallel, or occult Saturn initially points to a high degree of suppression and/or repression of our woundedness.

Saturn's task is to keep us grounded—to regulate our evolutionary pace. The mythical Icarus made himself wings and flew toward the Sun, but getting too close, his wings melted and he fell back to the ground. Like Icarus, we need to stay between acceptable limits of awakening and sleeping, in accordance with our present rate of evolution of consciousness. When we get too elated or move too quickly, Saturn steps in and brings us back to Earth.

Saturn conjunct Chiron says to us that we need to solidify the foundations of our journey of healing and evolution of consciousness—to become accountable, responsible, and serious and to strive for mastery—before we can take our rightful place in the higher realms, so to speak. Although we may feel held back, suppressed, repressed, limited, and restricted, there is important work to be done in this space. Our wounds serve us *as they are* until we are truly ready to transcend them.

From one point of view, this is a most difficult aspect and tends to make us extremely judgmental of ourselves and of our perceived weaknesses. We seek to maintain ultimate control of ourselves and of our lives, yet we are subservient to our reactions (that have their origins in our wounds and issues). Our wounds and issues will rule us until we learn their lessons and learn to love them for their service to us.

The preceding can also manifest as a need/desire to control others, and/or it can make us repressive, harsh, cruel, domineering, overly strict and disciplinary, and/or uncompromising.

From another point of view, this aspect is a gift inasmuch as it forces us to stay in the one place—unable to run away from our wounds and issues until we deal with them, methodically and thoroughly.

When combined with other "easier" and significant Chiron aspects, this aspect can be a welcome addition to the charts of people wishing to pursue a healing path—for themselves and/or for others.

With more evolved persons, this aspect can also be a tacit indication of considerable work already done in past lives on healing and evolution of consciousness.

Interestingly, Chiron was conjuncting Saturn when the original series of *Star Trek* was approved for production. (Details of the significance of *Star Trek* in relation to Chiron and our collective healing journey can be found at http://www.martinlass.com/library.htm#issues.)

Opposition

After Chiron conjunct Saturn, Chiron opposition Saturn is perhaps the most difficult of the Chiron-Saturn aspects. Saturn's power to hold us in one place (until we begin to take responsibility for our lives and attend to our healing journey) is somewhat broken down here. The reason for this is that the opposition aspect gives us a place we can run to when things get too difficult or painful, gives us an alternative, and gives us the power to challenge, reject, and/or disagree with what is thrown our way.

In practice, when things get too difficult or painful, we tend to run in the opposite direction—in this case, toward Saturn. We batten down the hatches, taking up conservative values, acting conservatively, and opting for conservative situations. We tend to fall back on what we know works, even if it is stifling to do so. After a time, though, finding ourselves too limited, restricted, held back, held down, and suppressed in our life's expression, we run the other way again—in this case, back into our wounds and issues. This tick-tocking catalyzes and facilitates our healing and evolution of consciousness by ever impelling us to look at our issues and wounds.

On the one hand, we may tend to see our limitations, restrictions, suppression, and repression as being caused by others—for example, the expression of "father" and/or authority issues. Here, our path requires the healing of blame and judgment by seeing how these things served us in many ways, not the least of which was to contribute to us being who we are today.

On the other hand, we may tend to hold *ourselves* back—to restrict, limit, and repress ourselves—because the alternative is having to deal with our wounds, which we are not necessarily ready to do. This latter case can lead to conservatism, pragmatism, and hard-nosed attitudes toward others and ourselves. We can tend to be hard taskmasters, in which case we are effectively becoming our "fathers."

Either way, if we are willing to work with our wounds and issues, Saturn offers unparalleled support. Saturn is the gatekeeper, guarding the entrance to the outer planets—even guarding the doorway to Chiron until we are ready to take responsibility for our lives. This said, the key to this aspect's resolution lies in giving up blame and in taking personal responsibility for our lives, our issues, and our wounds.

When combined with other "easier" and significant Chiron aspects, this aspect can be a welcome addition to the charts of people wishing to pursue a healing path—for themselves and/or for others.

Trine

Chiron trine Saturn confers the increased potential for serious, intentioned, and responsible work toward our healing and evolution of consciousness. With this aspect, we tend to understand innately that we need to be as disciplined, serious, responsible, practical, and hard working in this area of our lives as we are in any other.

Consequently, this is perhaps the most blessed of the Chiron-Saturn aspects. It does not make it easy; it just makes it seem more profitable to embark upon the healing journey to begin with. Moreover, we are better placed to approach our healing and evolution of consciousness methodically, seriously, and persistently.

On the negative side, due to our constant attention to matters concerning our wounds and issues (and our attempts to work through these), we may tend to limit, restrict, repress, and otherwise hold back other areas of our lives. Alternately, we may continually resist and/or repress our wounds and issues, as this is the line of least resistance. (Trines, although considered gifts in the chart, are not always appreciated and/or honored, so can lead to laziness).

This aspect can be a tacit indication of considerable work already done on healing and evolution of consciousness in past lives.

When combined with other "easier" and significant Chiron aspects, this aspect can be a welcome addition to the charts of people wishing to pursue a healing path—for themselves and/or for others.

Interestingly, Chiron was trining Saturn when the film *Close Encounters of the Third Kind* was released. (Recall the main character's obsessive persistence in trying to find the answers to inexplicable urges and visions arising from within him.)

Square

Chiron square Saturn represents a kind of double dose of blockage and repression of our wounds and issues. If this square forms part of a T-square aspect or another larger planetary pattern, a healing path will almost certainly be evident. Otherwise, it will be very difficult to gain access to these areas of our lives.

This aspect formed a major feature of the years between 1935 and 1952 and for those born at the time. It contributed to what the youth of the 1960s called the Establishment. The economic and technological growth of the twentieth-century world arose, in part, out of this aspect. Uranus's opposition to Chiron in 1952 finally broke down the Chiron-square-Saturn aspect of 1935–52. In this lies the clue to working with this aspect in the chart: *look for, and work with, Uranus aspects and transits to Chiron and Saturn,* as these will offer the best healing possibilities.

Otherwise, this aspect renders us prone to emotional backlashes, violence, frustration, desire to control others, and/or deep self-depreciation. Attaining mastery of the material world—physically, emotionally, mentally, financially, politically, in terms of resources, and/or in terms of people and populations—seems the only defense against our wounds and issues. And, paradoxically, in this lies the gift/blessing of this aspect—i.e., that the only answer to our woundedness may be to defer to trying to master the material world. Consequently, this aspect can be found in a statistically significant number of charts of rich, powerful, and/or famous people.

The preceding illustrates an important point: whether we heal our wounds and resolve our issues or not—whether we are put in the position of being *able* to heal our wounds and resolve our issues or not—we are nonetheless still being driven toward our divine design. The world needs people attending to a spiritual path as well as people attending to a material path; one complements, supports, and defines the other; one cannot exist without the other. Moreover, by working toward material mastery, we are simultaneously gaining the very same tools we require for spiritual mastery; the material and the spiritual are mirror reflections.

This is not to say that Saturn square Chiron, when unaspected to any other planets, is impossible to work through, heal, and transcend. On the contrary, it is simply that the challenge is magnified immensely (as are the gifts of meeting that challenge). As previously suggested, aspects and transits of Uranus can offer a way of consciously working through the wounds and issues reflected in this aspect.

As part of a T-square or other such larger planetary pattern, this aspect may be a welcome addition to the charts of persons wishing to pursue a path of healing—for themselves and/or for others.

Sextile

Chiron sextile Saturn confers increased potential for seriousness, responsibility, discipline, and hard work in relation to our journey of healing and evolution of consciousness. As with all sextiles, though, we must activate this aspect with our wish and intention. When we do, this aspect confers the capacity to work through our wounds and issues in an organized, thorough, systematic, and complete fashion.

In the absence of such a wish/intention, this aspect remains mostly benign.

Quincunx

Chiron quincunx Saturn produces a niggling, nagging, irritating, unsettling, and persistent sense of responsibility for our healing and evolution of consciousness. This is often mirrored in our efforts and impulse to help others get on with their lives.

As long as we are attending to our wounds and issues, we will feel more or less satisfied. If we fail to attend to these things, though, we will feel constantly irritated, uneasy, and incomplete, and we will tend to beat ourselves up for not doing enough in the direction of sorting out our lives. By projection, we may tend to beat up on others for their perceived laziness, inaction, lack of discipline, and lack of organization with respect to their healing paths.

With this aspect, the healing path lies in attending to our issues and wounds *as they arise;* otherwise, the cumulative effect becomes overwhelming. Part of the healing path lies in acknowledging the efforts we *do* make, because we tend to be quite hard on ourselves; we need to see the other side of the picture.

Whether combined with other significant Chiron aspects or not, this aspect can be a welcome addition to the charts of people wishing to pursue a healing path—for themselves and/or for others.

If this aspect is part of a larger pattern—particularly a yod, a kite, or a square/quincunx/trine triangle (such as in the chart of Sai Baba)—it can confer increased healing ability and focus and would be a welcome addition to the chart of a person called to heal as a life's path.

Chiron in Aspect to Uranus

Chiron-Uranus aspects have a very long cycle due to the long orbits of each of these planets. During the twentieth century, we did not experience Chiron conjunct Uranus at all. Sextiles occurred only during 1939–40. Trines occurred only during 1945–46 and 1994–95. Squares occurred only during 1943 and 1997. Quincunxes occurred only during 1948–49 and 1992–93. Oppositions of Chiron and Uranus, on the other hand, were more prolific during the twentieth century than for thousands of years prior to this—forty-one occurrences spanning the years 1952–89.

From the point of view of consciousness, Uranus's theme is *awakening*, i.e., attaining a higher level of consciousness with respect to any given issue. Uranus seeks to resolve paradoxes, synthesize opposites, transcend conflicts, resolve disagreements, and take discords into concord. It does all this by showing us how the seemingly separate and opposing pieces of our lives—and of the world around us—are actually connected in a larger picture/plan. For this reason, Uranus is associated with genius.

Uranus shines a light on the issues and themes of the planets it aspects. In Chiron's case, Uranus shines a light on our wounds and their attendant issues, impelling and encouraging us to strive for a higher perspective on these things. It brings that which lies within our darkness into the light, so that we may then have an opportunity to heal. Its mission is to reveal to us the lessons, blessings, benefits, and gifts inherent in the events, circumstances, and aspects of our lives about which we have misperceptions, illusions, judgments, and blame. In short, it seeks to show us the perfection of our lives.

Chiron in aspect to Uranus represents a revolution in consciousness as well as a revolution in healing. Put these together and we have the healing journey of consciousness, and, as the Chiron Paradigm asserts, healing is synonymous with the evolution of consciousness.

Chiron-Uranus aspects also rule the exploration, discovery, and development of radical new ideas and technologies for healing, many of which are energetic in nature—such as radiology, acupuncture, bio-electro-magnetic therapy, spiritual healing, color therapy, and so forth.

Conjunction, Parallel, Contraparallel, Occultation

Chiron conjunct, parallel, contraparallel, or occult Uranus last occurred in 1898. The next time will be in 2042–43 and 2066–67. For those born with this aspect, there is a continual light shone upon their wounds and issues. It takes a highly evolved person to bear this continually. This aspect, when combined with other significant aspects of Chiron, will tend to produce a highly sensitive and powerful healer capable of delving into the very nature of wounding, healing, and the human psyche. Psychic and mystical experiences are possible here. This would be particularly so if the two planets are occulting. This aspect also confers a high degree of creativity, particularly in music.

Collectively speaking, this aspect heralds a new and revolutionary consciousness concerning our now-favorite themes of wounding and healing (taken, as always, in their broadest sense), as mirrored in every aspect of our collective, cultural, and individual lives.

This aspect can be a tacit indication of considerable work already done on healing and evolution of consciousness in past lives.

The power of this aspect is apparent when we look at people who have it in their charts: Emanuel Swedenborg (occultation—1689, mystic), Johann Sebastian Bach (occultation—1685, famous composer), George Friedrich Handel (occultation—1685, famous composer), Domenico Scarlatti (occultation—1685, famous composer), Queen Anne, Ernest Hemingway, Fred Astaire, George Gershwin, Rene Magritte (Belgian painter), François Poulenc (French composer), and Antonio Vivaldi (1678, famous composer).

Notice the proliferation of famous composers. Music is a great healer.

Opposition

Chiron opposition Uranus shines a light—a challenge, in a sense—upon our wounds and issues. By illuminating these, we are given the ultimate opportunity to deal with them as they come to the fore.

This aspect is the most *active* of the Chiron-Uranus aspects barring the conjunction. Initially, it causes us to run away from our wounds and issues. In doing so, we bump into Uranus, who tries to show us a higher perspective on these wounds and issues. When Uranus's truth—the vastness and brightness of its perspective—becomes too confronting and/or painful to handle, challenging us beyond our comfortable and consensual beliefs, ideals, and values, we retreat again to Chiron and our woundedness. Here, having gleaned a little higher understanding and perspective from our Uranus adventure, we may find new ways of attending to and dealing with our wounds and issues. When things become too confronting and/or painful again, we run away again and find ourselves bumping into Uranus once more. On goes the tick-tocking journey of healing and evolution of consciousness. The universe certainly had a sense of humor when it invented this aspect! It reminds one of rats in a cage!

If we are unable to deal with the wounds and pain that arise, nor the expanded perspectives offered by Uranus, then we find ourselves stuck in a kind of nightmare of constant running. Consequently, we will tend to try anything to "blank out" and not have to deal with our wounds and issues—alcohol, drugs, sleep, work, music, and all other types of escapism and avoidance. If this goes on for too long, though, it is inevitably reflected in our bodies through illness, disease, and general malaise. It seems that there is no escape or avoidance.

This all-or-nothing kind of psychology is the very reason why Chiron opposition Uranus (and Chiron opposition Pluto, as we shall see later) is an aspect that confers healing ability and/or focus in our lives. We cannot avoid it; we cannot run away from it; it follows us wherever we go. This is why the generations of people born between 1952 and 1989 have altered the consciousness of the planet via the healing modalities (taken in their broadest sense). The mid-1960s represented the fulcrum point for a mass movement of consciousness. The late 1970s represented the culmination. The 1990s represented the peak—particularly as this time encompasses not only Chiron's perihelion and perigee but also Chiron's own half-Return.

It is interesting that a statistically significant number of athletes possess this aspect, not the least of which are Martina Navratilova, Chris Evert Lloyd, Kathy McMillan (American track and field champion), and Ed Moses (American athlete, a hurdler who won Olympic gold at Montreal in 1976 and at Los Angeles in August 1984). Perhaps they are literally trying to run away from their wounds and issues. This may sound implausible; however, consider that (1) our outer activities mirror our inner state, and (2) one of the means we use to avoid having to sit down and think deeply about our issues is to stay busy and physically active all the time.

In the whole, this aspect tends to confer healing ability and focus, particularly when combined with other significant Chiron aspects that offer alternate ways of dealing with the opposition.

Trine

The last two Chiron-Uranus trines occurred in 1945–46 and 1994–95—both instances occurring very close to Chiron's perigee and perihelion (closest point to the Earth and the

Sun, respectively) in Libra (in 1945 and 1996). This makes it difficult to separate the interpretation of this trine from the interpretation of the perigee/perihelion in Libra.

In general, though, Chiron trine Uranus brings our wounds and issues into sharp focus, much the way the Chiron-Uranus opposition does. However, it does so in a more harmonious way inasmuch as it offers us easier access to Uranus's higher perspectives—to the underlying logic behind our wounds and issues.

Having said this, though, this trine combined with Chiron's perigee/perihelion can make us feel naked—our wounds and issues exposed and vulnerable. The result is that we tend to run away from our wounds and issues and toward Uranus—toward technology, global networking and communications, and humanitarian themes; if we cannot fix ourselves, we try to fix the world and make it a "better" place in which to live, driven by our individual and collective feeling of inadequacy. (The general modern view that humans are messing up the planet is an example of this psychological tendency.)

This trine gives us an enormous opportunity to delve into our wounds and issues. Whether we take advantage of the opportunity or not will depend on the other aspects in our charts and upon our general willingness (or not) to attend to our wounds and issues.

Persons born during the 1945–46 trine represent the advance scouts, so to speak, of the coming shift of consciousness of the 1960s. Many were actively involved in this shift, being, as they were, in college at the time during the mid-1960s.

In a sense, those born during this trine (1945–46) fell dramatically into two camps. The first camp consisted of the advance scouts of the coming "new age" (Chiron in Libra); the second camp consisted of those who birthed the technological, information, and communications eras (Uranus in Gemini).

Those born during the 1994–95 trine have yet to blossom into measurable trends and patterns. We can predict, however, that these children will contribute, in their later years, to two vastly polarized trends as we approach the next Chiron apogee/aphelion of 2020–21. Some will turn toward a fresh new age movement. They will gravitate back to spirituality and global consciousness; this time, however, it will have a more practical basis than the previous New Age (Chiron in Libra again and, to a lesser degree, Uranus in Capricorn/Aquarius). Others will favor the practical and economic path (Uranus in Capricorn/Aquarius) and will seek to solidify, secure, and protect the material, economic, social, and political state of the world as it becomes increasingly global in outlook.

This aspect can be a tacit indication of considerable work already done on healing and evolution of consciousness in past lives.

It can also be a welcome addition to the charts of those wishing to pursue healing as a life's path—for themselves and/or for others.

Square

With Chiron square Uranus (1943 and 1997), the possibility of a deeper understanding of our wounds and issues tends to be blocked initially, creating accentuated feelings of separateness and disconnectedness. This, in turn, tends to *increase* our drive to grow, heal, and evolve.

If, by virtue of other Chiron aspects in our charts (or the lack thereof), we are unable or unwilling to deal with our wounds and issues as they arise, we will *still* be driven toward our divine design. (All things serve the larger plan of the world.) In this case, though, our wounds and issues will tend to act as a powerful, but *unhealed,* motive force, similar to Chiron square Saturn. In this case, possible avenues of expression include technology, the information age, space, invention, and innovation—each as a defense against, avoidance of, and/or escape from, having to bear or deal with our issues and woundedness (in particular, those born around 1943)—alternately, as a substitute for the healing for which we innately wish.

If, on the other hand, we are willing to attend to our wounds and issues, we are driven on a healing path—one that *also* takes us to our divine design. Naturally, the healing "flavor" of our divine design will vary from that of others, depending on the other features of our chart. Although this aspect remains very challenging, the balancing rewards are worth pursuing.

If this aspect is part of a T-square or other planetary pattern, then this can facilitate the healing process; this would also be a welcome addition to the charts of those wishing to pursue healing as a life's path—for themselves and/or for others.

If this aspect is a person's only aspect of Chiron, then look for transits to Chiron and/or Uranus—particular Uranus transits—to offer a potential healing path. Alternately, look for concordant synastry aspects (conjunction, parallel, contraparallel, trine, sextile) between the native and the person or persons with whom they are closest (in terms of relationship)—in particular, concordant synastry aspects involving Chiron and Uranus or Chiron and Mercury. In short, such a close personal partner or friend can often offer the native greater understanding of, and perspective on, their wounds and issues as well as on their life's path and purpose.

Sextile

Chiron sextile Uranus (1939–40) confers the increased possibility of seeing the higher meaning, logic, and plan behind our wounds and issues. Like all sextiles, however, it must be activated, consciously and intentionally, by our wish for, and efforts toward, our healing and evolution of consciousness. Otherwise, this aspect remains mostly benign.

In any case, it is a welcome addition to the charts of people wishing to pursue healing as a life's path—for themselves and/or for others—whatever the specific modality of healing might be.

Quincunx

The influence/effect of Chiron quincunx Uranus (1948–49 and 1992–93) is almost the same as Chiron opposition Uranus, but with two differences. The first difference is that the influence of the quincunx is not as acute, challenging, or confronting as the opposition. The second is that the quincunx produces a constant nagging feeling, uneasiness, irritation, unsettledness, and restlessness—feelings arising from the (misplaced) belief that we are never doing enough toward our healing and evolution of consciousness.

This aspect ever prods us to attain a higher understanding—a new level of consciousness—of our wounds and their attendant issues.

In the charts of persons wishing to pursue healing as a life's path—for themselves and/ or for others—this aspect is a welcome addition.

Moreover, this aspect can confer healing ability and focus, particularly when combined with other significant Chiron aspects.

Chiron in Aspect to Neptune

Due to Neptune's slow orbit, aspects of Neptune and Chiron are rare, having global significance as well as making an extreme personal impact in our natal charts.

In general, in its highest expression, Neptune is about our potential return to spirit, oneness, and unconditional love. Its wordless messages "speak" of a divine order beyond ideas, images, concepts, and logic—even beyond *meaning,* as such. Its influences are *felt* in the spiritual heart and *known* in the soul.

In its earthly expression and manifested in our lives, Neptune can seem strange, mysterious, confusing, illusive, and ethereal. Its influences, refracted by our fragmented consciousness, can create confusion, delusions, fantasies, irrationalities, and disassociative states of consciousness.

Either way, Neptune constantly challenges us to acknowledge spirit, the divine, and the love that lies behind our existence and at the root of all creation.

When aspecting Chiron, Neptune seeks to bypass our intellect, rationalizations, justifications, and protective mind-games in order to help us access, recognize, acknowledge, embrace, and finally love our wounds and issues. Through Chiron, Neptune (the call of spirit) encourages us to move through our wounds and issues by seeing all sides of the otherwise negatively judged events and circumstances of our lives. The goal is unconditional love—for ourselves, for others, and for our lives; the steps are recognition, acknowledgment, forgiveness, acceptance, inclusion, and, beyond forgiveness, oneness and unconditional love. The ultimate message of Chiron aspecting Neptune is that love is the greatest healer.

Conjunction, Parallel, Contraparallel, Occultation

Chiron conjunct, parallel, contraparallel, or occult Neptune (1879–80, 1945, and 2010) produces a resonant channel between our soul (and its experience of unconditional love) and our lower nature (and its attendant wounds and issues).

Depending on our level of healing and evolution of consciousness, this can affect us in one of two ways (or a proportional balance of both ways):

In its lowest expression, it can entirely disassociate us from reality and make it virtually impossible for us to touch the ground, so to speak. The result will tend to be escapist patterns and behavior. It may result in indulgence in drugs, alcohol, and other mind-numbing pursuits; it may manifest as social misconduct and/or dysfunction; it may cause us to seek out sectarian religions, cults, and fringe groups; and/or it may result in psychopathy.

In its highest expression, this aspect can confer extraordinary healing ability and focus. It can be the mark of a mystic, saint, or prophet. It can also be the mark of genius, because, if we can bear our wounds and issues, we are directly connected to our soul. Such assertions are evidenced by the fact that Edgar Cayce (the "Sleeping Prophet"), Albert Einstein, and Michelangelo share this aspect.

The less evolved we are, the more likely this aspect will manifest its lower expression. Conversely, the more evolved we are, the more likely this aspect will manifest its higher expression. In truth, each of us will have both higher and lower expressions, manifesting to differing degrees in different areas of our lives.

Ultimately, this aspect creates a deep need to connect with spirit as an answer to our woundedness. Through this aspect, Neptune encourages us to unconditionally love our wounds and issues—love the lost, disowned, denied, and otherwise negatively judged pieces of ourselves—and bring them lovingly back into the light.

This aspect can be a tacit indication of considerable work already done on healing and evolution of consciousness in past lives.

In the charts of persons wishing to pursue healing as a life's path—for themselves and/or for others—this aspect is a welcome addition.

Moreover, this aspect can confer extraordinary healing ability and focus, particularly when combined with other significant Chiron aspects.

Opposition

With Chiron opposition Neptune (1900–1901, 1990, and 2048–55), we initially tend to try to escape our wounds and issues—escapism, avoidance, drug use, fantasy, illusion, delusion, self-deceit, and/or imagination. Psychologically speaking, this might cause us to create alternate or virtual realities within the mind as a haven from our wounds and issues.

If, however, we are able and willing to deal with our wounds and issues (this may be supported by other aspects of Chiron in the chart), then the effect of this aspect is to encourage us constantly to look into our darkness and love what we find there. In this way, the pieces of ourselves are brought back into the fold.

In this latter case, a foundation built from our efforts toward healing and evolution of consciousness is required. Otherwise, Neptune's messages remain inexplicable and confusing. This illustrates that Neptune, like Chiron, can only be reliably accessed via Saturn—through hard work, discipline, seriousness, resolve, persistence, and so forth.

When combined with other significant Chiron aspects (particularly trines and sextiles), this aspect is a welcome addition to the charts of persons wishing to pursue healing as a life's path—for themselves and/or for others—and it can be the mark of a person called to heal as a life's path/purpose/calling/destiny.

Trine

Chiron trine Neptune (1895, 1920–26, 1963–68, and 1994–95) indicates that our deepest wounds and issues resonate with our longing for a return to spirit, oneness, and love.

This will tend to find expression through creative, artistic, and/or spiritual pursuits, even if we do not attend, consciously and intentionally, to our wounds and issues. Alternately, it might lead to the exploration of, and experimentation with, altered states of consciousness. Both of these manifestations were the hallmark of the explosion of creativity and experimentation during the Chiron-Neptune trines of the 1960s.

If we choose to attend to our wounds and issues, we may lean toward spiritual, healing, and creative pursuits; if we do not, then we may lean toward escapist and/or consciousness-altering or dulling pursuits and devices. Either way, as always, our divine design is expedited, consciously or unconsciously.

This aspect can be the tacit indication of considerable work already done on healing and evolution of consciousness in past lives.

When combined with other significant Chiron aspects, this aspect is a welcome addition to the charts of persons wishing to pursue healing as a life's path—for themselves and/or for others—and it can be the mark of a person called to heal as a life's path/purpose/calling/destiny.

Square

With Chiron square Neptune (1849–50, 1893, 1935–37, 1954–55, 1996–97, and 2042), we initially tend to feel cut off from soul/spirit/divinity/home/source/God. We can feel abandoned by spirit—left in a world without love, compassion, meaning, or connection.

Our reaction to this can take two forms: either we are more impelled to seek out spirit, meaning, connection, and love, or we tend to deny spirit entirely and seek an existentialist and/or atheistic life. In practice, we generally live somewhere between these two extremes, expressing one side while repressing the other.

This aspect bears a lot in common with Chiron in Pisces inasmuch as it makes us feel as though the universe has betrayed and/or abandoned us. In response, we may try to shut the door to our soul. Even in shutting the door, though, our path takes us on a journey—events and circumstances—upon which we will ultimately rediscover the love that lies behind all things. As Chiron says, through the darkness lies the light.

If this aspect forms part of a T-square or other such planetary pattern, the healing path is more easily facilitated. In this case, it would be a welcome addition to the charts of persons wishing to pursue healing as a life's path—for themselves and/or for others—whatever the modality of healing might be.

Sextile

Chiron sextile Neptune (1891, 1940–41, 1950, 1999, and 2038–39) offers a healing conduit between our woundedness and our soul/spirit. As with all sextiles, however, we must activate/use this conduit, consciously and intentionally, by attending to our wounds and issues. In this case, this means actively trying to unconditionally love each of our lost, denied, disowned, and/or otherwise negatively judged parts. Such efforts will be quickly supported by this aspect. Otherwise, this aspect remains mostly benign.

This aspect would be a welcome addition to the charts of persons wishing to pursue healing as a life's path—for themselves and/or for others.

Quincunx

With Chiron quincunx Neptune (1897–98, 1905–7, 1981–84, 1992–93, and 2046–47), we find ourselves seeking a new level of understanding/consciousness with respect to our wounds and issues. Through this aspect, Neptune tries to help us love our dark, repressed, unacknowledged, denied, disowned, ignored, unseen, negatively judged, and otherwise unloved parts, reminding us that all things are a service of love.

This aspect will tend to produce the nagging, niggling, irritating, and unsettling feeling that, behind the things we currently judge, blame, and/or condemn, there is an unseen meaning and providence. This will tend to impel us to seek a higher understanding of the people, events, and circumstances of others' and our lives.

If we do not consciously heed the call of this aspect, then, as a substitute, we will tend unconsciously to try to fix, change, and/or rescue others—to "save" them from their wounds and issues. To this end, we may unconsciously create, imagine, and/or project an evil force, against which we are fighting. This, in turn, can lead us to extreme religious beliefs and practices.

Alternately, we may express this aspect by vehemently seeking to "disprove" spirit or by reacting violently against spirit in some way.

If we heed the call of this aspect, it can be a welcome—if at times exasperating—partner on our journey of healing and evolution of consciousness. We will never be completely satisfied unless we are attending to our wounds and issues, which is a blessing in disguise.

When combined with other significant Chiron aspects, this aspect is a welcome addition to the charts of persons wishing to pursue healing as a life's path—for themselves and/or for others—and it can be the mark of a person called to heal as a life's path/purpose/calling/destiny.

Chiron in Aspect to Pluto

Pluto represents death and rebirth, ends of old cycles and beginnings of new cycles, transformation, transmutation, nuclear energy, quantum physics, and so forth. In terms of consciousness, Pluto represents the potential for the transformation of consciousness and understanding from one octave to the next.

If we have not done sufficient work toward our healing and evolution of consciousness, we cannot yet move up the octave, so to speak, and Pluto turns us back. This sometimes entails "plowing in" old forms that have outlived their usefulness and/or have become stuck in their evolution. Such plowing in prepares the soil of consciousness for the growth of new forms that will better serve our future healing and evolution of consciousness.

Chiron-Pluto aspects challenge, confront, and stir up our longest-standing and most deeply ingrained wounds and issues more intensely, more mercilessly, more ceaselessly, and more violently than any other aspect. To make sense of such uncompromising and seemingly cruel influences, we must remember that spirit will do everything it can to ensure our ultimate healing and evolution of consciousness. We are not allowed by the laws of the universe to remain static for too long. We must be moving either toward or away from the light—evolution or involution.

Ultimately, the choice is ours to make or not make. In this, Pluto, when aspecting Chiron, forces our hand, impelling us to choose our direction. If we choose to attend to the issues and wounds brought up by Chiron-Pluto aspects, then we can release and gain access to unparalleled power for the transformation of consciousness—our own consciousness as well the consciousness of the planet.

Conjunction, Parallel, Contraparallel, Occultation

Chiron conjunct, parallel, contraparallel, or occult Pluto (1883–84, 1941, and 1999) puts the maximum pressure upon our wounds and issues, challenging us to attend to them and attain new levels of consciousness. Alternately, if we are not yet ready for this quantum leap, Pluto wipes away the old forms of the preceding cycle and initiates a fresh tack—still dealing with the same wounds and issues, but in different forms.

With this aspect, a person is constantly challenged to make every moment a turning point. There seems to be no stability, safety, security, comfort, or safe haven. This can be an untenable state of affairs or an extraordinary gift, depending on the evolution, preparedness, and willingness of the native.

If we are unprepared or unwilling to attend to our issues and wounds, we may project these outwardly, taking them out on the world in violent ways. Alternatively, we may seek to change the world to such a degree that, if successful, might make recompense for the woundedness we feel inside. Still further, we may become self-destructive in our effort to escape from the pain of our wounds and issues.

The negative power of Chiron conjunct Pluto can be seen in its last two occurrences: in 1941 (in the midst of World War II) and at the end of 1999 (heralding a new wave of worldwide terrorism and the resurgence of Middle East conflicts).

If we are, to a degree, prepared and willing to attend to our wounds and issues, this will enable major leaps of healing and evolution of consciousness. The key to healing this aspect lies in recognizing that our violent and destructive tendencies and reactions arise from a genuine impulse/desire/need for healing and evolution of consciousness. Instead of directing these reactions/tendencies toward others (destructiveness) or toward ourselves (self-destructiveness), the question is: What lies, illusions, misperceptions, misunderstandings, judgments, expectations, conditions, and outmoded ways of thinking and living must die in us in order to make way for a new way of being?

The mastery of this aspect would produce a gifted healer of extraordinary ability, but one who might frighten others with their power and intensity. Even if not mastered, the hand of fate/destiny works through this aspect, creating people who are destined to turn the world upside-down in some way, often violently and irrevocably.

Examples of people with this aspect illustrate its power: Bruce Lee, Karl Marx, Benito Mussolini, John Maynard Keynes (economist), Riccardo Muti (conductor), and Walt Whitman.

This aspect—if tempered with caution, reserve, and wisdom—would be a welcome addition to the charts of people wishing to pursue healing as a life's path—for themselves and/or for others. If combined with other significant Chiron aspects, this aspect would be the mark of an extraordinary healer called to pursue healing as a life's path/purpose/calling/destiny—whatever form that might take.

This aspect can be a tacit indication of considerable work already done on healing and evolution of consciousness in past lives.

Opposition

If the Chiron-Uranus opposition is difficult to deal with, then the Chiron-Pluto opposition is even more so. In particular, those born in the early to mid-1960s with this aspect have taken considerably longer to come to terms with their issues and wounds than might have been the case without this acute aspect—more so than those with only other Chiron aspects. Having said this, those persons born with *both* the Chiron-Uranus opposition and the Chiron-Pluto opposition (1962–67) have had a fairer chance of coming to terms with their issues and wounds, because Uranus offers higher understanding and perspective.

This aspect acts in a similar way to Chiron opposition Uranus, but much more acutely and intensely. (Natives born in 1966 with Chiron-conjunct-Saturn opposing Pluto-conjunct-Uranus received a double blow.) The depth of inner pain mirrored in this aspect has caused people to try every imaginable way—positive and negative, constructive and destructive—of burying, avoiding, ignoring, and/or denying their wounds and issues. The lateness of the 1st Chiron square in these persons' personal Chiron cycles has a lot to do with this, too.

Here, resisting or failing to attend to our wounds and issues may lead to extreme violence and destructiveness—toward ourselves and/or toward others—creating a collective challenge for humanity.

With the opposition aspect, we tick-tock between the two planetary poles—in this case, between Chiron and Pluto. When our wounds and issues become too painful or difficult, we run toward Pluto. Here, Pluto engenders change, violence, conflict, war, challenge, confrontation, and death—within us and/or outside us. Finding Pluto too painful and/or difficult to deal with, we retreat once more into our woundedness. Finding no relief from Chiron, we bounce back toward Pluto, and so the game proceeds—a game that *demands* that we eventually attend to our wounds and issues. If we cannot, we lash out, self-destruct, and/or retreat within.

On the other hand, when we address, work through, and heal the wounds and issues illuminated by this aspect, we gain access to unparalleled power of healing and transformation for ourselves and for others. People who work through this aspect will emerge as major healers of the planet in the first decades of the new millennium.

Either way—attending or not attending to our wounds and issues—the inexorable movement of the evolution of the consciousness of the planet is expedited.

When combined with other significant Chiron aspects (particularly trines and sextiles), this aspect is a welcome addition to the charts of people wishing to pursue healing as a life's path—for themselves and/or for others. It would also be the mark of an extraordinary healer called to pursue healing as a life's path/purpose/calling/destiny—whatever form that might take.

Trine

Chiron trine Pluto (1895, 1909–10, 1950, 1989–90, and 2037–38) confers natural powers of healing and transformation with respect to our wounds and issues. However, as with Chiron conjunct Pluto and Chiron opposition Pluto, this aspect can manifest in several different ways.

In the first case, it can cause us to actively lash out against, and/or seek to change, the outside world as an answer to our woundedness. In the second case, we lash out against ourselves, attempting to self-annihilate or "blank out." In the third case, it can give us the gift of personal healing and evolution of consciousness to a degree paralleled only by the conjunction and opposition.

The difference in the preceding will be determined by how we use this aspect—i.e., how we attend to our wounds and issues; we must still do the work. (Trine aspects can engender laziness in the areas of our talents and gifts.)

Overall, this aspect is more harmonious than the conjunction and opposition.

This aspect can be the tacit indication of considerable work already done on healing and evolution of consciousness in past lives.

When combined with other significant Chiron aspects, this aspect is a welcome addition to the charts of people wishing to pursue healing as a life's path—for themselves and/or for others. It would also be the mark of an extraordinary healer called to pursue healing as a life's path/purpose/calling/destiny—whatever form that might take.

Square

With Chiron square Pluto (1893, 1919–21, 1947, 1992–93, and 2028–30), we may initially be unable to deal with or transform our wounds and issues; our evolutionary path appears blocked. However, Pluto will constantly try to break through to us with new understanding. In a square aspect (Saturnian influence), it does this by bringing crises that force us to sit down and reassess our lives; it keeps tripping us up until we "get it" and higher understanding is born.

If we refuse to attend to our wounds and issues, Pluto will continue to mirror these in the external calamities of our lives. Ensuing negative reactions will be similar to those experienced with Chiron conjunct Pluto, Chiron opposition Pluto, and Chiron trine Pluto. (See these aspects for details.) However, our reactions will tend to be more focused toward *controlling* others and the world around us, rather than destroying or transforming it.

If, on the other hand, we choose to work in a positive way with Pluto's calamitous demonstrations (and with our wounds and issues, as always), we will reap the fruits of accelerated healing and evolution of consciousness. The healing path consists of transforming our perspectives and illusions, i.e., of seeing our wounds and issues and their associated events and circumstances in a new light, of seeing a larger picture, of seeing the balance, harmony, perfection, and love behind every aspect.

When combined with other significant Chiron aspects (particularly trines, sextiles, or in a T-square), this aspect is a welcome addition to the charts of people wishing to pursue healing as a life's path—for themselves and/or for others. It could also be the mark of a healer called to pursue healing as a life's path/purpose/calling/destiny—whatever form that might take.

Sextile

With Chiron sextile Pluto (1891, 1931–32, 1945, 1995, and 2012–14), we are given the possibility of consciously directing our powers of healing and transformation—for our own healing and/or for the healing of others. As with all sextiles, though, we must consciously activate this aspect with our effort and wish/intention for healing. We simply have to take the steps, and our healing journey will be facilitated and supported. Otherwise, this aspect remains mostly benign.

When combined with other significant Chiron aspects, this aspect is a welcome addition to the charts of people wishing to pursue healing as a life's path—for themselves and/or for others.

Quincunx

Chiron quincunx Pluto (1897, 1903, 1953–54, 1981–85, and 2041–42) creates incessant, nagging, irritating, unsettling, and frustrating feelings that impel us to heal our wounds and issues and transform our consciousness. It impels us to see the hidden blessings, benefits, lessons, and gifts of our wounds and issues—to see the flip sides of people, events, and circumstances that we might otherwise judge only negatively.

If we fail to attend to the call of this aspect, we will tend to take out our criticisms, negativity, frustration, and irritation upon others. We will tend to seek to fix, change, harm, and/or destroy others and their lives; or we will unconsciously "stir the pot," seek to upset/disrupt the balance of things, and/or wantonly needle others for no other reason than to discharge our negative feelings. Alternately, we may take it out on ourselves in self-depreciating and self-destructive ways.

On the other hand, if we turn the power of this aspect inward and attend to our wounds and issues, this aspect can be a constant blessing, never failing to provide new material for our spiritual growth. Here, the healing path consists of attending to each wound and issue *as it arises.* Otherwise, the cumulative effect gradually becomes unbearable.

Overall, this aspect requires us to seek new perspectives, new understandings, and/or new levels of consciousness about the issues behind our wounds (the specific nature of which can be seen, as always, in the sign and house placements of Chiron).

A statistically high number of noted athletes have this aspect, not the least of which are Chris Evert Lloyd and Venus Williams. The nervous energy of this aspect is discharged physically through their sport.

Statistics also show that the unresolved/unhealed nervous energy of this aspect may also be discharged sexually in unusual and nonconsensual ways—homosexuality, bestiality, sadomasochism, fetishes, and so forth.

When combined with other significant Chiron aspects, this aspect is a welcome addition to the charts of people wishing to pursue healing as a life's path—for themselves and/or for others.

Chiron in Aspect to the Midheaven

Chiron aspects to the Midheaven (MC) indicate that, in some way, we are destined to express our journey of healing and evolution of consciousness before the eyes of others, for the benefit of others, and/or through our chosen vocation. This does not necessarily presuppose a vocation in healing per se, although many vocations not generally considered healing/medical professions are indirectly healing to others—such as music.

Alternately, Chiron-MC aspects may indicate that we are destined to play out our wounds and issues through our chosen vocation/career and/or before the eyes of others.

In reality, we will probably play out each side at different times—now the wounding, now the healing. Whatever the case may be and depending on the other aspects in the chart, it will tend to become a public affair and/or a thread in our vocation, whether the "audience" is small or large.

Ultimately, our vocation and public image are exterior expressions of who we are, why we are here, where we come from, and where we are going. As such, they are destined to reflect our life's path/purpose/calling/destiny—the essence of this path reflected from the Moon's nodes, its expression reflected from the Sun, its exterior masks reflected from the Ascendant, its lower emotional issues reflected from the Moon, and its inherent wounds reflected from Chiron.

As we evolve, our personal/inner path becomes increasingly an outward path of service to others, and, as it does, this is reflected through our vocation and through our public persona.

In truth, the distinctions we make between our life's path, its essence, its expression, its arena of execution, its masks, our wounding and healing journey, our career, and our public persona *are illusory distinctions. All are part of our total divine design.* Chiron-MC aspects merely illuminate this truth by bringing our journey of healing and evolution of consciousness into greater alignment with our vocation and/or public persona.

Conjunction (Simultaneously Opposing the IC)

With Chiron conjunct the MC, our journey of healing and evolution of consciousness is potentially in perfect alignment with our vocation; this is a call to heal, and more than likely in a public way.

Initially, though, and depending on the other features of our chart, our career path will tend to be fraught with difficulties, false starts, and disappointments until we align it with our healing path. This may result in numerous career changes early on. We may also feel as though we are not getting the recognition we deserve.

If we fail to attend to our wounds and issues, we will tend to play out our wounds and issues in our chosen vocation, particularly if that vocation is not yet in alignment with the eventual expression of our life's path/purpose/calling/destiny.

Conversely, if we do attend to our wounds and issues, we will find ourselves gravitating toward the vocation most fitting our life's path/purpose/calling/destiny.

Either way, our journey will tend to be played out before the eyes of others, whether the audience is small or large. We will tend to seek approval, recognition, status, kudos, and standing—ironically, for our woundedness and/or for our healing efforts. We will tend to have an innate wish for others to hear and see our story, even if we initially shun the limelight and even if public attention frightens us.

This aspect can be a welcome addition to the charts of persons wishing to pursue a healing as a life's path—for themselves and/or for others. When combined with other significant Chiron aspects, it can be the mark of a healer called to heal as a vocation, conferring healing ability and focus.

It can also be the indication of substantial work done in the past and/or in past lives on healing and evolution of consciousness.

Opposition (Simultaneously Conjuncting the IC)

Chiron opposition the MC tends to reflect wounds and issues relating to the past, parents, grandparents, heredity, genetics, and so on.

With this aspect, we tend to try to escape from and/or avoid the aforementioned wounds and issues by burying ourselves in our careers and/or by seeking a public life. Consequently, our wounds, issues, and the healing journey these inspire will tend to become a part of the career or public image we strive for, even if our career is not, strictly speaking, a career in healing.

This aspect may also lead to unexpected and uncomfortable public airing of our deepest wounds and issues. Or we ourselves may play out their drama in dramatic, sometimes violent, and often public ways.

Alternately, this opposition can create tension, conflict, and/or a dilemma between our vocation/career and our wounds and issues; one will necessarily aggravate the other. This, however, will impel us to attend to our wounds and issues. If we try to escape by putting all our energy and focus into our career, the same wounds and issues we tried to escape from will tend to emerge along the way anyway, still demanding attention.

If we choose to attend to our wounds and issues within the context of the vocation/career path, though, then this vocation/career path will almost certainly have a healing element, even if this is not the primary focus.

If accompanied by other significant Chiron aspects, this aspect is a welcome addition to the charts of people wishing to pursue healing as a life's path—for themselves and/or for others. Moreover, this may be the mark of a person called to heal as a life's path/purpose/calling/destiny.

Trine (Simultaneously Sextiling the IC)

With Chiron trine the MC, our wounds and issues and our vocation/career are inextricably intertwined. In a sense, our wounds and issues are put out front in a way that attracts others to our cause through empathy, sympathy, vulnerability, and a feeling of a common bond and/or cause.

While our wounds and issues remain unhealed, our reactions to these will tend to motivate us to visibly champion a cause, support underdogs and people who are down and out, and/or try to fix or change people and/or situations.

Conversely, when we attend to our wounds and issues, our actions will tend to manifest our healing journey through our vocation/career and/or in the public eye. In this case, this aspect can be the mark of a person called to heal as a life's path/purpose/calling/destiny.

This aspect can be an indication of substantial work done toward our healing and evolution of consciousness in the past and/or in past lives. It is also a welcome addition to the charts of people wishing to pursue healing as a life's path—particularly for the sake of others.

Interestingly, a statistically significant number of politicians and leaders (and their partners) have this aspect, or their lives have been influenced by it. For example, Chiron was trining the MC when Hitler gave his very first political speech in 1927.

Square (Simultaneously Squaring the IC)

Chiron square the MC indicates that our wounds and issues will initially block our vocation/career path and/or thwart our efforts to step out into the public eye.

Alternately, our wounds and issues may become a public affair and/or may create the circumstances for a career to be born, although, for all visible purposes, healing and resolution may never take place.

In the first case, we may not understand why our vocation/career and/or public life seem to be blocked or thwarted. Consequently, we may simply not develop this area of our lives. Our life's path/purpose/calling/destiny may lie elsewhere, our wounds and issues driving us there by seeming default. (In truth, it is all part of a larger plan).

In the second case, our wounds and issues become public property and may even give us a vocation/career in which we will play out the drama of these wounds and issues. In this case, it is likely that our wounds and issues will reflect those of the greater populace, and our journey will be played out upon a public stage.

A final case, leading on from the first case, is where, impelled by our frustrations about a blocked or thwarted career path or public life, we delve deeply into our wounds and issues in an effort to unlock this area of our lives. The result would be the expression, to a greater or lesser degree, of our healing path through our vocation/career and/or public life—for ourselves and/or for others.

This last case is most likely if there are other significant aspects of Chiron in our chart —particularly trines or oppositions. Moreover, when this aspect is combined with other significant aspects of Chiron, it can be the mark of a person called to heal as a life's path/purpose/calling/destiny as well as a vocation/career.

Sextile (Simultaneously Trining the IC)

Chiron sextile the MC gives us the possibility of attending to our wounds and issues and/or of plying a healing path through our vocation/career and/or in our public life. As with all sextiles, though, this aspect must be activated, consciously and intentionally, by our wish for, and attention to, our healing and evolution of consciousness. Otherwise, this aspect remains mostly benign.

When this aspect is combined with other significant aspects of Chiron (particularly trines and oppositions), it is a welcome addition to the charts of people wishing to pursue healing as a life's path—particularly for the sake of others. It can also be the mark of a person called to heal as a life's path/purpose/calling/destiny as well as a vocation/career.

Quincunx (Simultaneously Semisextiling the IC)

With Chiron quincunx the MC, our wounds and issues will tend to continually nag us, irritate us, unsettle us, and frustrate us by constantly poking their heads into our vocation/career and/or public lives.

The impulse for a vocation/career and/or public life may stem from our need for healing and resolution—as though career and/or a public life might help. Consequently, we may seem driven in our chosen careers or driven to stand out in the public eye, but with our uneasiness and unrest never completely allayed, even if we are consciously attending to our wounds and issues.

With this aspect, we are encouraged to find an outward expression for our wounds and issues—creatively, artistically, on the stage, in the public eye, in leadership situations, and so forth. Otherwise, we may find ourselves feeling scattered, incomplete, chaotic, disconnected, and frustrated.

If we fail to attend to our wounds and issues, we may find ourselves seeking to fix, rescue, and/or change others and the world around us in publicly demonstrative ways.

However, if we attend to our wounds and issues, our healing journey is likely to be expressed through our vocation/career and/or public life, whatever form that may take.

When this aspect is combined with other significant aspects of Chiron (particularly sextiles and trines), it is a welcome addition to the charts of people wishing to pursue healing as a life's path—particularly for the sake of others. It can also be the mark of a person called to heal as a life's path/purpose/calling/destiny as well as a vocation/career.

Chiron in Aspect to the IC

Quincunx (Simultaneously Semisextiling the MC)

Chiron quincunx the IC indicates that we will see our wounds and issues reflected in our past, our parents, grandparents, genetics, and general heredity. We may hearken back to bygone eras and/or expound the virtues of the past compared to the present as an unconscious way of trying to allay the pain of our woundedness. We may feel incomplete until we delve into our past, reveal its secrets, and resolve its issues, connecting all this with our present lives.

This aspect can make us feel as though the past often comes back to haunt us.

Because our wounds and issues ultimately have their origins in the past, this aspect is, from a healing perspective, eminently useful; as such, it may be a welcome addition to the charts of people wishing to pursue healing as a life's path—for themselves and/or for others.

(For all other aspects of Chiron to the IC, see Chiron in aspect to the MC.)

Chiron in Aspect to the Ascendant

The Ascendant is our window to the world. Initially, it represents the illusory ways in which we see ourselves and the ways in which we project these illusions out into the world. It is a mask that protects us from seeing too much about ourselves before we are ready. It is also a mirror in which we can see our issues and misperceptions when we are ready, giving us the opportunity to awaken and evolve.

As we attend to our wounds and issues, our masks become increasingly transparent. Moreover, we become increasingly able to use our masks, consciously and intentionally, in the fulfillment of our life's path/purpose/calling/destiny.

When Chiron aspects the Ascendant, we are destined in some way to act as a kind of *persona* for Chiron—an interface or emissary to bring Chiron's messages into the world. Chiron can be "seen" upon our countenance. Before attending to our wounds and issues, our woundedness will be seen; the more we attend to our wounds and issues, the more the healing journey will be seen.

Conjunction (Simultaneously Opposing the Descendant)

Chiron conjunct the Ascendant indicates that we are destined to personify Chiron in some way in our lives. In a sense, we unconsciously and continuously channel Chiron and its issues and messages.

Initially, our wounds and issues are worn upon our outer countenance, for all to see and feel, whether we are aware of it or not and whether others can consciously identify with it or not. We may find that others want to rescue us, wrap us up in cotton wool, nurture us, and soothe our woundedness. Alternately, they might want to slap us out of it.

Our own reaction, though, may be the antithesis of this—a total denial of our sensitive inner nature, a stoic posture, and/or a cynical, suspicious, or even atheistic attitude toward spiritual matters. We might come across as being as hard as nails.

Conversely, depending on the other aspects involved, we may play out the drama of our woundedness to the maximum, burdening others with our plight. (There is a Piscean element to this aspect.)

With this aspect, our woundedness tends to become our first mask—i.e., we unconsciously hide behind our wounds and issues. We may even believe that our wounds and issues *are* us, as opposed to being events and circumstances that happened to us.

When we consciously acknowledge and embrace this journey, we then *live* the healing journey in the first person—an example for all to see and aspire to; Chiron works its healing magic on the world through us. In this case, this aspect confers empathy, deep understanding, and an unconditionally loving manner.

When combined with other significant Chiron aspects, this aspect is a welcome addition to the charts of people wishing to pursue healing as a life's path—for themselves and/or for others. It may also be the mark of a person called to heal as a life's path/purpose/calling/destiny.

Opposition (Simultaneously Conjuncting the Descendant)

Chiron opposition the Ascendant indicates that we are poised to awaken to a larger picture of ourselves and of our lives.

This aspect tends to illuminate wounds and issues around relationship, the way others see us, and the way we see ourselves in relation to others. Chiron teaches us that others are a perfect reflection of us—mirroring all the things we have learned to love about ourselves and all the things we have yet to learn to love about ourselves. By having our relationship wounds and issues thrown in our faces, we are being impelled/encouraged to recognize that (1) we are not the center of some private world; (2) we are not so different from others; (3) what we see in others is us—the negative and the positive; (4) our image of ourselves may be distorted; and (5) ultimately, we are all connected and basically seeking the same thing, i.e., to awaken to our true nature.

This aspect is a welcome addition to the aspect set of people wishing to pursue healing as a life's path—for themselves and/or for others. If it is accompanied by other significant Chiron aspects, it can confer healing ability and focus, particularly in the area of healing relationships and wounds of self-worth/self-image.

Trine (Simultaneously Sextiling the Descendant)

With Chiron trine the Ascendant, our wounds and issues and our self-image are intimately connected. We will tend to wear these wounds and issues on our sleeve. For this reason, this aspect can confer a certain charisma, empathy, and sensitivity that others may find attractive, particularly if they are into trying to rescue, protect, care for, and/or heal others.

As with Chiron conjunct the Ascendant, this trine aspect indicates that Chiron is "channeled" through us and can be seen upon our countenance. In this way, we will tend to play out the wounding and healing journey in all our personal dealing with others, as well as in our daydreams, imagination, and fantasies about ourselves.

If we attend to our wounds and issues, this aspect can confer healing ability and focus and is a welcome addition to the charts of persons wishing to pursue healing as a life's path—particularly for the sake of others.

Square (Simultaneously Squaring the Descendant)

With Chiron square the Ascendant, our wounds and issues will initially tend to prevent us from being open—from sharing our innermost self with others. We may tend to be overly shy and fearful of contact with others in an effort to hide and/or avoid our sensitive and wounded inner nature.

Conversely, the way we see ourselves in relation to others may thwart access to our wounds and issues. In this case, we tend to mistake our masks/personas for our true nature, believing our own publicity, so to speak. This can drive us—consciously or unconsciously —to create masks/personas that protect us from our wounds and issues and/or hide our true nature from others. This could be a blessing for those wishing to go into show business, politics, or the media.

On another tack, we may tend to see the world in terms of woundedness, pain, and despair, seeing little possibility of healing or reconciliation. This can lead to disillusionment, loss of energy and inspiration, negativity, fatalism, existentialism, and even atheism.

This aspect poses the question, *Who I am really?* The ultimately dissatisfying nature of our masks/personas engenders the wish to connect with something truer, more permanent, and closer to spirit. If we rise to this call, attending to our wounds and issues, our masks/personas will eventually lose their grip/attraction, and we will be inspired to show a truer face to the outside world. In this case and/or if this aspect is accompanied by other significant Chiron aspects, this aspect would be a welcome addition to the charts of people wishing to pursue healing as a life's path—for themselves and/or for others.

Sextile (Simultaneously Trining the Descendant)

With Chiron sextile the Ascendant, we are given the possibility of directly working with our masks/personas, self-image, and public image for our healing and evolution of consciousness.

If we activate this aspect, consciously and intentionally, by our wish for healing, our wounds as well as our healing will tend to be visible upon our countenance. Otherwise, this aspect remains mostly benign.

Due to the simultaneous trine with the Descendant, this aspect can confer empathy, rapport, and sensitivity with others. We will tend to feel others' wounds and issues, and, if we are attending to our own healing and evolution of consciousness, we will be able to offer support, nurturing, and/or healing.

This sextile can be a welcome addition to the charts of those wishing to pursue healing as a specific life's path and purpose—for themselves and/or for others. If it is accompanied by other significant Chiron aspects, it can confer healing ability and focus, in which case it would be a welcome addition to the charts of people called to heal as a life's path/purpose/calling/destiny.

Quincunx (Simultaneously Semisextiling the Descendant)

With Chiron quincunx the Ascendant, our wounds and issues will tend to incessantly poke their heads into our interactions with others, into the way we see ourselves, and into the way others see us. This will tend to be frustrating, irritating, and unsettling unless we attend to our wounds and issues.

The simplest manifestations of this are self-doubt, low self-esteem, fear that others will see our incompleteness and/or faults, and a drive toward perfectionism. We may tend to feel that, at all costs, we must present our best face.

This aspect impels a new level of consciousness about who we are. What is our true essence as opposed to our masks/personas? And where is the line between the two? Until we attend to our wounds and issues, our uncomfortable and sometimes embarrassing interactions with others will ever prod us to take action toward our healing and evolution of consciousness.

If we do attend to our wounds and issues, not only will we be better able to show our true self, but we will tend to have a healing effect upon others. For this reason, this aspect would be a welcome addition to the charts of people wishing to pursue healing as a life's path—for themselves and/or for others. If this aspect is accompanied by other significant Chiron aspects, it could be the mark of a person called to heal as a life's path/purpose/calling/destiny. It would certainly confer healing ability and focus.

Chiron in Aspect to the Descendant

Quincunx (Simultaneously Semisextiling the Ascendant)

With Chiron quincunx the Descendant, we will tend initially to have nagging, frustrating, irritating, unsettling, and incessant self-doubts about our ability to have and maintain "normal" relationships with others. This can cause us to either beat ourselves up for our failings or judge others for theirs, making relationships difficult and uncomfortable at times. Moreover, we will tend to play out our wounds and issues in our relationships. On the positive side, though, relationships will be the arena where our healing and evolution of consciousness can take place, particularly with the right partner.

With this aspect, if Chiron sits in the 1st or 12th house, natives will tend to be prone to self-sabotage and/or abuse by others (which is a mirror of our own self-depreciation). (See Chiron in the 1st house or Chiron in the 12th house, accordingly, in chapter 8.)

The path of healing lies in learning to love all aspects of ourselves, as each aspect manifests in our relationships and is mirrored in our partner(s). Our drive for perfectionism—whether directed toward ourselves or others—is really a drive to see that we are already perfect as we are.

This aspect would be a welcome addition to the charts of people wishing to pursue healing as a life's path—for themselves and/or for others. If this aspect is accompanied by other significant Chiron aspects, it could be the mark of a person called to heal as a life's path/purpose/calling/destiny. It would certainly confer healing ability and focus, particularly if Chiron sits in the 1st house.

(For all other aspects of Chiron to the Descendant, see Chiron in aspect to the Ascendant.)

CHAPTER TEN

Chiron in Planetary Patterns

Chiron in a T-square

In a T-square (an opposition of two planets with a third planet squaring both the first two), the planet at the junction of the two squares serves as the vehicle for the reconciliation of the issues of the opposing planets. Simultaneously, the two opposing planets serve as the catalysts for raising our consciousness around the issues associated with the squaring planet. In this way, where Chiron is situated in a T-square will determine its role in the pattern.

If Chiron is one of the opposing planets, then the squaring planet will offer aid and assistance in healing and resolving our wounds and issues as indicated by Chiron and as illuminated and challenged by the opposing planet. At the same time, Chiron and the opposing planet will act as catalysts in the raising of our consciousness around the issues of the squaring planet. Let's take an example, ignoring house placements for the sake of simplicity.

Let's suppose we have Chiron in Pisces opposition Uranus in Virgo, both squaring Venus in Gemini.

Chiron in Pisces indicates a wound of feeling as though the universe/God has betrayed and/or forsaken us, indicating possible early childhood happenings or circumstances that seemed unforgivable. Uranus in Virgo acts as a light shining upon our wounds and issues, encouraging us to see them in the greatest possible detail and to attend to them in a healing way. Venus in Gemini might assist the healing and resolution of these wounds and issues by giving some intellectual objectivity to our emotional nature. Furthermore, it may influence us toward having multiple relationships instead of getting stuck in the potential stagnation of a single relationship. In this way, we will reap the benefit of a variety of perspectives that will tend to help us see a bigger picture of our lives. This, in turn, will ultimately help us gain a greater consciousness around those things that we previously judged in solely negative ways, i.e., those things that constitute the reasons why we feel the universe/God betrayed or forsook us. In short, Venus, in this case, will give us perspective and objectivity.

In addition, Chiron in Pisces and Uranus in Virgo will act as catalysts to bring our Venus issues to a higher level of consciousness. The lower octave of Venus in Gemini can be fickleness in relationships, shallowness of the heart, and a lack of perseverance and loyalty when things get difficult. Venus squaring Chiron indicates that we may be like this as a defense against people getting too close to us and thereby having our woundedness exposed. It can also be that we are unwittingly betraying and forsaking others (another interpretation of the fickleness of Venus in Gemini) as an unconscious revenge against the universe/God for doing this to us. *We must become what we condemn in order to learn to love it.* Uranus, squaring Venus and illuminating our wounds and issues through Chiron, seeks to show us a different picture. What we call being betrayed and forsaken has hidden blessings, benefits, lessons, and gifts. We will unconsciously play out our wounds and issues through relationship, repeatedly and in many different circumstances (Venus in Gemini), until the penny begins to drop. As it does and we gradually resolve our issues and heal our wounds, our sensitive inner nature will be revealed, our spiritual heart opened, and our true *self* allowed to shine through.

If Chiron in a T-square pattern is at the junction of the two squares, then, on the one hand, Chiron will help us resolve the issues around the opposing planets. At the same time, the opposing planets will act as catalysts for the healing and resolution of our wounds and issues indicated by Chiron. That is, the opposing planets will help bring our wounds and issues into a higher state of consciousness. Again, let's take an example.

Let's say we have the Sun in Cancer opposition Mercury in Capricorn, both squaring Chiron in Libra.

The issues of the Sun in Cancer opposing Mercury in Capricorn may be that we wish to be caring, nurturing, loving, and kind to others (Sun in Cancer). However, our head tells us that this is being too soft, wishy-washy, sentimental, and easily swayed by others' emotional problems (Mercury in Capricorn). Furthermore, we may be extremely practical, pragmatic, responsible, and unemotional in our way of thinking (Mercury in Capricorn), but we tend to sabotage this by following random emotional impulses (Sun in Cancer). Chiron in Libra will help us overcome this dilemma by showing us the hidden blessings, benefits, lessons, and gifts that each way of being affords us. It will help us connect head and heart, realizing that each represents but a part of the greater whole of ourselves.

Chiron in Libra may represent a wound of feeling alone and/or incomplete without another with whom to share our life. Mercury in Capricorn squaring Chiron initially represents an intellectual fortress of protection against our woundedness. However, it will seek to give us a more down-to-earth understanding of our predicament, also inspiring us to get practical, organized, and serious about dealing with our wounds and issues. The Sun in Cancer squaring Chiron will initially cause us to pine away, feeling as though the wound of aloneness can never be filled. However, it will also seek to show us that, ultimately, the love, nurturing, and care that we may seek from companionship are already within us. In short, it will try to teach us to love ourselves. It will try to awaken us to the truth that there is nothing missing within us. Head (Mercury) and heart (Sun) will join in this T-square to teach us that balance and wholeness already exist in the world and in our lives and that, most importantly, we are never truly alone.

Chiron in a Grand Trine

In a grand trine, three planets make mutual trines, generally within one element—earth, water, air, or fire. They mutually enhance each other, the sum greater than the parts. A grand trine represents some gift or other in our lives, the nature of which is determined by the element, sign, and house placements of each planet and by the other aspects made to these three planets.

When Chiron is involved in a grand trine, the specific themes of wounding and healing become emphasized in the areas of life indicated by (1) the other two planets, and (2) by the element, sign, and house positions of all three planets. A grand trine involving Chiron would generally tend to indicate specific healing themes in our lives. It may also indicate substantial work done on our healing and evolution of consciousness in the past and/or in past lives. It will also tend to confer healing ability and focus. Let's give an example of a grand trine involving Chiron.

Let's say we have Chiron in Aquarius trine the Moon in Gemini trine Jupiter in Libra. In isolation, Chiron in Aquarius may indicate a wound of feeling isolated, cut-off, disconnected, and/or alienated from society. The Moon in Gemini may indicate talkativeness and a chameleonesque emotional nature. Jupiter in Libra may indicate an obsessive need for balance and companionship arising from Inner Child issues around feeling alone.

Chiron in Aquarius trining the Moon in Gemini may indicate a talent for being able to see our woundedness from others' perspectives, to put ourselves in their shoes, and to share our understandings with them. Chiron in Aquarius trining Jupiter in Libra may indicate the potential for a healing return to the childlike wisdom of the Inner Child that knows that we are never truly alone. Jupiter in Libra trining the Moon in Gemini may indicate a capacity for networking on a large scale.

Taken together, these three planets in the Grand Trine might indicate a potential gift for large-scale sharing with others the journey of the Inner Child—the journey from aloneness and isolation back to a feeling of togetherness and connectedness. How this might manifest in practical terms would be seen in the house placements of the three planets involved, particularly Chiron's house placement.

Chiron in a Triangle of a Trine and Two Sextiles

This planetary pattern represents a kind of miniature grand trine. (Refer to the notes on grand trines in the previous section.) The planet at the junction of the two sextiles is doubly enhanced by the two trining planets and forms the focal point of the pattern. In addition, the focal planet will further enhance the trining planets.

If Chiron is the focal planet, then our journey of healing and evolution of consciousness will be enhanced by the trining planets. For example, if Chiron, as the focal planet, sextiles Saturn and the Moon, our healing journey will be enhanced by a sense of seriousness and responsibility (Saturn). It will also be enhanced by a direct connection between our deepest hidden wounds and our visible lower emotional nature (Moon). Conversely, enhanced control (Saturn) of our lower emotional nature (Moon) will aid our journey of healing and evolution of consciousness (Chiron).

If Chiron is one of the trining planets, then, in combination with the other trining planet, it will help us see the benefits, blessings, lessons, and gifts that are hidden within the issues of the focal planet. For example, if Chiron is trining Venus and both are sextiling the Sun, Chiron and Venus will enhance the Sun. In practical terms, this might mean that Chiron will help us reveal, acknowledge, embrace, and finally love our sense of self, our creativity, our willpower, and our willingness to let ourselves shine. Venus will help us express beauty, balance, warmth, and harmony. Chiron trine Venus indicates a close connection between our journey of wounding and healing and our emotional nature, i.e., our capacity to love and be loved. This can tend to enhance the openness of our self-expression and our potential for the free expression of our inner light and love.

Chiron in a Grand Cross

A grand cross consists of two planets opposing each other and squaring two other planets also opposing each other. Each opposition pair of planets represents a catalyst for the raising of consciousness around the issues of the planets in the other opposition.

In general, the grand cross initially represents an *impasse* of consciousness. For a transcendence of this planetary pattern, the issues of all four planets involved must be attended to relatively simultaneously. If this is done, the potential for healing and evolution of consciousness is unparalleled.

This being so, when Chiron is involved in a grand cross, it is almost an irrevocable requirement that we attend to our woundedness in order to free up our lives and in order to fulfill our life's path/purpose/calling/destiny. Of course, this can be difficult. We must attend not only to our woundedness, represented by Chiron in this pattern, but also simultaneously to the issues raised by the other three planets. An understanding of the mechanics of this planetary pattern can assist greatly. Even without such understanding, these mechanics will tend to impel us in a certain direction, unconsciously driving the journey of healing and evolution of consciousness. Let's take an example, ignoring house and sign positions for the sake of simplicity.

Let's say we have a Chiron-Uranus opposition squaring a Mercury-Jupiter opposition. First, the Chiron-Uranus opposition indicates that our wounds and issues are constantly being illuminated, encouraging us to attain a new level of consciousness about them. The Mercury-Jupiter opposition will act as a catalyst for the attainment of this aim. In this case,

Mercury opposition Jupiter indicates a dilemma between the childlike and seemingly naïve but ultimately wise knowings of the Inner Child and our adult mental attitudes and thinking. This opposition will give two opposing but complementary perspectives to the issues brought up by the Chiron-Uranus opposition. The Jupiter side will encourage us to delve into our childhood issues and see a greater wisdom thereof; it will encourage a broader perspective, beyond our small concerns and narrow views. The Mercury side will help us develop objectivity and see all sides of the issues that we previously judged primarily negatively. In this way, the Jupiter-Mercury opposition will help us attend to the wounds and issues illuminated by Uranus.

From the other angle, the Jupiter-Mercury opposition, as we have said, indicates a dilemma between the childlike and seemingly naïve but ultimately wise knowings of the Inner Child and our adult mental attitudes and thinking. The Chiron-Uranus opposition might assist the resolution of this dilemma by showing us ways in which these seemingly opposing views are actually connected. It might show us how they both serve us in different ways to come to a more complete picture of reality, closer to truth. In other words, Chiron and Uranus will show us that these two ways of viewing the world are *complementary.*

Chiron in a Star of David

The Star of David planetary pattern consists of six planets (or more, if there are conjunctions involved) in a necklace of six sextiles. It is a highly balanced pattern allowing open correspondence between the issues of our lives in six different areas. Whether we make use of this psychological grid of interconnections is up to us.

Chiron's presence in a Star of David pattern would indicate that conscious access to our journey of wounding and healing would be increased sixfold, with five extra planets offering assistance. The conscious journey of healing and evolution of consciousness would be an integral part of our lives, whether we called it "healing" or not. Moreover, we would tend to have a natural and unforced healing effect upon others.

This pattern would tend to indicate that we have done substantial work on our healing and evolution of consciousness in the past and/or in past lives.

Chiron in a Yod

The yod planetary pattern (also referred to as "the finger of God") consists of a triangle formed from two quincunxes and a sextile. The focal point of the yod is the planet at the junction of the two quincunxes. The two sextiling planets assist in bringing our consciousness around the issues of the focal planet into a higher state.

When Chiron is involved in a yod pattern, the elements of healing and evolution of consciousness are emphasized. Chiron's role in the pattern will change according to its placement.

If Chiron is the focal point, the two sextiling planets will impel us to attain a higher state of consciousness around our specific wounds and issues as indicated by Chiron. For example, if Jupiter sextiles Mars and they both quincunx Chiron, then Jupiter and Mars will impel us to attend to our wounds and issues. Jupiter will tend to impel us to see the hidden perfection and wisdom that lie behind our wounds and issues, i.e., to see the benefits, blessings, lessons, and gifts. Mars will give us an extra kick—an extra impulse—to get on with the journey.

If Chiron is one of the sextiling planets, then, in combination with the other sextiling planet, it will impel us to attain a new level of consciousness concerning the issues of the focal planet. For example, if Chiron sextiles Saturn and they both quincunx Venus, Chiron and Saturn will impel us to raise our consciousness around the issues of earthly love, relationships, beauty, balance, harmony, etcetera. (Any other aspect that Venus might make in the chart as a whole will modify these issues.) In this example, Chiron will impel us to heal wounds of relationship, the feelings of being loved or not, and the feelings of being able to love or not. Saturn will encourage us to get serious about these same issues and to take responsibility for their healing and resolution.

Chiron in a Triangle of a Trine, a Square, and a Quincunx

This triangular mixture of aspects has the best of all possible worlds. It contains a blockage or limitation to overcome (square), an enhancement to aid us on our journey (trine), and an impelling force to drive us to attend to that journey (quincunx). When Chiron is involved in this pattern, then the themes of healing and evolution of consciousness will be apparent in the pattern's issues. Moreover, this pattern will tend to confer healing ability and focus and would be a welcome addition to the charts of people wishing to pursue healing as a life's path—for themselves and/or for others.

The first step in interpreting this pattern is to interpret each individual aspect separately. Then we can look at the pattern as a whole. The focal planet is the planet at the quincunx-trine junction. This planet will assist in the breaking down of the *impasse* of consciousness reflected in the issues of the squaring planets. This focal planet will assist in bringing about a new level of understanding and awareness.

If Chiron is the focal planet, it will help us see all sides of the issues of the squaring planets, revealing the hidden benefits, blessings, lessons, and gifts of each. In this way, it will help us heal the issues that otherwise maintain the impasse of consciousness indicated by the square.

If Chiron is one of the squaring planets, the focal planet will assist us in healing and resolving our wounds and issues, enabling us to unlock the higher potential of the other squaring planet.

Chiron in a Triangle of an Opposition, a Trine, and a Sextile

The opposition in this planetary pattern is already resolved to a degree by the trining/sextiling planet. The trining/sextiling planet—the focal planet—will assist in further integrating the issues of the opposing planets and bringing about a higher, more unified understanding and awareness.

If Chiron is the focal planet, then the integration and resolution of the opposition issues are dependent on our journey of healing and evolution of consciousness. The opposition issues will impel us to attend to this journey.

If Chiron is one of the opposing planets, then the focal planet will offer assistance on the journey of healing and evolution of consciousness, called to action by the planet opposing Chiron.

This pattern generally confers healing ability and focus and is a welcome addition to the charts of persons wishing to pursue a life of healing—for themselves and/or for others.

Chiron in a Kite Pattern

The kite pattern is one of the most advanced of planetary patterns and is rarely seen. It consists of a grand trine where one of the trines is also part of a trine-and-two-sextiles pattern. It can also be viewed as two opposition-trine-sextile patterns placed back to back, their respective focal points also trining.

The focal point of the kite pattern is the tip of the kite, i.e., the planet at the junction of the two sextiles, simultaneously opposing the junction of two of the three trines. The planet that opposes the focal planet will be the major catalyst in this pattern, challenging and confronting us to attain a new level of consciousness at the focal-point planet. The three trining planets will represent an inherent gift we bring into this lifetime. The two trining planets sextiling the focal planet will focus this gift into the focal planet.

If Chiron is the focal planet, then the journey of healing and evolution of consciousness will be one of the major focuses of our life, whatever external form that may take. This would be the mark of a person "called" to heal in some way, conferring healing ability and focus.

If Chiron is the planet opposing the focal point, it will act as the catalyst to inspire new levels of consciousness expressed through the focal planet. Said another way, our wounds and issues will drive us along the healing path, which, in turn, will help us open up the expression of the focal planet.

If Chiron is one of the two trining planets that sextile the focal point, then it will serve to bring healing and resolution to the issues of the focal planet, thus allowing the focal planet's fullest expression.

In all cases, Chiron's presence in this pattern indicates that the themes of healing and evolution of consciousness will be strong in our lives, whether consciously acknowledged or not. As such, it would be a welcome addition to the charts of people wishing to pursue healing as a life's path—for themselves and or for others. Moreover, this pattern would tend to indicate that we have done substantial work on our healing and evolution of consciousness in the past and/or in past lives.

CHAPTER ELEVEN

Chiron in Transit

It is important to note that a transited planet's natal aspects will tend to determine the "flavor," intensity, and specific effect of any given transit. The transit of a natal singleton will be less significant than the transit of a planet with multiple aspects in the natal chart. However, having said this, transits offer natal singletons their only opportunity to become significantly active in our lives. This makes transits of singletons worthy of special attention when reading the chart.

Note also that the house and sign placements of the planets involved in any given transit will give the generalized influences and themes of the transit a practical context in day-to-day life. Due to limitations of space, however, we will restrict our definitions to the generalized influences and themes, leaving the context of house and sign placements to the reader to work out and integrate. The themes and keywords of each of the signs and houses can be found in any basic astrology book.

The Psychology of Retrograde and Multiple-Pass Transits

Particularly in the case of the outer planets, a transit may occur more than once, due to the retrograde (apparent backward) motion of the transiting planet. The transiting planet will make the first pass in direct (forward) motion, the second pass in retrograde motion, and the third and final pass in direct motion once more. (Five passes are also possible if the transiting planet goes retrograde twice.)

Multiple-pass transits are much more powerful in their final effect due to the increased length of the overall transit.

When Chiron is involved in a multiple-pass transit *as the transiting planet,* the first pass will tend to bring to the surface our wounds and issues pertaining to the natal planet transited in its essence, sign, house, and natal aspects—giving us our first opportunity to attend to these things. Conversely, when Chiron is involved in a multiple-pass transit *as the natal planet transited,* the first pass will tend to bring to the surface our wounds and issues, as indicated by natal Chiron's sign, house, and natal aspects, again giving us our first opportunity to attend to them.

In both cases, the second (retrograde) pass will go even deeper, potentially exacerbating the wounds and issues brought up in the first pass; during this phase, healing and resolution will tend to be blocked or restricted, impelling us to introspect. The third pass will open the door again for deeper healing and for the final resolution of the attendant issues.

Transits of Chiron

Conjunct, Parallel, Contraparallel, Occult

In general, these transits are the most powerful and have the most obvious effects in our lives as they directly activate the transited planet and the natal planets in aspect to it. When Chiron is the transiting planet, it acts as a catalyst for the healing and evolution of consciousness of the issues around the transited planet and its aspecting companions, as played out through their respective signs and houses.

As always, occulting transits are the most powerful and focused.

Chiron Conjunct, Parallel, Contraparallel, Occult the North Node

Wounds, regrets, failings, and unresolved issues around our life's path and purpose are brought to the surface, impelling us to clear the way for a more conscious pursuit of that path and purpose.

Chiron Conjunct, Parallel, Contraparallel, Occult the South Node

Wounds and issues from the past and/or past lives surface during this transit, encouraging us to finally heal and resolve them, moving forward on our life's path and purpose.

Chiron Conjunct, Parallel, Contraparallel, Occult the Sun

Residual feelings of shyness, fear of self-expressing, ego wounds, loss or lack of willpower, thwarted or repressed creativity, etcetera, surface, encouraging healing and resolution of these.

Chiron Conjunct, Parallel, Contraparallel, Occult the Moon

Old wounds, regrets, self-depreciation, and negative feelings about our emotional protective patterns and about the reactions and emotional habits of our lower nature surface. Chiron's light encourages us to bring our emotional nature into a higher octave, closer to love.

Chiron Conjunct, Parallel, Contraparallel, Occult Mercury

Residual wounds, regrets, negative feelings around our ability to communicate, interact with others, express ourselves and/or think clearly, and/or being unintelligent are brought to the surface, impelling us to attend to these issues.

Chiron Conjunct, Parallel, Contraparallel, Occult Venus

Residual wounds, regrets, self-depreciation and negative feelings around being loved or not, being able to love or not, and around relationships and issues of companionship are brought to the surface. This will occur most often within our current relationships, encouraging us to attend to these issues in this area of our lives.

Chiron Conjunct, Parallel, Contraparallel, Occult Mars

Residual wounds, regrets, self-depreciation, and negative feelings around actions, decisions, and intentions we have had in the past and/or that we have failed to act upon surface during this transit. We are encouraged to see the reasons behind our past manifestations and to take appropriate action now. What stops us from activating our lives?

Chiron Conjunct, Parallel, Contraparallel, Occult Jupiter

Jupiter encourages us to see a bigger picture with respect to our wounds and issues, to see the hidden benefits, blessings, lessons, and gifts within those issues that we previously judged solely negatively. Jupiter coaxes us to return the childlike but wise view of the world being the best of all possible worlds with everything in its right place and serving a larger plan. This is a medium-strength healing transit.

Chiron Conjunct, Parallel, Contraparallel, Occult Saturn

Saturn, via the circumstances of our life, forces us to sit down and stay seated in some way until we begin to take stock, becoming serious and responsible about our journey of wounding and healing. This is a call to get serious and to face our inner nature. This is a major healing transit.

Chiron Conjunct, Parallel, Contraparallel, Occult Chiron

See "The Chiron Return" in chapter 5.

Chiron Conjunct, Parallel, Contraparallel, Occult Uranus

Residual wounds, regrets, self-depreciation, and negative feelings surface. Issues and areas include (1) our failure to expand our minds, (2) our network of friends and contacts, (3) our view of the world and our lives, (4) our inability to choose a direction in life and stick to it, and (5) past major changes in our lives that we judge primarily negatively. Chiron encourages us to see the perfection and plan in all these issues and to embrace the changes as a vehicle for our healing and evolution of consciousness.

Chiron Conjunct, Parallel, Contraparallel, Occult Neptune

Residual wounds, regrets, self-depreciation, and negative feelings surface. Issues and areas include our spiritual life or lack thereof, our sense of aloneness, and/or feeling abandoned by the universe/God, etcetera. We are encouraged to reach out to spirit, to reach inward to our spiritual heart and soul, and to see the divine in all things in our lives, past, present, and future.

Chiron Conjunct, Parallel, Contraparallel, Occult Pluto

Residual wounds, regrets, self-depreciation, and negative feelings surface. Issues and areas include losses, endings, major upheavals, major crises, major changes, and deaths we may have had in our lives, metaphoric and actual. We are encouraged to move beyond these illusions and see the new forms that these things now take in our lives. This transit is a call to emerge into a new cycle of our lives, activating our innate powers of transformation of consciousness.

Chiron Conjunct, Parallel, Contraparallel, Occult the MC
Residual wounds, regrets, self-depreciation, and negative feelings around career and public image issues arise during this transit. We are encouraged to link our life's path and purpose—our inner passion—with our chosen vocation. We are also encouraged to heal our wounds and issues around what others think of us, around being seen by others, and/or around being on show, so to speak.

Chiron Conjunct, Parallel, Contraparallel, Occult the IC
Residual wounds, regrets, self-depreciation, and negative feelings surface. Issues and areas include past wounds and issues of family—parents, grandparents, great grandparents, and other older relatives, in particular. We are encouraged to heal the past so that we can move forward into the future more freely and openly.

Chiron Conjunct, Parallel, Contraparallel, Occult the Ascendant
Residual wounds, regrets, self-depreciation, and negative feelings surface. Issues and areas include our self-image, our self-confidence, our self-appreciation, our view of ourselves, and the way others see us. We are encouraged to see and love ourselves just as we are, *masks and all,* for it all serves others and us in ways that we may not initially see.

Chiron Conjunct, Parallel, Contraparallel, Occult the Descendant
Residual wounds, regrets, self-depreciation, and negative feelings surface. Issues and areas include (1) our relationship with others, (2) our separation from others, (3) our seemingly scattered psyches, (4) our state of health (physical, emotional, mental, and/or spiritual), and/or (5) our deep wish and need for companionship. We are encouraged to attend to these issues in a healing way.

Opposition
In general, opposition transits shine a light on the natal planet they oppose, challenging and confronting us to achieve new consciousness around the issues of the natal planet. When Chiron is involved in opposition transits, the themes of healing and evolution of consciousness become part and parcel of the issues raised.

Chiron, as the transiting planet, brings up residual wounds, regrets, self-depreciation, and negative feelings around the issues of the transited natal planet. This is similar to a conjuncting transit, but is more challenging and confronting because it illuminates the flip sides of issues that we may be reluctant to see and acknowledge.

Chiron Opposition the North Node
See Chiron conjunct the South Node.

Chiron Opposition the South Node
See Chiron conjunct the North Node.

Chiron Opposition the Sun
Residual wounds, regrets, self-depreciation, and negative feelings surface. Issues and areas include failure to express ourselves, to honor our creativity, to exercise our willpower, and/or to allow ourselves to shine. These are illuminated and thrown back in our faces, challenging us to deal with them.

Chiron Opposition the Moon
Residual wounds, regrets, self-depreciation, and negative feelings around our lower-natured emotional reactions and protective devices surface. These are thrown back at us, challenging us to learn to love these aspects of ourselves for the service they have afforded us in keeping us safe until we are ready for greater truth.

Chiron Opposition Mercury
Residual wounds, regrets, self-depreciation, and negative feelings surface. Issues and areas include failure to express ourselves clearly, communication difficulties in general, difficulty in making friends, feeling unintelligent, and/or feeling out of touch. These are brought to the fore and thrown back at us, challenging us to attend to these feelings.

Chiron Opposition Venus
Residual wounds, regrets, self-depreciation, and negative feelings around perceived failure(s) in relationships, feeling not loved, feeling unable to love, and our emotional nature in general are thrown back in our faces. Chiron challenges us to attain a new consciousness concerning these issues and concerning our feelings around them.

Chiron Opposition Mars

Residual wounds, regrets, self-depreciation, and negative feelings surface. Issues include things we have done or not done in the past and around perceived failure(s) to take action, make an intention, and/or carry out a resolve. These are thrown back in our faces, challenging us to come to a new level of consciousness, ultimately seeing how inaction is a form of action, appropriate to certain circumstances and situations.

Chiron Opposition Jupiter

Residual wounds, regrets, self-depreciation, and negative feelings surface. Issues and areas include (1) perceived failure to acknowledge and listen to the wisdom of our Inner Child/ spiritual heart/soul, (2) our excessive negativity, (3) our excessive nature that swings from one extreme to another, and/or (4) our perceived failure(s) to attend to the details of things we turn our attention to. These are thrown back in our faces, challenging us to attend to these issues and our feelings about them.

Chiron Opposition Saturn

Residual wounds, regrets, self-depreciation, and negative feelings surface. Issues and areas include (1) feeling restricted, limited, repressed, and/or oppressed; (2) authority, discipline, seriousness, and/or responsibility in our lives; and/or (3) the issue of blame. These are thrown back in our faces, challenging us to take responsibility for our lives and to get serious about our journey of healing and evolution of consciousness.

Chiron Opposition Chiron

See "The Opposition" in chapter 5.

Chiron Opposition Uranus

Residual wounds, regrets, self-depreciation, and negative feelings surface. Issues and areas include (1) major changes in our lives, (2) our inability to set a direction and stick to it, (3) feeling unable to fit in with others or be a part of groups, and/or (4) feeling different from others. These are thrown back at us during this transit, challenging us to find new perspectives on these issues. We are challenged to see the hidden benefits, blessings, lessons, and gifts in these issues in terms of our potential healing and evolution of consciousness.

Chiron Opposition Neptune

Residual wounds, regrets, self-depreciation, and negative feelings surface. Issues and areas include (1) neglect of our spiritual life, (2) feelings of betrayal by the universe/God, (3) feeling abandoned by those who "should" have loved us more, (4) our own rejection of spiritual matters, and/or (5) our seemingly irrational and incommunicable feelings. These are thrown back in our faces, challenging us to see things differently and challenging us to acknowledge the presence of love, oneness, and spirit around us and within us.

Chiron Opposition Pluto

Residual wounds, regrets, self-depreciation, and negative feelings surface. Issues and areas include loss, endings, radical changes, major crises, major upheavals, and/or death in our lives. These are thrown back in our faces violently and forcefully. We are challenged to transcend our old perspectives and biases around these issues. We are challenged to see the new forms taken by those things in our lives that we felt we lost. Chiron challenges us to see the benefits, blessings, lessons, and gifts in crises and calamities. This is a major healing transit.

Chiron Opposition the MC

See Chiron conjunct the IC.

Chiron Opposition the IC

See Chiron conjunct the MC.

Chiron Opposition the Ascendant

See Chiron conjunct the Descendant.

Chiron Opposition the Descendant

See Chiron conjunct the Ascendant.

Square

In general, squaring transits bring to a head the issues of the transited planet. They do this by somehow stopping us in our tracks—by causing us to have to take stock, think deeply, and try to understand the nature of the issues at hand. In this way, square aspects and squaring transits are related to Saturn.

When Chiron is the transiting planet, the wounds and issues around the natal planet are triggered. They are brought to the fore, in some ways suspending the free flowing of the affairs of that planet until we sit down and reassess, take stock, and think deeply about the issues at hand.

Chiron Square the North Node

See also Chiron square the South Node.

Our life's path and purpose are seemingly thwarted and brought into question by residual wounds, regrets, self-depreciation, and negative feelings concerning our path and purpose.

Chiron Square the South Node

See also Chiron square the North Node.

The transiting square of Chiron to the South Node brings our past wounds and issues into view, encouraging us to take stock, reassess, and examine the ways in which these have thwarted our life's path and purpose.

Chiron Square the Sun

Our free expression, creativity, willpower, and ability to shine are seemingly thwarted or limited by the surfacing of woundedness around these Sun themes. We are encouraged to take stock of, reassess, and think deeply about, these wounds and issues.

Chiron Square the Moon

Chiron questions our lower-natured emotional reactions, patterns, and habits and their role in keeping us from healing and resolving our wounds and issues. We may find that our emotional reactions during this transit keep us from functioning normally in our lives, impelling us to question, take stock of, reassess, and examine our emotional life.

Chiron Square Mercury

Chiron questions the wounds and issues around (1) our mental life, (2) our ability to communicate with others, (3) feeling out of touch, and (4) our feelings of being unintelligent, encouraging us to delve into these issues. We may find ourselves seeking solitude and silence during this time.

Chiron Square Venus

Chiron brings our wounds and issues around relationships, being loved or not, being able to love or not, and our need for companionship into focus. This can take the form of impasses in dealings with others close to us. It can also indicate the surfacing of long-past issues—i.e., resentments, regrets, blame, hurt, and so forth—particularly in long-term relationships.

Chiron Square Mars

Chiron will tend to bring us to a halt in our lives. It will do this in order to impel us to delve into the reasons why we might thwart, sabotage, limit, interfere, and repress our life's activity, drive, momentum, intentions, and actions in general.

Chiron Square Jupiter

Chiron will bring to the fore wounds and issues around (1) our Inner Child, (2) our sense of injustice in the world, (3) our doubts about there being a larger plan, and/or (4) our failure to attend to the details of things to which we turn our attention. We may find that we lose a sense of meaning and joie de vivre during this time, inspiring us to search for meaning, a larger picture of life, and a broader perspective.

Chiron Square Saturn

Chiron will bring our wounds and issues around restrictions, limitations, repressions, oppressions, authority, responsibility, and discipline to the fore. This will put the brakes on our lives in some way, impelling us to take stock, reassess, and reexamine our lives—past, present, and future. It encourages us to ask the questions *Who am I? Where do I come from? Where am I going?* and *Why am I here?* It encourages us to see the ways in which Saturn's issues have served us, despite their frustrating nature and their sometimes-painful processes.

Chiron Square Chiron

The 1st Square
See "The 1st Square" in chapter 5.

The 2nd Square
See "The 2nd Square" in chapter 5.

Chiron Square Uranus

Chiron will tend to thwart higher understanding during this time, impelling us to search for deeper meaning and connections in our wounds and issues. It will encourage us to attend to our woundedness around (1) radical change in our lives, past and present, (2) being a part of society and community, (3) our place within groups, (4) feeling different from others, (5) fitting in or not fitting in, and/or (6) not feeling as though we can access a higher meaning in the seeming chaos of our lives.

Chiron Square Neptune

Chiron will tend to bring our woundedness to the surface. Issues and areas include (1) spirituality or lack thereof; (2) the nature and existence of love; (3) our misperceptions and illusions of our lives, inner and outer; (4) the fantasies and escapisms of our inner life; and/or (5) any feeling of betrayal or abandonment in our lives. It will tend to give us pause and a reason to ponder these important issues.

Chiron Square Pluto

Chiron will bring wounds and issues to the surface. Issues and areas include loss, endings, death, major crises, major upheavals, and radical change in our lives. This will tend to stop us in our tracks via some outer or inner circumstances. This, in turn, will tend to impel us to break through our judgments, blockages, and wounds around these issues. Chiron and Pluto will work together to birth a new level of consciousness—one that sees that new forms are birthed from what we initially perceived as loss, endings, death, major crises, major upheavals, and radical change.

Chiron Square the MC

See also Chiron square the IC. See also Chiron conjunct the Ascendant or the Descendant, accordingly, if in orb.

Chiron will bring up our wounds and issues around vocation and/or our public persona. It will tend to put the brakes on these areas of our lives. It will impel us to think more deeply about the things in our lives that have been holding us back from fully activating and expressing these areas.

Chiron Square the IC

See also Chiron square the MC. See also Chiron conjunct the Ascendant or the Descendant, accordingly, if in orb.

Chiron will tend to bring up issues to do with the past, family, parents, grandparents, and other older relatives. These things may slow us down during this transit, impelling us to delve into these wounds and issues more deeply than we might otherwise be inclined.

Chiron Square the Ascendant

See also Chiron square the Descendant. See also Chiron conjunct the MC or the IC, accordingly, if in orb.

Chiron will bring to the surface wounds and issues in the areas of self-image, sense of self, how we see ourselves, and/or how we think others see us. We may find ourselves asking who we really are as opposed to the masks/personas we tend to wear and project. We may experience shyness, reticence, fear of what others think of us, and/or low self-confidence during this transit. It may also bring up past and/or forgotten wounds around these same issues.

As a reaction to the preceding, this transit may cause us to feel it necessary to exaggerate our masks, personas, and/or public image in order to hide our wounds, issues, and even our true nature from others. In extreme cases, we may even begin to believe our own publicity, so to speak, in an unconscious effort to hide our wounds, issues, and even our true nature from *ourselves*.

If Chiron is in the lower hemisphere, internal issues will be emphasized. If Chiron is in the upper hemisphere, external issues will be emphasized.

Chiron Square the Descendant

See also Chiron square the Ascendant. See also Chiron conjunct the MC or the IC, accordingly, if in orb.

Chiron will bring to the fore our wounds and issues around (1) relating to others, (2) being in relationships, (3) being alone, and/or (4) health and disease (physical, emotional, mental, and/or spiritual). We will tend to be impelled to attend to these things during this transit.

If Chiron is in the lower hemisphere, internal issues will be emphasized. If Chiron is in the upper hemisphere, external issues will be emphasized.

Trine

In general, trining transits represent a time of increased opportunities, possibilities, meetings, connections, and affinities. Things will just seem to fall into place during this time in the areas indicated by the transiting and natal planets.

When Chiron is the transiting planet, it will bring about increased opportunities, possibilities, meetings, connections, and affinities in relation to the healing and evolution of consciousness of the issues pertaining to the natal planet. (This may still be uncomfortable.)

Chiron Trine the North Node

Chiron will inspire increased opportunities, possibilities, meetings, connections, and affinities in relation to our journey of healing and evolution of consciousness and in relation to our specific life's path and purpose.

Chiron Trine the South Node

Chiron will assist us in the healing and resolution of woundedness around the past, past lives, and/or our unfulfilled life's path and purpose. It will assist us by bringing increased opportunities, possibilities, meetings, connections, and affinities to illuminate past issues that may have become hidden or been forgotten.

Chiron Trine the Sun

Chiron presents us with increased opportunities, possibilities, meetings, connections, and affinities for the healing and resolution of wounds and issues around self-expression, creativity, willpower, and allowing (or not allowing) ourselves to shine.

Chiron Trine the Moon

Chiron illuminates our lower emotional nature—i.e., our lopsided perspectives, misperceptions, judgments, biases, illusions, and lies. It does this via increased opportunities, possibilities, meetings, connections, and affinities that bring our emotional patterns, habits, and reactions into view, giving us the opportunity to heal and resolve these issues.

Chiron Trine Mercury

Chiron assists us in the healing and resolution of our woundedness around communication, networking, thinking processes, and feeling unintelligent. It does so by offering us increased opportunities, possibilities, meetings, connections, and affinities for exchange, interaction, communication, and mental stimulation.

Chiron Trine Venus

Chiron offers us increased opportunities, possibilities, meetings, connections, and affinities for the healing and resolution of our wounds and issues around loving, being loved, relationship, companionship, aloneness, harmony, and/or peace.

Chiron Trine Mars

Chiron provides increased opportunities, possibilities, meetings, connections, and affinities for the healing and resolution of our woundedness around what we have done or not done in our lives, our past and present actions and reactions, and/or our past and present decisions and intentions.

Chiron Trine Jupiter

Chiron creates increased opportunities, possibilities, meetings, connections, and affinities for the healing and resolution of our woundedness around (1) childhood, (2) our Inner Child, (3) our feelings of meaninglessness, (4) our loss of faith in a divine plan, and/or (5) our lack of close attention to our life's meaning and purpose.

Chiron Trine Saturn

Chiron assists in offering increased opportunities, possibilities, meetings, connections, and affinities for the healing and resolution of our wounds and issues around "father" issues, authority, responsibility, repressions, limitations, restrictions, seriousness, and discipline.

Chiron Trine Chiron

The 1st Trine
See "The 1st Trine" in chapter 5.

The 2nd Trine
See "The 2nd Trine" in chapter 5.

Chiron Trine Uranus

Uranus brings about abrupt and increased opportunities, possibilities, meetings, connections, and affinities for the healing and resolution of our specific woundedness, as indicated by natal Chiron. It inspires us to delve deeper into the higher meanings behind those things in our lives that we have been judging primarily negatively and have been blaming for our life's predicaments. It inspires us to see a larger plan behind the seeming chaos of our lives. This is a major healing transit.

Chiron Trine Neptune

Chiron awakens increased opportunities, possibilities, meetings, connections, and affinities for the healing and resolution of our woundedness around (1) our spirituality, (2) loss or absence of faith in divinity, (3) the seeming absence of love in our lives, and/or (4) our emotional nature that longs for a return to oneness and love. It inspires us to pursue spiritual matters, higher understanding, and/or solace for the spiritual heart and soul.

Chiron Trine Pluto

Chiron creates increased opportunities, possibilities, meetings, connections, and affinities for the healing and resolution of our woundedness around radical change, loss, endings, and death in our lives. It inspires a deep and intense search for higher meaning and understanding around these issues. Ultimately, it seeks to show us how and where births and new forms arose from the perceived losses, deaths, endings, major crises, major upheavals, and radical changes in our lives.

Chiron Trine the MC

Chiron creates increased opportunities, possibilities, meetings, connections, and affinities for the healing and resolution of woundedness around our vocation and around our public persona. It inspires us to make connections between our specific life's path and purpose and our career/vocation. It encourages us to see the ways in which our specific woundedness in these areas has served us on our healing journey.

Chiron Trine the IC

Chiron opens up increased opportunities, possibilities, meetings, connections, and affinities for the healing and resolution of woundedness around the past, past lives, genetic history, family, parents, grandparents, and other older relatives. It inspires us to delve into this past, make peace with our relatives, and heal past issues. It encourages us to identify issues that have been holding us back from pursuing our life's path and purpose—in particular, ones related to vocation and to our public persona.

Chiron Trine the Ascendant

Chiron brings increased opportunities, possibilities, meetings, connections, and affinities for the healing and resolution of our woundedness around self-image, sense of self, the way we see ourselves, and how we think others see us. It inspires a new appreciation for who we are, as we are, beyond the illusions of our masks and beyond illusions about ourselves.

Chiron Trine the Descendant

Chiron opens up increased opportunities, possibilities, meetings, connections, and affinities for the healing and resolution of our woundedness around (1) relating to others, (2) relationships in general, (3) our feeling of aloneness, and/or (4) the issues of health and disease. It inspires us to make peace with others, resolve our differences, make new contacts and connections, and attend to our general health (physical, mental, emotional, and/or spiritual).

Sextile

In general, sextiling transits open up possibilities in our lives, like windows of opportunity. Whether we take these opportunities is up to us. Otherwise, sextiling transits are mostly benign. For this reason, they can come and go with or without our noticing them.

When Chiron is the transiting planet, it will open up possible avenues of healing and evolution of consciousness for the affairs pertaining to the natal planet being transited.

Chiron Sextile Chiron

The 1st Sextile

See "The 1st Sextile" in chapter 5.

The 2nd Sextile

See "The 2nd Sextile" in chapter 5.

Quincunx

In general, quincunxing transits tend to impel us to raise our consciousness of the affairs of the natal planet to new levels. They impel us to leave behind our old ways of seeing things, much in the same way as an opposition transit. However, quincunxing transits are not so challenging and confronting, although they tend to be nagging, irritating, frustrating, unsettling, and insistent. In this way, the quincunxing transit, particularly when made by

Chiron or the outer planets, is akin to a kind of miniature Pluto transit. It also has an affinity with the zodiac sign of Virgo.

When Chiron makes a quincunxing transit to a natal planet, it impels us in the aforementioned way to raise our consciousness to new levels around the wounds and issues pertaining to the affairs of the natal planet (taking into account the planet's own sign, house, and aspects).

Chiron Quincunx Chiron
The 1st Quincunx
See "The 1st Quincunx" in chapter 5.

The 2nd Quincunx
See "The 2nd Quincunx" in chapter 5.

Transits to Chiron

When Chiron is the planet transited, the transiting planet (depending on, and according to, its essential energy and the sign and house of its transit) aids the healing and evolution of consciousness of our specific wounds and issues (as indicated by natal Chiron and its aspecting companions, and played out through their respective signs and houses).

North Node
North Node Conjunction, Parallel, Contraparallel, or Occult Chiron
This is a call from our destiny to attend to our wounds and issues, so that we might more faithfully honor our life's path/purpose/calling/destiny.

North Node Opposition Chiron
See South Node conjunct Chiron.

North Node Square Chiron
See also South Node square Chiron.

Our specific wounds and issues, as indicated by natal Chiron, are brought into question. We are encouraged by the North Node (and the South Node) to examine the ways in which these wounds and issues have thwarted the discovery and fulfillment of our life's path/purpose/calling/destiny.

North Node Trine Chiron

The North Node will bring increased opportunities, possibilities, meetings, connections, and affinities for the healing and resolution of our specific wounds and issues, as indicated by natal Chiron. It will help us heal and resolve those particular wounds and issues that have been holding us back in our life's path/purpose/calling/destiny.

South Node

South Node Conjunction, Parallel, Contraparallel, or Occult Chiron

The past comes back to haunt us, triggering our wounds and issues, as indicated by natal Chiron, impelling us to finally heal and resolve them.

South Node Opposition Chiron

See North Node conjunct Chiron.

South Node Square Chiron

See also North Node square Chiron.

Old wounds and issues are brought into focus. We are encouraged to take stock, reassess, and examine the ways in which our specific woundedness, as indicated by natal Chiron, has thwarted our life's path/purpose/calling/destiny.

South Node Trine Chiron

The South Node awakens old wounds and issues around the past, past lives, and/or our possibly unfulfilled life's path/purpose/calling/destiny, bringing increased opportunities, possibilities, meetings, connections, and affinities for their healing and resolution.

Sun

Note: Sun transits are short-term, lasting only a few days at the most.

Sun Conjunction, Parallel, Contraparallel, or Occult Chiron

The Sun activates and illuminates our wounds and issues, encouraging us to express them and attend to them.

Sun Opposition Chiron

The Sun illuminates and activates our wounds and issues, as indicated by natal Chiron, challenging us to see, acknowledge, express, and attend to them.

Sun Square Chiron

The Sun encourages us to express our wounds and issues, as indicated by natal Chiron. However, our ego, self-will, and pride may get in the way, causing us to question these aspects of ourselves and their role in keeping our wounds and issues unhealed and unresolved.

Sun Trine Chiron

The Sun helps us express, heal, and resolve our wounds and issues by bringing increased opportunities, possibilities, meetings, connections, and affinities to illuminate our darknesses. By darknesses, we mean our repressions, wounds, blockages, judgments, biases, blame, and so forth. The Sun inspires us to exercise our will and self-determination toward the goal of healing and evolution of consciousness.

Moon

Note: Moon transits are very short, lasting only hours at the most.

Moon Conjunction, Parallel, Contraparallel, or Occult Chiron

This transit indicates transient (monthly) lower-natured expression and exacerbation of our inner wounds and issues. Brought to conscious light, we are encouraged to attend to these wounds and issues.

Moon Opposition Chiron

Our wounds and issues are brought to the fore through our lower-natured emotional reactions, protective patterns, habits, and impulses. Illuminated in this way, we are challenged to attend to these wounds and issues.

Moon Square Chiron

The Moon will trigger our wounds and issues, as indicated by natal Chiron. It will stop us for a short time from functioning normally, encouraging us to introspect, question, take stock, reassess, and examine our emotional life.

Moon Trine Chiron

The Moon, in this short transit, awakens our wounds and issues, as indicated by natal Chiron. It does this via increased opportunities, possibilities, meetings, connections, and affinities that illuminate these wounds and issues through the vehicle of our lower (Moon) nature.

Mercury

Mercury Conjunction, Parallel, Contraparallel, or Occult Chiron

This is a time of greater potential to be able to express, communicate, and mentally understand our wounds and issues, as indicated by natal Chiron.

Mercury Opposition Chiron

Mercury challenges us to gain a greater understanding of our woundedness, as indicated by natal Chiron. It challenges us to make connections between the seemingly confusing aspects of these wounds and issues and to communicate our understandings to others around us.

Mercury Square Chiron

Mercury will tend to hijack our mental processes, causing us to think more deeply about our wounds and issues, as indicated by natal Chiron. We may seem preoccupied during this time, seeking solitude and silence.

Mercury Trine Chiron

Mercury gives us increased opportunities, possibilities, meetings, connections, and affinities for the healing and resolution of our wounds and issues, as indicated by natal Chiron, creating an enhanced environment for exchange, interaction, communication, and mental stimuli.

Venus

Venus Conjunction, Parallel, Contraparallel, or Occult Chiron

Venus encourages us to express our feelings arising from our wounds and issues, to share them with others in close personal relationship, and to trust the resultant healing process. We may meet someone special during this transit.

Venus Opposition Chiron

Venus challenges us to love our wounds and issues. It challenges us to love those around us—past and present—who have had anything to do with those wounds and issues. It challenges us to see ourselves in the mirror of relationship, warts and all. Someone may come into our lives during this time and challenge our wounds and issues.

Venus Square Chiron

Venus, through relationship, will tend to trigger our woundedness, as indicated by natal Chiron. This will force us to pause for a moment. It will force us to take stock, reassess, and examine the role of woundedness in our relationships. It will cause us to question our ability or inability to give and receive love.

Venus Trine Chiron

Venus gives us increased opportunities, possibilities, meetings, connections, and affinities for the healing and resolution of our specific wounds and issues, as indicated by natal Chiron. It shows us how to love ourselves a little more and how to accept the love of others, most often through the vehicle of relationship.

Mars

Mars Conjunction, Parallel, Contraparallel, or Occult Chiron

This transit is a call to action with respect to our journey of wounding and healing.

Mars Opposition Chiron

Mars calls us to action in the tasks of healing and evolution of consciousness, bringing up the most acute aspects of our wounds and issues, challenging us to make a decision to deal with them.

Mars Square Chiron

Mars calls us to action by triggering our wounds and issues, as indicated by natal Chiron. We may find ourselves getting angry with others (and ourselves) for apparently thwarting our attempts to get on with our lives, to get certain things done, and to make certain decisions. We will be impelled to understand the ways in which our wounds and issues hold us back and why they do so.

Mars Trine Chiron

Mars opens up increased opportunities, possibilities, meetings, connections, and affinities for the healing and resolution of our specific woundedness, as indicated by natal Chiron. It inspires us to make resolutions and to take action toward our journey of healing and evolution of consciousness.

Jupiter

Jupiter Conjunction, Parallel, Contraparallel, or Occult Chiron

Jupiter encourages us to see a bigger picture with respect to our wounds and issues, to see the hidden benefits, blessings, lessons, and gifts within those issues that we previously judged solely negatively. Jupiter coaxes us to return a childlike but wise view of the world—a view that considers this world the best of all possible worlds, with everything in its right place and serving a larger plan. This is a medium-strength healing transit.

Jupiter Opposition Chiron

Jupiter challenges us to see a bigger picture with respect to our wounds and issues. It challenges us to see a larger plan, to see the inherent "rightness" of all that befalls us, and to see the service that even our woundedness affords us and others on the journey of healing. Jupiter says that, despite our judgments of the past, all's right with the world and there is a guiding hand at work.

Jupiter Square Chiron

Jupiter will inspire us during this time to seek a broader perspective—to recognize that there is larger plan behind our wounds and issues, as indicated by natal Chiron. It will seek to expand our consciousness—to awaken us to the guiding hand in our lives and to the "rightness" of all that transpires in our lives. We may not be able to concentrate on the details of these things during this time, as Jupiter seeks to help us see the whole picture at a glance.

Jupiter Trine Chiron

Jupiter creates increased opportunities, possibilities, meetings, connections, and affinities for the healing and resolution of our specific woundedness, as indicated by natal Chiron. It draws our attention to a larger picture of our lives. It seeks to reveal the meaning and purpose behind those things in which we previously saw no meaning and purpose. It seeks to awaken the knowing and wisdom of the Inner Child that knows that all's right with the world.

Saturn

Saturn Conjunction, Parallel, Contraparallel, or Occult Chiron

Saturn, via the circumstances of our life, forces us to sit down and stay seated in some way until we begin to take stock, becoming serious and responsible about our journey of wounding and healing. This is a call to get serious and to face our inner nature. This is a major healing transit.

Saturn Opposition Chiron

Saturn challenges us to get serious about, disciplined toward, and responsible for, our wounds and issues by throwing these back in our faces, forcing us to sit down and take stock. This is a major healing transit.

Saturn Square Chiron

Saturn impels us, during this transit, to (1) take stock, (2) accept responsibility, (3) cease blaming, and (4) start attending to and working seriously with our wounds and issues, as indicated by natal Chiron. It will tend to create events and circumstances that will impel us to do these things. This represents a time to think, reflect, ponder, plan, and make resolutions. This is a relatively major transit.

Saturn Trine Chiron

Saturn brings about increased opportunities, possibilities, meetings, connections, and affinities for the healing and resolution of our specific woundedness, as indicated by natal Chiron. It does so by inspiring seriousness and a sense of responsibility toward our journey of healing and evolution of consciousness.

Chiron

Chiron Conjunction, Parallel, Contraparallel, or Occult Chiron

See "The Chiron Return" in chapter 5.

Chiron Opposition Chiron

See "The Opposition" in chapter 5.

Chiron Square Chiron

The 1st Square
See "The 1st Square" in chapter 5.

The 2nd Square
See "The 2nd Square" in chapter 5.

Chiron Trine Chiron

The 1st Trine
See "The 1st Trine" in chapter 5.

The 2nd Trine
See "The 2nd Trine" in chapter 5.

Chiron Sextile Chiron

The 1st Sextile
See "The 1st Sextile" in chapter 5.

The 2nd Sextile
See "The 2nd Sextile" in chapter 5.

Chiron Quincunx Chiron

The 1st Quincunx
See "The 1st Quincunx" in chapter 5.

The 2nd Quincunx
See "The 2nd Quincunx" in chapter 5.

Uranus

Uranus Conjunction, Parallel, Contraparallel, or Occult Chiron

Uranus shines a light upon our woundedness, as indicated by natal Chiron, encouraging us to attend to what we see. It encourages us to bring our consciousness regarding our wounds and issues into a higher state, seeing the perfection and plan behind it all. This is a major healing transit.

Uranus Opposition Chiron

Uranus shines a challenging light upon our wounds and issues, as indicated by natal Chiron. It impels us to attend to these things, encouraging us to see them in a different light, from different angles, and from a more inclusive vantage point. This is a major healing transit.

Uranus Square Chiron

Uranus impels us to seek a higher consciousness around our specific wounds and issues, as indicated by natal Chiron. It will tend to create unexpected blockages, restrictions, limitations, and closed doors in an effort to get us to introspect. It will encourage us to see larger connections, to see the flip sides of things, and to see the overall plan behind these things. This offers us a way of moving beyond the apparent blockages of this square. This is a relatively major transit.

Uranus Trine Chiron

Uranus brings about abrupt and increased opportunities, possibilities, meetings, connections, and affinities for the healing and resolution of our specific woundedness, as indicated by natal Chiron. It inspires us to delve more deeply into the higher meanings behind those things in our lives that we have been judging primarily negatively and that we have been blaming for our life's predicaments. It inspires us to see a larger plan behind the seeming chaos of our lives. This is a major healing transit.

Neptune

Neptune Conjunction, Parallel, Contraparallel, or Occult Chiron

This transit represents a time when Neptune encourages us to love ourselves just as we are—to love those parts of us that have been wounded, fragmented, separated, judged negatively, and/or condemned. Neptune also encourages us to love our woundedness as well as the people involved in our woundedness for the service they have afforded us and others in the larger loving plan of life. This is a major healing transit.

Neptune Opposition Chiron

Neptune challenges us to love ourselves unconditionally—all of ourselves, including the light and the dark, the "good" and the "bad," and the hidden and the visible. It challenges us to see the divine plan that lies behind those things that we have been judging primarily negatively in our lives, past and present. It challenges us to open our spiritual eyes and hearts and allow ourselves to be healed by the love that is always around us. This is a major healing transit.

Neptune Square Chiron

Neptune will act in a mysterious and unpredictable way upon our wounds and issues, as indicated by natal Chiron. We are being called to stop and go within, to hear the small voice within our spiritual hearts, to hear our soul/spirit, and to acknowledge the guiding hand of love in our lives. We are being impelled to see the love that lies hidden within our wounds and issues. This love drives us constantly toward our ultimate healing and evolution of consciousness and toward a return to oneness and love. Ultimately, the wound is a gift of love. This is a relatively major transit.

Neptune Trine Chiron

Neptune opens increased opportunities, possibilities, meetings, connections, and affinities for the healing and resolution of our specific woundedness, as indicated by natal Chiron. It inspires deep thought, pondering, meditation, a quest for spiritual and/or psychological advice, and, ultimately, the wish to love the whole of ourselves as we are. This is a major healing transit.

Pluto

Pluto Conjunction, Parallel, Contraparallel, or Occult Chiron

Pluto most violently and forcefully shakes our wounds and issues, bringing them to the surface in ways we cannot ignore, impelling us to attend to these things immediately or suffer major upheavals in our lives, internally or externally. Pluto encourages us to alter our preconceptions, illusions, misperceptions, biases, and lopsided attitudes toward those things that we feel created our wounds and issues. It encourages us to see the other side of the picture and to acknowledge the loving service behind all things, people, events, and places. This is a major healing transit.

Pluto Opposition Chiron

Pluto violently and forcefully shakes up our wounds and issues, challenging us to attend to them immediately or suffer further feelings of loss, endings, crises, death, and change. In opposition, Pluto shines a light on the flip sides of our wounds and issues in an effort to wipe away our lopsided illusions, misperceptions, and lies that merely perpetuate our woundedness. Pluto seeks to evolve our consciousness in dramatic ways. This is a major healing transit.

Pluto Square Chiron

Pluto will forcefully bring our wounds and issues, as indicated by natal Chiron, to our immediate attention. This will tend to stop us in our tracks by sometimes-radical external circumstances. This, in turn, will tend to force us to delve into our woundedness and find new ways of breaking though old impasses of consciousness. This is a major transit.

Pluto Trine Chiron

Pluto brings swift and sometimes drastic occasions of increased opportunities, possibilities, meetings, connections, and affinities for the healing and resolution of our specific woundedness, as indicated by natal Chiron. It inspires us to shift our consciousness concerning these issues. It inspires us to leave behind old illusions, to allow judgmental attitudes to die, to see the flip sides of these issues, and to end old cycles in our lives. In this way, we are making room for the birth of higher consciousness. This is a major healing transit.

Chiron Transits of Houses

In general, Chiron transiting a house will tend to bring up our wounds and issues around the affairs of that house. During the transit, we are encouraged to attend to these wounds and issues—to expand our consciousness concerning the affairs of the given house.

Chiron Transiting the 1st House

See also Chiron in transit to the Ascendant, particularly conjuncting the Ascendant.

Chiron transiting the 1st house will tend to bring to the surface our woundedness around (1) our self-image, our sense of self, how we see ourselves, and how we feel others see us; (2) issues of physical health and disease; and/or (3) issues of past and/or present physical abuse.

The healing path consists of seeing, acknowledging, embracing, and finally loving ourselves just as we are.

Chiron Transiting the 2nd House

Chiron transiting the 2nd house will tend to bring to the surface our woundedness around (1) our material affairs (and our psychological transference and projection of material affairs to our emotional life); (2) material and/or emotional security, safety, comfort, and values; and/or (3) being loved, cared for, and looked after.

The healing path consists of seeing, acknowledging, embracing, and finally loving the ways in which we are being looked after by the universe. It also consists of discovering that the ultimate place of security, safety, trust, and abundance is within us—in our hearts.

Chiron Transiting the 3rd House

Chiron transiting the 3rd house will tend to bring to the surface our woundedness around (1) issues around our mental affairs, (2) our ability to communicate, network, and interact with others, (3) feeling smart or stupid, and/or (4) our capacity or inability to remain focused on one thing at a time. It can also bring up issues around siblings, early learning, gossip, and publicity.

The healing path consists of discovering where the special form of our intelligence lies. In addition, it consists of seeing, acknowledging, embracing, and finally loving the unique way(s) in which we communicate and share ourselves and our inner wisdom with others. Lastly, it consists of seeing where we *do* have superior focus, attention, and intention.

Chiron Transiting the 4th House

See also Chiron in transit to the IC, particularly conjuncting the IC.

Chiron transiting the 4th house will tend to bring to the surface our woundedness around our family life. This can mean woundedness around immediate family, extended family, community, humanity, Earth (Gaia), nature, heritage, roots, our children, our parents, and/or our spouse.

The healing path consists of (1) learning how to care for and nurture ourselves, (2) seeing how we are cared for and nurtured by others but in ways we might not be seeing or acknowledging, and/or (3) discovering the form of our "family" beyond the usual definitions.

Chiron Transiting the 5th House

Chiron transiting the 5th house will tend to bring to the surface our woundedness around our expression of self. Issues and areas include self-expression, ego, child within, love, romance, sexuality, creativity (including children as the product of our creation), willpower, and self-determination, and/or allowing or not allowing ourselves to shine.

The healing path consists of acknowledging where we *do* shine, particularly in the eyes of others. Furthermore, it consists of allowing ourselves to be who we are, without fear or guilt—to celebrate our creation and our lives through our own creations, whatever form they may take.

Chiron Transiting the 6th House

Chiron transiting the 6th house will tend to bring to the surface our woundedness around work, service to others, methods of doing things, ingrained habits, and/or health and disease (physical, mental, emotional, and/or spiritual).

The healing path consists of seeing and acknowledging how our specific ways of approaching and doing things are serving a larger plan—a plan that serves both our lives personally as well as the world at large. In short, there are no right and wrong ways of approaching and doing things, only ways, each of which is perfect in its own context.

We tend to think there is something wrong with us, with others, and/or with the world. The healing question is, what are the benefits, blessings, lessons, and gifts of these supposedly "wrong" things?

Ultimately, we seek perfection in the world around us and in ourselves, because this is the secret of creation—i.e., attending to ever finer detail—and it is our destiny to become co-creators of the world.

Chiron Transiting the 7th House

See also Chiron transiting the Descendant, particularly conjuncting the Descendant.

Chiron transiting the 7th house will tend to bring to the surface our woundedness around relationship—aloneness, companionship, marriage, social life, social justice, our place in society, and/or our psychology in general.

The healing path consists of realizing that we already have everything we wish for in another; this is why we seek a partner with certain attributes—so we can see ourselves in the mirror of relationship. This does not mean that relationship then becomes redundant; on the contrary, it allows us to celebrate the sacredness of relationship even more.

Chiron Transiting the 8th House

Chiron transiting the 8th house will tend to bring to the surface our woundedness around loss, death, endings, major crises, major upheavals, major changes in our lives, joint finances, sexuality, taxation, and/or some spiritual matters (metaphysics, life after death, esotericism, and the occult).

The healing path consists of realizing where deaths have brought births, where losses have brought gains, and where major calamities have been new beginnings. Moreover, it consists of recognizing that behind the veil of material forms lies eternal and incorruptible spirit, and it is ultimately going to be our task to give spirit its forms.

Chiron Transiting the 9th House

Chiron transiting the 9th house will tend to bring to the surface our woundedness around education, philosophy, religion, spirituality in general, morals, ethics, racism, travel, adventure, and sources of wisdom in general.

The healing path consists of gradually seeing, acknowledging, embracing, and finally loving our own inner wisdom. Initially, we seek this wisdom outside us—through teachers, education, travel, religions, and so forth; we are looking for the big picture. However, all this is but a reflection of the inner wisdom we are learning to trust. The universe is within us.

Chiron Transiting the 10th House

See also Chiron transiting the MC, particularly conjuncting the MC.

Chiron transiting the 10th house will tend to bring to the surface our wounds and issues around vocation, career, work, status, station, being seen in public, public persona, and public image, and/or around being recognized, appreciated, respected, and/or acknowledged for our achievements.

The healing path consists of seeing, acknowledging, embracing, and finally loving all the things within us that drive us to seek these things. All things serve our evolution of consciousness and, ultimately, are leading us inexorably toward our divine design.

Chiron Transiting the 11th House

Chiron transiting the 11th house will tend to bring to the surface our woundedness around fitting into society or not, collective expression, humanitarian ideals, networking, extended family, hopes and dreams, technology and progress, feeling different from others, feeling like a stranger or an alien, and/or feeling lost in the crowd.

The healing path consists of seeing, discovering, embracing, and finally loving where we fit into the puzzle of life—our personal place, our family place, our community place, and our place in the larger picture of humanity. Our individual gifts and talents have a place—a context—in which they are designed to shine the brightest.

Chiron Transiting the 12th House

Chiron transiting the 12th house will tend to bring to the surface our wounds and issues around (1) feeling abandoned and/or betrayed by the universe/God; (2) feeling victimized and/or covertly manipulated (by secret enemies); (3) our inner life, dreams, fantasies, and dark secrets; (4) past lives and subconscious impulses (karma); and/or (5) our feelings of being exiled, separate, closed-in, locked-up, and/or incarcerated.

The healing path consists of delving into the recesses of our psyche—of walking into our own darkness without flinching—and learning to love what we find there. It consists of bringing all our disowned, lost, denied, condemned, and negatively judged parts back into the fold. Chiron says that no part of us is unlovable or unloved—the dark, the light, the good, the bad, the beautiful, and the ugly . . . all parts are embraced by the universe's love.

CHAPTER TWELVE

Chiron & Past Lives

Chiron and Past-Life Symbolism

How do we determine if Chiron in the natal chart indicates past-life wounds and issues? The answer, when considered from a certain perspective, is simple: *it always does.* In order to understand why this is so, we need to understand what wounds are, even beyond what we have already asserted. From Chiron's perspective, *wounds mirror areas of our life that we have not yet learned to love unconditionally.*

According to the Chiron Paradigm, the only things we take from lifetime to lifetime are those things we have learned to love unconditionally. The rest represents a kind of un-awakened void—our wounds in an unconscious, embryonic state.

Having said this, though, if we have not worked through a particular issue in a given lifetime, learning how to love it unconditionally, *it is bound to show up in our future lifetimes as a wound until we learn to love it.* However, unlike the things we *have* learned to love un-conditionally, it will not necessarily show up in subsequent lifetimes in the same *form* as in previous lives—and certainly not in the same circumstances.

The areas of our life that we have not yet learned to love will show up in the planetary patterns of our natal horoscope until we have transcended them. The *essence* of our wounds and issues shows up in our Chiron *aspects*; however, the *house* and *sign* determine the exact *forms* in which our wounds and issues will manifest, *which may not be the same from lifetime to lifetime.*

The reasons for this are energetic and metaphysical. Without getting too technical, the planetary energies themselves (particularly of the outer planets) and their angular aspects relate more to our higher nature—the more permanent part of us that incarnates from lifetime to lifetime. Conversely, the signs and houses (combined with the Moon, the inner planets, the Ascendant, and the MC) relate more to our lower nature—the garb of personality that we don afresh each time we incarnate—*which dies at the death of the body, after each incarnation.*

Nothing of the *personality* remains after physical death. It breaks down and disperses in the same way as the physical body. What remains is our *essence,* enlightened to a greater or lesser degree by the things we have learned to love.

This is why we do not remember our past lives. What we *can* remember, as we become more evolved, is memories of what we have learned to love unconditionally. *We do not remember traumas, crises, calamities, pain, suffering, abuse, and so on, because these things are judgments made by our lower nature—our personalities—that do not survive from lifetime to lifetime.* If we *do* remember these things, it is only because we have loved them and no longer see them as negatives, but as loving aspects of a larger plan of perfection. (No hate mail, please!)

So, what about past-life regression? Doesn't this prove that we remember past lives? Yes and no, I say. In my studies of Chiron, I have researched, conducted, and personally experienced past-life regression therapy. Again, I say that the only things we take from lifetime to lifetime—*the only things we remember from lifetime to lifetime*—are the things that we have learned to love unconditionally.

Memories of past lives that come up in a past-life regression therapy session that invoke the deep and uncommon experience of unconditional love are likely to be *real* past-life memories. Such real memories may be our own memories *or they can be others' memories that we are tuning in to, because we are resonating at a similar frequency.* All other so-called past-life memories that engender any other emotions aside from unconditional love are not real past-life memories. If this is so, then what are they? There are several possibilities.

Past-life memories (that are not memories of moments of unconditional love) can be symbolisms of our minds, giving form to our wounds and issues in ways we can more easily relate to. In this way, past-life regression therapy—let's now simply call it *regression therapy*—represents a perfect Chiron-based therapy.

The other possibility is that we are connecting, psychically, to the wounds and issues of other people (past or present) resonating at a similar frequency to us—we are connecting to the collective consciousness.

The "memories" that arise from regression therapy are mostly *symbols* of our wounds and issues—mirroring the things we have not yet learned to love unconditionally. In exactly the same way, *our real-life events and circumstances are also the symbols of what we have not yet learned to love unconditionally.* From this perspective, symbolic memories arising from regression therapy and the real circumstances of our present lifetimes *are mirroring the same wounds and issues.*

If the preceding is true, then why would we need regression therapy? There can be several answers to this. First, regression therapy gives us a *different perspective* on wounds and issues upon which we may have become stuck. Second, regression therapy puts *distance* between us and our wounds and issues, allowing, perhaps, an easier approach in order to begin the healing process. Last, in cases where we are in extreme denial about our responsibility and participation in our own woundedness—i.e., we are in blame and judgment—*regression therapy gives us the chance to place blame outside our present lives,* again giving us a chance to begin the healing process where it was previously blocked. Although placing blame outside us may seem like a negative step, sometimes we need to take a step back in order to find a new way forward.

It is important to note the similarity between so-called past-life memories and dreams. Like regression therapy, dreams also offer us a symbolic window into the depths of our psyche. Dream images/symbols and regression images/symbols are often very similar; moreover, each can be used as tools in the healing process. In both cases, the barrier of the critical mind is temporarily removed.

How to Work with Past-Life and Dream Symbols/Images

One way to work with past-life and dream symbols/images is to identify which one (or more) touches us emotionally the deepest. Then, we can "sit" with the symbol/image(s), allowing whatever comes up in us to bubble to the surface. We are advised to resist judging what comes up at this time or trying to figure out the whys and wherefores of it all, but simply to watch, listen, and feel. Then, we can begin looking for the balancing flip sides of the scenario and of the emotions the scenario may bring up. In short, we can ask ourselves the following questions:

1. What are/were the blessings, benefits, lessons, and gifts of the scenario and of the emotions it initially engendered/engenders?

2. What are the alternate (positive) ways of seeing the scenario?

3. What aspects of the scenario might we be missing, misperceiving, judging one-sidedly, ignoring, and/or failing to acknowledge?

4. In what ways might the scenario (and its reflection in the real events and circumstances of our lives) have contributed in positive ways to who we are today—to the manifestation of our divine design (as best we understand it at the moment)?

Always remember Chiron's perspective: There is a gift in every wound.

Past-Life and Dream Symbol/Image Examples

Although further discussions of regression therapy and dreams per se go beyond the scope of this book, in this chapter I offer some symbolic past-life/dream scenarios that are designed to bypass the critical mind and touch our wounds and issues directly. These scenarios may trigger new perspectives and thus allow the healing process to proceed. They are a compilation of the many symbols, dreams, and past-life memories of those with whom I have worked over the years, including my own.

Note that some of the symbols appear in more than one sign or house, as the symbolisms are often complex and cross the boundaries of established definitions. In addition, do not feel limited to reading just your own Chiron sign. From the holographic perspective, each one of us has within us the seed of every aspect of every planet, every sign, and every house in every possible pattern. In this way, we each have all possible wounds and are connected to all possible past lives—our own and others'.

Although Chiron in each person's chart mirrors their individual wounds and issues, Chiron's essence is more universal, encompassing all wounds and issues that keep us confined to the inner planets, as well as all healing and evolution of consciousness that will take us to the outer planets and beyond. In the same way that our individual wounds and issues represent universal Chiron seen through the prism of the zodiac signs and houses, the following dream/past-life scenarios represent our universal spirit/soul seen through the prism of the dream and past-life symbols and images of the psyche. Each offer unparalleled insight into the deepest recesses of our being.

Lastly, note that although the following symbols/images are each gender-specific, they can apply to any of us, male or female; after all, we may have been the opposite sex in a previous life.

Chiron in Aries or in the 1st House

- A person is beaten, robbed, raped, and/or left for dead.
- A person is kidnapped, sold as a slave, and worked to the point of death.
- A child is constantly told that he is useless, worthless, and no good.
- A person is sacrificed by the tribe, for the tribe, to appease the gods.
- A person, having committed a "crime," lives her life trying to make up for it.
- A person is unintentionally responsible for another's death and/or loss.
- A child is abandoned by his parents and lives in the streets.
- A person is born into the lowest untouchable caste of society.
- A person is exiled and left for dead, due to leprosy or the plague.

Chiron in Taurus or in the 2nd House

- A natural disaster destroys a person's home, village, city, or nation.
- A family cannot afford their child and adopts her out.
- A person loses everything he owns through litigation.
- A child feels like a burden to her struggling parents and family.
- A person's closest love is killed. Or a person loses her parents.
- A person experiences a revolution where all previously accepted values are wiped away.
- Famine creates starvation in a person's village.
- An aristocrat loses everything in a revolution.

- A rich person dies rich but unhappy and unloved.
- A person is left out of an inheritance.

Chiron in Gemini or in the 3rd House

- A person with a speech impediment is deemed a moron by society.
- A person is wrongly accused in a foreign country and cannot explain his innocence due to a language barrier.
- A person's public statement is misinterpreted and she becomes a laughingstock.
- A breakdown in communications leads to loss of lives.
- A war refugee loses touch with his friends and family.
- A gossip's machinations backfire, causing disgrace and dishonor.
- A war captain, under sudden attack, cannot think fast enough to save his men.
- A person, misunderstood and different from others, is deemed by the local people to be the village idiot.
- Twins or siblings are separated at birth or in early childhood.
- A politician is destroyed by a slanderous media campaign.

Chiron in Cancer or in the 4th House

- A person's parent's die and she is raised under duress by close relatives.
- A shy person keeps to himself, feeling as though love will never come.
- A person's children are slaughtered in full view.
- A person's mother emotionally tortures him throughout childhood.
- A native witnesses the felling and burning of her forest homeland.
- A conservationist, trying to save a species, is defeated by poachers.
- A person's baby dies in her arms of an unknown disease.
- A child wishing for love is raised in a cold, disciplinary, and cruel environment.
- A person is forcibly exiled from his homeland.
- A person's spouse dies. He remarries and his second spouse dies, too.
- A person falls in love with another who is unattainable by marriage, station, class, age, race, and/or distance.

Chiron in Leo or in the 5th House

- Draconian parents prevent a child from pursuing her creativity through art and/or music.

- An orphaned child loses his sense of individuality in an orphanage.

- Heavy expectations from parents and teachers cause a person's breakdown and/or abandonment of her creative expression.

- A person is required to subjugate himself to the needs of family and/or community in times of hardship, sickness, and/or crisis.

- A person is passed over in the selection process for awards or a position of accolade, public recognition, special privileges, and/or leadership.

- A person sees others of lesser talent and worthiness gaining exponentially more fame, fortune, and success.

- A person lives in the shadow of her siblings' success and accolades.

- An artist's creations are condemned and/or misunderstood by society.

- A gambler is unable to curb his addiction and dies in abject poverty.

Chiron in Virgo or in the 6th House

- A person leaves her life's work unfinished due to terminal illness.

- A child is broken in spirit by his parents' incessant criticism and unattainable expectations.

- A woman's partner leaves her, despite still loving her, unable to live up to her unreasonable standards.

- A doctor is unable to save his patients from an unknown disease.

- A social/political/green activist is condemned, imprisoned, and/or exiled for trying to change the status quo.

- An underling is beheaded for criticizing or questioning the king/queen.

- A person admits himself into a psychiatric institution for depression and confusion. He is subsequently drugged and given electroshock therapy, losing his critical faculties in the process.

- A person's sense of completeness and stability is shattered by war, and her family is scattered as refugees.

- A person wastes his life in hedonism and bohemianism.
- Venereal disease or Alzheimer's leaves a person confused and unable to function in her life.

Chiron in Libra or in the 7th House

- Family, partner, and/or friends die in a plague or war, leaving a person utterly alone.
- A society with rigid social expectations ostracizes and/or exiles a person for not fitting in.
- A person is imprisoned and/or condemned to die for taking a stand.
- Physical deformity prevents a person from ever having a partner.
- A person's spouse dies slowly of a terminal illness, and then he himself dies of heartbreak.
- Soul mates recognize each other, but one is very young and another is very old, making consummation impossible.
- The story of Romeo and Juliet.
- A person following her inner calling is hated by all, condemned by society, and ostracized by those close to her, leaving her feeling alone.
- Conflict between a person and his spouse or family creates unrest and disharmony. The person's unresolved and unexpressed issues and wounds in this area turn into cancer.

Chiron in Scorpio or in the 8th House

- A person loses her family and friends in the plague or in war.
- A person witnesses the massacre of his village.
- Drought and famine forces a person out of work.
- A person's wealth is confiscated by the monarchy, church, or state.
- Twins are separated and lost from each other.
- A person's mentor/teacher/guardian/parent passes away, leaving her feeling empty and forlorn.

- A mother loses her young baby.
- A person suffers sexual mutilation at the hands of a ritualistic cult.
- A "happy" period of life is abruptly ended.
- A long marriage ends abruptly in divorce.
- A person realizes that he has been secretly used and manipulated for years.

Chiron in Sagittarius or in the 9th House

- Bombarded by a lifetime of calamities, a person gives up trying to understand why.
- Living in the wake of heavy religious dogma and ritual, a person's spiritual heart languishes, starved for personal contact with the divine.
- A person feels unenlightened, living in the shadow of the great wisdom and divine inspiration of a society governed by a religious order, e.g., ancient Tibet.
- A person who, as a child, wished to adventure far and wide over the globe, lives and dies in a small and remote village.
- A person feels thwarted from expanding her life by repressive people and/or circumstances.
- A person has a vision or dream that others cannot relate to and so discards it peremptorily.
- A person's adventure/exploration to new lands ends in failure, death, loss, and/or disgrace—think Everest, Antarctica, or outback Australia.
- A person feels his life is meaningless, and withers away, physically, mentally, emotionally, and/or spiritually.

Chiron in Capricorn or in the 10th House

- A person's achievements are not respected, recognized, or valued in her own lifetime.
- A person is silenced for sociopolitical reasons.
- A person's need for power and recognition leads him to sacrifice his own morals, ethics, and values, leading ultimately to disgrace and disrespect.
- Economic recession puts a person's life into chaos and disorder.

- A person raised in a religious/spiritual order feels disconnected from the real material world, longing to be "normal."
- A person seeking to help others is thwarted from gaining the power and authority to do so.
- A child is ignored, being just one of dozens of others vying for attention in an orphanage.
- A person watches helplessly as events beyond her control dissect her life and the lives of those close to her, one piece at a time.
- A person freed from prison after countless years cannot cope on his own, his life a shambles.

Chiron in Aquarius or in the 11th House

- A person is locked up and left to die for speaking her inner truth.
- A person is left alone after his family and/or tribe has been destroyed.
- A person is ostracized from society for being different.
- A person is burned at the stake for her blasphemous viewpoints and occult practices.
- A person's new invention is boycotted, condemned, and ridiculed.
- A person is born in an unpopulated wasteland, having to eke out a meager existence.
- A person is born of two conflicting cultures and is ostracized by both.
- A long voyage takes a person to a strange new land, cut off from all she has known.
- A strange person lives in a dark, overgrown house, feared and teased by children, ignored by adults, and forgotten by the world.

Chiron in Pisces or in the 12th House

- After invaders ransack the village/nunnery/monastery, a person relinquishes his or her faith in God.
- A person is institutionalized, unable to get a grasp of reality and unable to function in the normal world.
- A person, having been deemed by a narrow-minded society to have committed a crime, is left in the remote wilderness to die.

- Unscrupulous confidence tricksters take advantage of a person, causing him to lose everything.
- A person, wounded in love, vows never to open her heart again.
- A person of great psychic ability loses touch with normal living.
- A person who is maimed/raped/mugged sees her aggressor get off scot-free in legal proceedings.
- A person's secret enemies bring about his demise.
- A person opens her entire inner life to another, only to be used, abused, and discarded.
- The story of Jesus Christ: accusation, trial, and crucifixion. "Eli, Eli, lama sabachthani?" That is to say, "My God, My God, why hast thou forsaken me?"[1]

1. Matthew 27:46.

CHAPTER THIRTEEN

Example Chart Delineation

For guidance purposes in the interpretation of Chiron in the natal chart, we offer an example natal chart delineation, read from a healing and spiritual perspective. The chart we have chosen is rich in Chiron aspects, as this gives us the greatest possibility of seeing how Chiron works in a "focused" chart.

The chart we have chosen is that of a real person, whom we will call "Milly." We have changed her name and omitted her birth details for reasons of privacy. We have included her own feelings and thoughts and have correlated these with the various details of her chart. We have also correlated some of Milly's important life events with specific Chiron transits.

Milly

Milly is a healer, singer, midwife, and mother (chart 2). Her expressed purpose in life is to bring personal healing and change to a large number of people. She has worked on personal and planetary healing since the age of fourteen. Her passions include healing, music, writing, art, nature, and learning.

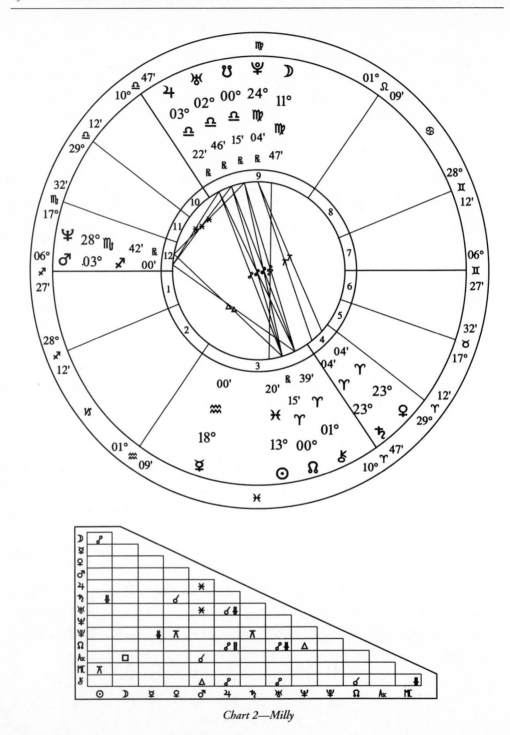

Chart 2—Milly

The first thing to look at is the life's path/purpose/calling/destiny, seen in the nodes of the Moon. All other features of the chart revolve around this.

The North Node in Aries indicates a life's path of finding, acknowledging, and affirming a strong sense of *self.* The South Node indicates that Milly comes from a background (past-life or otherwise) of denying self and of giving away her power to others.

Initially, she has unconsciously tended to place more importance and value on others than on herself. She tends to have an underlying low self-esteem and has spent much time in the beginning depreciating herself. There is also a tendency toward people-pleasing. In addition, there is a tendency to take the line of least resistance and to opt for greatest safety, particularly when in social settings. Furthermore, there is the tendency to avoid conflict, to try to keep the peace, and to seek out smooth waters. This tends to make her dependent on the whims and tastes of others. When she does this for too long, she ends up becoming resentful and beating herself up for it.

Milly's journey is about the acknowledgement of *self;* it is a journey toward true self-worth. Her task in this lifetime is to create personal solidity, stability, and presence—a tangible core of self-awareness. It is about focusing her attention and concentration inward, ultimately realizing that everything that she does for herself simultaneously benefits those around her. To be spiritually selfish is the highest altruism. Committees and the consensus can only go so far toward co-creating the world. Individual effort and inspiration are also necessary. As time goes by, Milly will be increasingly encouraged, even impelled, by the events and circumstances of her life to "go it alone."

Furthermore, Milly will find herself increasingly *wishing* to go it alone. There is a place in the world for positive ego. The expression of positive ego is a sacred act of acknowledging the light within—of allowing ourselves to shine in the world, without guilt, fear, or self-depreciation.

Milly's North Node in the 3rd house indicates a lifetime aimed toward communicating and sharing the innate wisdom, knowledge, and experience that she brings with her from other lives. Initially, though, she will find it difficult to relate to society and difficult to find a way of communicating her inner knowledge. She will tend to feel like an outsider at first. (Martin Schulman describes this placement as "an invitation to join society."[1]) Moreover, her inner knowledge will not always be in line with the consensus. For these reasons,

---

1. Martin Schulman, *Karmic Astrology,* volumes 1–4 (York Beach, ME: Samuel Weiser, 1984).

Milly's task is to find a way of sharing what is inside of her in ways that others can relate to; she must learn the language of current-day society.

In a sense, Milly is the adventurer who has traveled the world and experienced life in the raw. Now, in this lifetime, she returns to the "ordinary" world to share her tales of adventure—share the jewels of wisdom she has picked up along the way.

To find a language with which to communicate this tale, it will be necessary for Milly to gather much information and data across a wide field of knowledge. Like all of us, Milly already has all the answers within; the challenge is to discover the language, framework, and context in which to put them. As she gathers information/data, she will gradually recognize the place of each piece in the jigsaw puzzle of the universal plan. When sufficient information is synthesized into this picture, she will gradually understand how to communicate it, enabling her to share her inner knowledge.

When taken together, the North Node in Aries and in the 3rd house summarize Milly's path/purpose/calling/destiny: to acknowledge and validate her true self and her inner knowledge, and to share and communicate this with others. Her sense of self-worth is intimately connected with these two aspects; when we fail to acknowledge and honor our inner knowledge/wisdom and/or fail to share this with others (if it is our calling to do so), always giving in to the wishes, ideas, and opinions of others, we beat ourselves up.

It is important to recognize that we gather knowledge and data not just to increase our knowledge, understanding, and wisdom, but so we can "remember" what we already know wordlessly inside. Milly's life is about remembering who she is and awakening to her inner knowledge/wisdom.

Note that Milly's nodes aspect Chiron, Jupiter, Uranus, Neptune, and Mars. We will deal with these aspects shortly.

Next, we will look at the way Milly *expresses* her life's path/purpose/calling/destiny; we will look at the Sun, its sign, its house, and its aspects.

With the Sun in Pisces, Milly expresses her life's path primarily through the emotions. Initially, she has tended to feel like the victim of her life and to be prone to every shift of the wind. She is extremely sensitive to the energy environment and, on the one hand, is ruled by the slightest change of emotion around her.

On the other hand, her sensitivity gives her enormous powers of perception. She is able to feel what others are feeling, without words. This ability can be a burden at times, though, when she cannot seem to shut out the outside world. This in turn can cause a retreat into the inner safety of a virtual world, making Milly a dreamer. Around the dreamer, though, can be a hard shell that masks her inner sensitivity.

Milly has a tendency to take on the wounds and causes of others—to support and champion underdogs, lost causes, and people who are down and out. Her deepest wish, whether acknowledged or not, is to reconnect with the love and oneness of her divine origins. She sometimes loses herself in this wish, allowing others to encroach and take advantage of her. Then, she feels victimized and has a tendency to indulge in self-pity. However, these, too, are necessary steps upon her path. Milly's challenge is to try to retain her individual sense of self while listening to the inner voice that speaks from her spiritual heart; individuality and a sense of belonging to the greater whole are both equally necessary.

The 3rd-house placement of Milly's Sun indicates that she will express her Piscean traits in the areas of communication, media, writing, intellectual pursuits, and so forth. She has a message to share, and this is in perfect alignment with her life's path/purpose/calling/destiny (nodes). The *way* she will share it will depend on the other astrological considerations of her chart.

Note that Milly's Sun opposes her Moon. We will look at this aspect in a moment.

Now we will look at Milly's Chiron—the force that drives her along her life's path/purpose/calling/destiny (nodes) and colors its expression (Sun).

Milly's Chiron in Aries indicates that her deepest void or wound, around which all her other wounds and voids revolve, is a profound loss of self-worth. Some event, circumstance, or issue, very early in her life (mirroring things she brought into this lifetime that she has yet to love unconditionally), convinced her that she was entirely worthless and/or unworthy of love—perhaps even that she was undeserving of life itself. The healing journey is about finding self-worth.

Milly's original perceptions of worthlessness were, in the final analysis, *misperceptions,* but the gift of these has been the journey upon which they have taken her. She is who she is—with her unique divine design—because of this journey.

The journey toward true self-worth (as opposed to illusory self-esteem) consists of discovering the *essence*—the spirit or soul—that lies behind and beyond all manifestations of *personality.* It consists of dissolving the illusion that we are our masks/personas. Our masks/personas are impermanent and, as such, offer no true safety or security—they come, they go, they can be lost, and they can change. Most importantly, our masks/personas *are* our wounds and issues.

However, the gift in our wounds and issues is that they impel us toward healing and higher consciousness—they impel us toward our divine design.

Milly's Chiron in the 3rd house indicates that her deepest wounds, aforementioned, are played out in the area of knowledge and understanding, creating deep feelings of not knowing or not being worthy to know, of being stupid, slow, ignorant, or uneducated, and/or of being unable to communicate what is inside of her—as though there is nothing inside her worth communicating.

Chiron drives Milly's pursuit of knowledge, understanding, and wisdom—driving her to find out all she can about all subjects to which she feels connected. In this process, she will gradually realize, by the reflection of that knowledge, that, somewhere deep inside her, she knew it all already. This placement is about seeing, acknowledging, and embracing her inner knowing and wisdom.

Milly's 3rd-house Chiron also drives her to try to find ways of feeling worthy of sharing/communicating what is inside of her—of feeling as though she has something worth sharing/communicating—despite her fear and low self-esteem.

The ultimate gift of Chiron in the 3rd house is the discovery and sharing of our deepest inner knowledge and wisdom in ways that society can relate to.

Taken as a whole, Milly's Chiron in Aries in the 3rd house tends to cause her to equate knowledge, understanding, and wisdom with self-worth. If she is stupid and/or uneducated, then she is worthless and useless to the world. So, as compensation, she seeks knowledge, understanding, and wisdom in order to feel worthy to exist, in order to feel worthy to have something to say, and in order to feel worthy to participate in life.

Ultimately, Milly will realize that the knowledge, understanding, and wisdom gained from the world around her is pale in comparison to that which already lies in her spiritual heart. This realization is the birth of true self-worth.

The journey will not be in vain, though, because, in the process, she will have learned how to share/communicate her inner knowledge/wisdom in ways others can relate to. The essence of her message will be, *we already know it all inside—our journey is about remembering.*

Let's now consider the Moon in Milly's chart and its place as the outer face of Chiron.

Milly's Chiron in Aries expresses, as we have said, her wound of deep loss or lack of self-worth. The external face of the Virgo Moon is the perfectionist. It represents the person for whom nothing is ever good enough, who can never be happy or satisfied with the performance of self or others, and/or who can never be happy or satisfied with the status quo. The Virgo Moon takes solace and refuge in criticism of self and others.

All this derives, in Milly's case, from never being happy or satisfied with herself, her performance, and/or with who she is at any given moment. Can we see how Chiron and the Moon are psychologically connected here? Naturally, this will ever impel her to try to improve herself. Ultimately, though, it will ever drive her to love herself for being exactly who she is.

Now let's widen our perspective of Milly's chart by considering some of the important aspects, beginning with the Chiron-North Node conjunction.

North Node conjunctions point to special planetary guides in our lives. In this lifetime, Chiron is Milly's special planetary guide—one of the reasons we have chosen to delineate her chart in this chapter. Chiron not only guides her life, but her path/purpose/calling/destiny is to do Chiron's work—to do healing in some form or other.

With this conjunction sitting in the 3rd house, Milly's primary task is to communicate and express the messages of Chiron. Further, it is to communicate and express these messages in a highly personal way. And the messages are about acknowledgment of self, about allowing herself to shine, and about learning to freely share her inner knowledge/wisdom.

Milly's Chiron opposes the South Node conjunct Uranus and Jupiter. Aside from the Chiron-North Node conjunction, this is one of the more important features of her chart. The opposition of Chiron and Uranus (covered in chapter 9) was a feature of many born between 1952 and 1989. Its manifestation tends to fall somewhere between two extremes. On the one hand, we can react with escapism, avoidance, and self-destructive behavior. On the other hand, if we take up the challenge and attend to our wounds and issues, it can confer increased healing ability and focus.

In the latter case, Chiron opposition Uranus can be the mark of the healer. Unable to escape or hide from her woundedness, like Chiron in the myth, Milly ever seeks to learn all she can about healing, healing others as she goes along.

Jupiter is involved in this planetary pattern, too—conjunct the South Node and Uranus and opposing Chiron. Jupiter represents the Inner Child that knows in its spiritual heart that all is right with the world. Milly's Inner Child lies hidden behind her wounds, calling out to be heard and driving her to the healing path. Jupiter opposition Chiron seeks to show Milly the big picture—the origin, context, meaning, and purpose—of her wounds and unresolved issues. Jupiter promises her the freedom of awakened consciousness if she can dissolve the illusions of her lower nature that constitute her wounds and issues.

The Chiron-North Node conjunction opposing the Uranus-South Node-Jupiter conjunction forms a trine/sextile triangle pattern to the Neptune-Mars conjunction in Sagittarius in the 12th house.

Mars, from a spiritual perspective, represents action, reaction, intention, and motivation. Neptune represents the striving for oneness, spirit, and love. Taken together, they represent the potential for active, conscious, and intentional pursuit and expression of spirit. Initially, however, when we are primarily *reactive,* this can cause us to act in mysterious and irrational ways, particularly in the 12th house. Milly is being given the opportunity to delve—actively, consciously, and intentionally—into her psyche, seeking the spirit within.

When Milly's Neptune-Mars conjunction is considered in relation to the aspects it makes with the nodes, Chiron, Uranus, and Jupiter, this gives her journey motivation, power, and drive from a *supraconscious* source—from higher self/spirit/soul/guides. When transits set off any of the planets involved in this pattern, all the other associated planets resonate, too. This triangle of planets is a powerful indicator of Milly's healing ability and focus, and probably indicates substantial work done in previous lives on healing and evolution of consciousness.

Milly's Pluto in Virgo represents a generation of people destined to revolutionize healing and healing methods. Being in a wide-orbed conjunction with the South Node and its attendant aspects, this indicates that Milly brings revolutionary healing ideas and abilities into this lifetime. It also indicates that she understands, intuitively, the metaphysics of healing and the evolution of consciousness.

Milly's 9th-house planets reflect the wisdom she brings through the South Node (past-life point), channeled through the 3rd-house planets, and activated and motivated by the 12th-house planets.

Returning our attention now to the aforementioned Sun-Moon opposition, this aspect keeps Milly balanced. It keeps her feet on the ground and her head in the heavens. Bless this aspect! It is her godsend. Aside from driving her toward self-improvement and toward learning to love herself, aforementioned, the Moon in Virgo is very pragmatic, positively skeptical, discerning, rigorously attending to detail, and is a doubting Thomas if there ever was one! Milly's innate emotional need for order, for knowing all the details, and/or for putting them in their proper place not only keeps her honest, but it gives her credibility. The Pisces Sun can then soar on the firm foundations that the Moon provides, without getting lost in the clouds.

This opposition of the Sun and Moon, as with all oppositions, provides an innate balance check; both sides of the equation demand consideration. This is what makes oppositions so difficult: they demand that we balance and/or synthesize things that initially seem opposite, at odds, incompatible, irresolvable, and irreconcilable.

Let's now turn to Milly's Saturn-Venus conjunction quincunx her Pluto-South Node conjunction. Normally, I would not allow such a wide orb for a quincunx (to the South Node). However, as the South Node conjuncts Pluto inside a six-degree orb, we will consider that it also quincunxes Saturn-Venus.

This planetary pattern means that Milly was destined to have her father, symbolically or actually, create dramatic and revolutionary change in her life. This was enacted most obviously in the real-life circumstance of her father "stealing" her away from her mother when she was five years old. In practical terms, this means that Milly's "father" will invariably show up in her every relationship until she learns to love every aspect of her father and her father issues.

In this pattern, Saturn's quincunx to the South Node implies a past-life connection between Milly and her father, with unfinished business to complete. Recall what we said about past-life symbolism, though. We should take this formulation as symbolic and not actual. We are *not* suggesting that her actual father in this lifetime was the same as her actual father in a past life. However, we *are* suggesting that her *father issues* are the same and will be played out in each lifetime through her actual fathers and/or through those in her life who mirror these father issues.

Given the preceding, Milly's journey goes a little like this: First, there were negative judgments and blame because of deeds "done to her" by a father/authority person or father/authority persons in a past life. Then, there was the failure to resolve (or complete) these issues in past lives. Next, through the metaphysical principles of attraction and resonance, Milly and this other person *(or a person of a very similar frequency)* were brought together in this incarnation. Then, there were the events and circumstances of Milly's early life that mirrored her innate wounds and issues. Next, there is the lesson of accepting what they "did to her." Then, the lesson of learning to forgive them. Finally, there will be the lesson of learning to love them unconditionally, knowing that no forgiveness was ever necessary and that everything that transpired between the two of them (and all other fathers, actual and metaphorical, in this lifetime and in past lifetimes) was part of a larger plan.

In short, this quincunx demands that Milly strive for a new perspective and understanding of unresolved past-life/symbolic issues through the vehicle of present-life interaction with her natural father and/or father/authority people in this lifetime. (Indications from Milly herself suggest that her natural *mother* in this lifetime played the father role we are suggesting here.)

When viewed in the context of her life's path/purpose/calling/destiny, the role of father in Milly's life takes on a higher meaning. The father in our lives is the one who challenges us (even if "father" is expressed through the physical mother or other extended family members). The father is the one who questions our self-worth, our right to exist, our beliefs, and our actions. The "father" is the mirror of the universe/God/creator/All/spirit, whereas the "mother" is the mirror of the creation/Goddess/mother/maintainer/world/matter.

Milly's father/authority issues (and interaction with father figures) exacerbate her wounds of self-worth. Paradoxically, though, her "father" and father issues will simultaneously impel her to ultimately assert, affirm, and empower herself. This is doubly emphasized by the fact that Venus and Saturn in her chart are, like Chiron, in Aries. These placements will tend to manifest as external restrictions, repressions, limitations, cruelty, harshness, coldness, abuse, and so forth, which, in turn, are designed to encourage her to stand up and say, "Enough is enough!" Furthermore, in the process, she will collect valuable gifts along the way—discipline, seriousness, perseverance, fortitude, determination, and so forth. The love of the Father comes in mysterious ways. The return to the love of the Father is the ultimate end of all healing.

Finally, we come to the singleton in the chart, i.e., Mercury. Normally, we would have dealt with Mercury earlier in the reading, after coming to its aspects to other planets, but when it is unaspected, it tends to get left until later.

Milly's Mercury in Aquarius and in the 3rd house, *unaspected to any other planets,* paradoxically adds weight to her purpose of communication. Initially, it remains isolated, and

Milly will tend to find it hard to give voice to her wisdom and understanding. Chiron, also in the 3rd house, further accentuates this. The gifts of Mercury's isolation and of its Aquarian stance are objectivity, distance, space, and perspective. It is the voice of reason, helping her sense a higher order in what her earthbound understanding initially perceives as chaos and injustice.

Milly's Libran Midheaven indicates that any career or public path she may take will need to offer her a sense of balance and be in line with her chosen life's higher purpose. This is particularly so as it lies so close to the conjunction of Jupiter, Uranus, and the South Node.

Milly's Sagittarian Ascendant initially indicates that she tends to see herself as an adventurer on the journey of life. She sees herself as a free spirit and wishes to embrace life with both hands. Whether she can do this depends on her willingness to attend to her wounds and issues. Effort toward healing is required. Moreover, there is a wide-orbed square between Milly's Sagittarian Ascendant and her Pisces Sun, indicating that her sensitive nature may initially be at odds with the adventurer spirit in her. All going well, Milly will tend to embrace her inner journey of healing with the same sense of adventure as a rock climber embracing their physical sport.

One of Milly's specific questions in the reading was about her relationships. Let's have a quick look at this, as it will also serve to illustrate assertions made previously with respect to Chiron and its place in relationship.

Recall that Milly's Saturn-Venus conjunction quincunxing the Pluto-South Node conjunction indicates that the "father" will tend to "show up" in her every relationship until she learns to love him. Moreover, by virtue of her wounds and issues (Chiron), Milly will tend to attract people who will beat her up, metaphorically or actually, until she stands up for herself. Initially, these people may have similar wounds and, therefore, an immediate empathy with Milly. However, as time goes by, they will tend to take out their own frustrations and woundedness upon Milly—and vice versa. Relationships are mirrors.

Recall also that our wounds and issues take us exactly to the place(s) we need to be in order to learn our lessons, heal our wounds, and resolve our issues.

Given the preceding, it now makes perfect sense that Milly would be attracted to people who would eventually challenge her self-worth by playing out their issues upon her.

The lesson of Chiron in Aries is learning to love *self*. Milly's actual relationship experiences have provided exactly this opportunity (and she herself sees and confirms this).

Now let's look at some of the facts, as related by Milly herself in the reading, and see how they fit in with the preceding delineation. We will concentrate on Chiron placements, aspects, and transits, as this is our theme in this book. Words in quotations are Milly's exact words.

Natal Placements

Chiron in Aries

Physical abuse in the earliest years (ages 1–5, according to Milly), continuing throughout childhood and into some adult relationships. Sexual abuse periodically. Prone to "energy crashing and over-giving." Tends to experience healing crises very physically. A need to share her "extraordinary" experiences with others, and to feel important and validated by virtue of having experiences that transcend and surpass (even if negatively) the normal experiences of others.

Chiron in the 3rd House

The expressed wish to heal. "A gifted child from a dysfunctional family who didn't achieve worldly academic potential." Concerning her stepmother, Milly relates: "The main way she wounded me was to make me feel unacceptable for being 'gifted.' The word 'brain' was a putdown in the family."

Milly also experienced wounds in relation to her siblings. Milly expresses a wish to write globally, inspired by her adversity. She also expresses a wish to work with people with schizophrenia and other mental "illnesses." She is a self-taught "psychologist" with a great interest in weighing up and exploring others' depths. All this has led to a deep understanding of healing and to an extended ability to communicate healing ideas.

Natal Aspects

Chiron Conjunct the North Node

An expressed deep wish to bring healing/change to as many others as possible. A feeling of destiny, having "worked on personal and planetary healing since awakening at age fourteen."

Chiron-North Node Conjunction Opposition
Uranus-Jupiter-South Node Conjunction
Path of the healer. Inner Child discovery. "Very deep thinker and lover of life's mysteries." Finds herself "unintentionally" working with abused children. Also learning "to love even the *wounder,* not just the wounded." (In addition, see Milly's expressed purpose in life, on the first page of this chapter and in the following paragraph.)

Chiron-North Node Conjunction Trine Neptune-Mars Conjunction in Sagittarius in the 12th House
Highly motivated individual in the area of personal and planetary healing. Expressed purpose: "To receive humility and initiation as a healer with unconditional love for All that is."

Chiron Transits
Early Life Abuse (Ages 1–4, According to the Transits)
It is interesting that Chiron went retrograde four months after Milly's birth and conjuncted natal Chiron in the tenth month *at the same time the North Node conjuncted the natal Sun.* Furthermore, Chiron and Uranus danced around Milly's natal IC and MC for the first few years of life. Her healing destiny and its imprint as a vocation are set here, with the wounds that will drive her healing journey in place.

Transiting Pluto-Uranus Conjunction Opposed Natal Chiron While Transiting the 9th House
Moved to Australia.

Transiting Chiron Conjunct the Natal Saturn-Venus Conjunction in the 4th House
Milly's father "stole" her away from her mother. In addition, Pluto was conjunct the natal Jupiter-Uranus conjunction. This indicates revolutionary change (Pluto) to Milly's Inner Child (Jupiter) and to her overall view of the world (Uranus).

Transiting North Node Square the Natal Chiron-North Node Conjunction and the Natal Uranus-Jupiter-South Node Conjunction
Milly relates that this was the time that she started her personal and planetary healing journey.

Transiting Chiron Opposition the Natal Neptune-Mars Conjunction

Personal and planetary healing journey given extra impetus. (This was the year and a half following the previously mentioned transit).

Milly's Children

——First Child

Transiting Jupiter conjuncted Milly's natal Sun, shortly after she rejoined with her own mother. Of her firstborn, Milly says, "I needed to be loved unconditionally, and she came to give me this."

——Second Child

First Chiron-square-natal Chiron transit. This second child was born to a different father than the first child. The father was "some sort of dark one, energy vortex, inward collapse, wolf in sheep's clothing." The purpose of the child's relationship with Milly is, in her own words, "to reflect my own wounds and search for truth."

——Third Child

Transiting Chiron was square Milly's natal Saturn-Venus conjunction during the second half of this pregnancy. This child has the same father as the second child. This child, as Milly puts it, "knows that persistence pays. His polarities aren't fully heterosexual. Also, I remembered my sexual abuse during this pregnancy."

——Fourth Child

Transiting Saturn conjunct natal Chiron, and transiting Chiron opposing the natal Saturn-Venus conjunction. This child has a different father from the other three children. Milly recalls that the father's "mental illness" manifested when this child was born. "His extremely traumatic childhood blew up in his face. He became 'paranoid schizophrenic.' He has continued to attack and attempt to wound me despite every loving effort." During the child's birth, Milly relates, "I made the noise I had always been afraid to make—the noise of my wound. I could never reproduce that sound and I feel the sadness even now as I recall it." Milly feels that she accessed tools during this birth and, subsequently, from this child that she could use in the future to defend herself.

First Chiron-square-Chiron Transit (Natal Chiron Conjunct the North Node)

Only months after this transit, Milly met spiritual teachers Ma Shivam Rachana and Daricha. Her healing journey began to gain momentum.

Transiting Uranus Square the Natal Chiron-North Node Conjunction

This was the period spent with the aforementioned spiritual teachers.

Transiting Chiron Opposition Natal Mercury (Singleton)

A guide came to Milly in the form of her English teacher. (Recall what was said earlier about the importance of transits to activate and resolve natal singletons.)

Transiting Jupiter Opposition the Natal Chiron-North Node Conjunction

A guide came to Milly. Of this encounter, she relates that it came "just in the nick of time, before I inwardly collapsed. This was my first quantum leap."

Nervous Breakdown/Transformation

This was a time of monumental spiritual emergency/emergence in Milly's life—between 1992 and 1993. In early 1992, the transiting North Node squared Milly's natal Chiron-North Node conjunction and Uranus-Jupiter-South Node conjunction. Transiting Chiron opposed Mercury in late 1992 and into early 1993. (Again, recall what was said about the importance of transits to activate natal singletons.) The fulcrum point was April 1993 when transiting Uranus squared the natal Saturn-Venus conjunction, while transiting Chiron opposed natal Mercury, while the transiting North Node squared natal the Sun and Moon, and while transiting Saturn squared the natal Neptune-Mars conjunction!

As we can see, healing crises are accentuated in people whose natal Chiron is involved in multiple planetary aspects. During this time, Milly relates, "I spent nine months under a [comforter] for 90 percent of my waking hours, not sleeping, not awake." She emerged afterward feeling reborn, "like a butterfly."

Transiting Chiron Conjunct Natal Pluto

In late 1994 and into 1995, Milly started writing "due to adversity," inspired to share her messages globally. Transiting Saturn conjuncted her natal Sun in February 1995. Later in 1995, transiting Chiron opposed the natal Chiron-North Node conjunction, while transiting Pluto conjuncted the natal Neptune-Mars conjunction.

Transiting Chiron Conjunct Natal Neptune

Experienced "increased spiritual awareness" in late 1998 and into September 1999. In August 1999, Milly experienced an enormous and cathartic healing crisis/cleansing, including "past-life recall." During this time, Barbara Hand Clow's book on Chiron came to her.

Transiting Chiron Conjunct Natal Mars

In October 1999, Milly experienced a period of activation and increased motivation for her personal and planetary healing. Although she acknowledges that she still has a long way to go, she has a conscious and powerful vision for the future.

In conclusion, it is important to be reminded that the degree of correlation between the planets and a person's actual life events and experiences, inner and outer, depends upon how focused—*how well aspected*—the chart is. Milly's chart is highly focused, so it presents the perfect vehicle for the exploration of planetary correspondences. We might find the chart of someone not so focused a little disappointing if we were expecting a similar result to the above.

Nonetheless, the influences of the planets are still there, whether manifest in obvious events in a person's life or not. In cases where the chart is less focused, the delineation must necessarily be more psychological and less concerned with relating actual events to planetary placements, aspects, and transits.

APPENDIX

Graphs

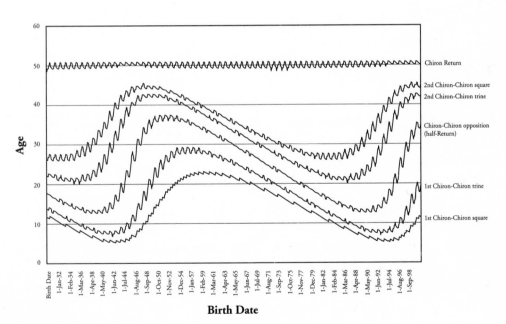

Birth Date

Graph 1—The Chiron Cycle

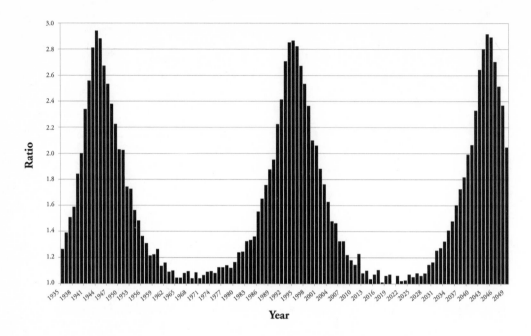

Graph 2—Year-by-Year Ratio of Chiron-Chiron Transits in the General Population

This graph was constructed by calculating all occurrences of Chiron-cycle aspects (conjunctions at and immediately following birth, as well as sextiles, squares, trines, quincunxes, the opposition, and the Return) in the "natal" charts for the first day of every month between 1890 and 2050 and then tallying these gross occurrences for each year. Note that this graph does *not* take into account population growth (which, for the purposes of this graph, is presupposed to be a steady ascending curve from one month to the next). When population growth is considered, we will naturally find that the ratio of Chiron-Chiron transits in the general population grows from one Chiron cycle to the next. Extrapolating from this, we can see that, as the general population grows, so the outer expression of all planetary energies grows. The most obvious reflection of this is in the increasing social tensions and intensity we find in growing cities and in global interrelations.

Glossary

divine design. The divine blueprint of our lives. Our special calling or mission. Our unique service to the creation. The thing we would most love to do with our lives when we have loved ourselves and loved our lives exactly as they are.

gift in the wound. Initially, the gift in the wound is each piece of the puzzle of our lives, revealed as we heal each wound and issue. Ultimately, it is the miraculous and perfect journey of our lives, leading to our divine design and expressing the "suchness" of omnipresent love.

healing, the. Our journey of consciousness toward truth, oneness, and love. Our journey home to spirit.

healing. Physical, emotional, mental, and spiritual healing, taken in its broadest sense, beyond mere medical boundaries. The process of integration, unification, merging, individuation, "wholing," balancing, awakening, revealing truth, raising consciousness, evolving, growing, and coming closer to love and oneness.

higher nature or higher self. Our consciousness, residing "between" the soul (our potentially unified/healed nature) and the lower nature (our polarized personas/emotions/perspectives) and partially awakened to truth, oneness, and love. The part of us we call "me" in enlightened moments and that is *relatively* wise and knowing. The part of us that cycles through incarnations, seeking healing and evolution of consciousness. The vehicle of the higher nature's physical expression is the voluntary nervous system. Its home is in the spiritual heart.

holographic. Describing that the smallest part of the universe reflects and contains the whole.

issues. Our polarized perceptions/perspectives of events, circumstances, and situations, often involving other people, that have thrown us off-center from a place of inner (and hence, outer) balance.

lower nature. Our dualistic animal nature that seeks pleasure and runs from pain and that protects our physical body. Summated in the autonomic nervous system. Its heart is in the solar plexus. Also, our manifested dualistic nature: polarized personas/emotions, judgments, blame, masks, charges, lies, illusions, and half-truths. The part of us that we call "me" in unenlightened moments of charge, bias, judgment, and blame.

Mysteries, the. Sacred and esoteric teachings passed down from the Avatars of the Mother Culture that is known today as Atlantis. The Mysteries were passed down through the Egyptian Mystery schools and through the Hermetic teachings of the early centuries AD.

Rainbow Bridge. A metaphoric and metaphysical device for bringing our fragmented and wounded consciousness (the many colors of the material creation) back into unity, balance, light, and love (the white light of spirit).

soul. The "keeper" of our divine design, represented simultaneously by the most expanded consciousness of the solar system (at the boundary, or *magnetopause,* of the solar system) and by the most focused consciousness of the Sun. Our true nature, beyond even our higher nature/self—unmanifest, pure, spaceless, timeless, omnipresent, and being the purest love.

wound. A sense of inner hurt, missingness, fragmentedness, injustice, unfairness, incompleteness, and so forth. The unresolved, undissolved, unreconciled, and/or unhealed issues that lie buried within our psyches, awaiting the healing process and arising from our early misperceptions and judgments of our lives and of the world around us.

wounding, the. Our journey into duality—into the material condition, illusion, ignorance, darkness, fragmentation, separation, isolation, and disconnectedness.

Bibliography

Bailey, Alice. *Esoteric Astrology.* Lucis Publishing Co., 1989. This text is available in its entirety at http://laluni.helloyou.ws/netnews/bk/astrology/toc.html.

Brennan, Barbara Ann. *Light Emerging: The Journey of Personal Healing.* New York: Bantam Books, 1993.

Campbell, Joseph. *The Hero with a Thousand Faces.* Fontana Press, 1993.

Demartini, John F. *Count Your Blessings: The Healing Power of Gratitude and Love.* Rockport, MA: Element Books, 1997.

Emerson, Ralph Waldo. *Nature and Other Writings.* Edited by Peter Turner. Boston: Shambhala, 1994.

Erdman, David V., ed. *The Complete Poetry and Prose of William Blake.* New York: Anchor Books, 1988.

Goodwin, Brian. *How the Leopard Changed Its Spots: The Evolution of Complexity.* New York: Charles Scribner's Sons, 1994.

Hand Clow, Barbara. *Chiron: Rainbow Bridge Between the Inner and Outer Planets.* St. Paul, MN: Llewellyn Publications, 1987.

The Hermetica: The Lost Wisdom of the Pharaohs. Translation by Timothy Freke and Peter Gandy. London: Judy Piatkus Publishers, 1997.

Jantsch, Erich. *The Self-Organizing Universe.* Oxford: Pergamon Press, 1980.

Jung, Carl G. *Archetypes of the Collective Unconscious.* Collected works, vol. 9, part i. 1934. Reprint, New York and London, 1959.

The Kybalion: A Study of the Hermetic Philosophy of Ancient Egypt and Greece, by Three Initiates. Chicago, IL: Yogi Publication Society, 1908.

Lantero, Erminie. *The Continuing Discovery of Chiron.* York Beach, ME: Samuel Weiser, 1983.

Nolle, Richard. *Chiron: The New Planet in Your Horoscope: The Key to Your Quest.* Tempe, AZ: American Federation of Astrologers,1983.

Ouspensky, P. D. *In Search of the Miraculous.* New York: Harcourt Brace Jovanovich, 1949.

———. *The Psychology of Man's Possible Evolution.* New York: Vintage Books, 1974.

Raleigh, A. S. *Occult Geometry and Hermetic Science of Motion & Number.* DeVorss Publications, 1991.

Reinhart, Melanie. *Chiron and the Healing Journey.* London: Arkana, 1989.

Roob, Alexander. *Alchemy & Mysticism: The Hermetic Museum.* New York: Taschen, 1997.

Rudhyar, Dane. *An Astrological Mandala.* New York: Vintage Books, 1974.

Schulman, Martin. *Karmic Astrology.* York Beach, ME: Samuel Weiser, 1984.

Stein, Zane B. *Essence and Application: A View from Chiron.* Originally published in 1985. The revised, 1995 edition is available to order on the author's website at http://www.geocities.com/SoHo/7969/page6.htm.

The Mountain Astrologer. Various issues, 1995-1998.

WellBeing Magazine Astrology Guide 2000. North Sydney, Australia: Wellspring Publishers, 2000.

Index

To Write to the Author

If you wish to contact the author or would like more information about this book, please write to the author in care of Llewellyn Worldwide and we will forward your request. Both the author and publisher appreciate hearing from you and learning of your enjoyment of this book and how it has helped you. Llewellyn Worldwide cannot guarantee that every letter written to the author can be answered, but all will be forwarded. Please write to:

Martin Lass
℅ Llewellyn Worldwide
2143 Wooddale Drive, Dept. 0-7387-0717-1
Woodbury, Minnesota 55125-2989, U.S.A.

Please enclose a self-addressed stamped envelope for reply,
or $1.00 to cover costs. If outside U.S.A., enclose
international postal reply coupon.

Many of Llewellyn's authors have websites with additional information and resources. For more information, please visit our website at http://www.llewellyn.com.

Free Magazine

Read unique articles by Llewellyn authors, recommendations by experts, and information on new releases. To receive a **free** copy of Llewellyn's consumer magazine, *New Worlds of Mind & Spirit,* simply call 1-877-NEW-WRLD or visit our website at www.llewellyn.com and click on *New Worlds.*

LLEWELLYN ORDERING INFORMATION

Order Online:
Visit our website at www.llewellyn.com, select your books, and order them on our secure server.

Order by Phone:
- Call toll-free within the U.S. at 1-877-NEW-WRLD (1-877-639-9753). Call toll-free within Canada at 1-866-NEW-WRLD (1-866-639-9753)
- We accept VISA, MasterCard, and American Express

Order by Mail:
Send the full price of your order (MN residents add 7% sales tax) in U.S. funds, plus postage & handling to:

Llewellyn Worldwide
2143 Wooddale Drive, Dept. 0-7387-0717-1
Woodbury, Minnesota 55125-2989, U.S.A.

Postage & Handling:

Standard (U.S., Mexico, & Canada). If your order is:
$49.99 and under, add $3.00
$50.00 and over, FREE STANDARD SHIPPING

AK, HI, PR: $15.00 for one book plus $1.00 for each additional book.

International Orders (airmail only):
$16.00 for one book plus $3.00 for each additional book

Orders are processed within 2 business days. Please allow for normal shipping time.
Postage and handling rates subject to change.

All Around the Zodiac
Exploring Astrology's Twelve Signs

Bil Tierney

A fresh, in-depth perspective on the zodiac you thought you knew. This book provides a revealing new look at the astrological signs, from Aries to Pisces. Gain a deeper understanding of how each sign motivates you to grow and evolve in consciousness. How does Aries work with Pisces? What does Gemini share in common with Scorpio? *All Around the Zodiac* is the only book on the market to explore these sign combinations to such a degree.

Not your typical Sun sign guide, this book is broken into three parts. Part 1 defines the signs, part 2 analyzes the expression of sixty-six pairs of signs, and part 3 designates the expression of the planets and houses in the signs.

0-7387-0111-4, 528 pp., 6 x 9   **$17.95**

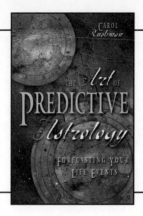

The Art of Predictive Astrology
Forecasting Your Life Events

CAROL RUSHMAN

Become an expert at seeing the future in anyone's astrological chart! Insight into the future is a large part of the intrigue and mystery of astrology. *The Art of Predictive Astrology* clearly lays out a step-by-step system that astrologers can use to forecast significant events including love and financial success. When finished with the book, readers will be able to predict cycles and trends for the next several years, and give their clients fifteen important dates for the coming year. An emphasis is on progressions, eclipses, and lunations as important predictive tools.

0-7387-0164-5, 288 pp., 6 x 9   **$14.95**

Astrology
Understanding the Birth Chart
(A Comprehensive Guide to Classical Interpretation)

KEVIN BURK

This beginning- to intermediate-level astrology book is based on a course taught to prepare students for the NCGR Level I Astrological Certification exam. It is a unique book for several reasons. First, rather than being an astrological phrase book or "cookbook," it helps students to understand the language of astrology. From the beginning, students are encouraged to focus on the concepts, not the keywords. Second, as soon as you are familiar with the fundamental elements of astrology, the focus shifts to learning how to work with these basics to form a coherent, synthesized interpretation of a birth chart.

In addition, it explains how to work with traditional astrological techniques, most notably the essential dignities. All interpretive factors are brought together in the context of a full interpretation of the charts of Sylvester Stallone, Meryl Streep, Eva Peron, and Woody Allen. This book fits the niche between cookbook astrology books and more technical manuals.

1-56718-088-4, 368 pp., 7½ x 9⅛, illus.   **$17.95**

To order, call 1-877-NEW-WRLD
Prices subject to change without notice

Astrology & Relationships
Techniques for Harmonious Personal Connections

DAVID POND

Take your relationships to a deeper level. There is a hunger for intimacy in the modern world. Astrology & Relationships is a guidebook on how to use astrology to improve all your relationships. This is not fortunetelling astrology, predicting which signs you will be most compatible with; instead, it uses astrology as a model to help you experience greater fulfillment and joy in relating to others. You can also look up your planets, and those of others, to discover specific relationship needs and talents.

What makes this book unique is that it goes beyond descriptive astrology to suggest methods and techniques for actualizing the stages of a relationship that each planet represents. Many of the exercises are designed to awaken individual skills and heighten self-understanding, leading you to first identify a particular quality within yourself, and then to relate to it in others.

0-7387-0046-0, 368 pp., 7½ x 9⅛   **$17.95**

To order, call 1-877-NEW-WRLD
Prices subject to change without notice

CHART INTERPRETATION
FROM A BUDDHIST PERSPECTIVE

BUDDHIST
ASTROLOGY

FOREWORD BY HIS HOLINESS THE DALAI LAMA

JHAMPA SHANEMAN & JAN V. ANGEL

Buddhist Astrology
Chart Interpretation From A Buddhist Perspective

Jhampa Shaneman and Jan V. Angel
Foreword by His Holiness the Dalai Lama

Use Buddhist wisdom and compassion to clarify your astrological readings.

Become your own astrological guru with the first book to apply Buddhist practice to Western astrology. Buddhist astrology bridges familiar astrological thinking with the ideas of karma, interdependence, and impermanence. What if we consciously choose the compassionate way as we traverse those high peaks of a Pluto transit or climb to the summit of a Saturn cycle? Does such a response set up an array of rippling effects?

While Buddhism is theologically and metaphysically compelling, it is also very practical. Within its tenets every psychological state is embraced, integrated, and brought to light. It is spirit-medicine for modern astrology.

0-7387-0315-X, 384 pp., 6 x 9   **$19.95**

To order, call 1-877-NEW-WRLD

Chiron
Transforming Bridge Between the Inner & Outer Planets

Barbara Hand Clow
(Revised edition with updated tables of Chiron in the houses)

Somewhere between Saturn and Uranus orbits a peculiar planetoid, Chiron. With its own unique elliptical orbit, Chiron separates the inner planets from the outer, giving astrologers new perspectives for interpretations. This book uncovers the fascinating truth about a planet that is revolutionizing modern astrology. Readers discover how Chiron rules Tarot reading, healing exercises, and initiation into the next level of awareness.

0-87542-094-X, 336 pp., 6 x9, illus., charts   **$16.95**

Electional Astrology
The Art of Timing

JOANN HAMPAR

Planning a wedding? Scheduling surgery? Buying a house? How do you choose a date and time that offers the best chance of success? The odds are in your favor when you plan life events using electional astrology—a branch of astrology that helps you align with the power of the universe.

Professional astrologer Joann Hampar teaches the principles of electional astrology—explaining the significance of each planet and how to time events according to their cycles. Readers will learn how to analyze the planetary alignments and compile an electional chart that pinpoints the optimal time to buy a diamond ring, adopt a pet, close a business deal, take a trip, move, file an insurance claim, take an exam, schedule a job interview, and just about anything else!

0-7387-0701-5, 216 pp., 6 x 9, charts   **$14.95**

To order, call 1-877-NEW-WRLD
Prices subject to change without notice

Llewellyn's New A to Z Horoscope Maker and Interpreter

LLEWELLYN GEORGE

A textbook . . . encyclopedia . . . self-study course . . . and extensive astrological dictionary all in one! More American astrologers have learned their craft from *Llewellyn's New A to Z Horoscope Maker and Interpreter* than any other astrology book.

First published in 1910, it is in every sense a complete course in astrology, giving beginners all the basic techniques and concepts they need to get off on the right foot. Plus it offers the more advanced astrologer an excellent dictionary and reference work for calculating and analyzing transits, progression, rectifications, and creating locality charts. This new edition has been revised and expanded by Stephanie Jean Clement, Ph. D., to meet the needs of the modern audience.

0-7387-322-2, 480 pp., 7½ x 9⅛ $19.95

Mythic Astrology
Internalizing the Planetary Powers

ARIEL GUTTMAN & KENNETH JOHNSON

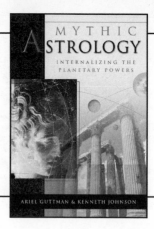

Enter a new dimension of spiritual self-discovery when you probe the mythic archetypes represented in your astrological birth chart. Myth has always been closely linked with astrology. Experience these myths and gain a deeper perspective on your eternal self.

Learn how the characteristics of the gods developed into the meanings associated with particular planets and signs. Look deeply into your own personal myths, and enjoy a living connection to the world of the deities within you. When you finally stand in the presence of an important archetype (through the techniques of dreamwork, symbolic amplification, or active imagination described in the book), you will have the opportunity to receive a message from the god or goddess.

0-87542-248-9, 400 pp., 7 x 10, illus.   **$24.95**

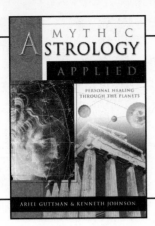

Mythic Astrology Applied
Personal Healing Through the Planets

ARIEL GUTTMAN &
KENNETH JOHNSON

The gods and goddesses of the ancient world are still with us today. They act out in our celebrities, the media, and most of all within our ourselves—often through our dreams and our own horoscopes. Through the planets in your chart you can discover the mythic dimensions of your own life. The authors of *Mythic Astrology* provide a way to do just that in their new book, *Mythic Astrology Applied*. Learn how to contact, work with, and bring harmony to the planetary archetypes within yourself.

This book might have you saying things like: "Now I know why I married a Vesta but really long for a Venus as my partner," or "Now I understand my relationship with my mother; she is a Demeter and I'm a Persephone."

0-7387-0425-3, 360 pp., 7 x 10, illus. $24.95